THE MYTH OF PROPERTY

THE MYTH OF PROPERTY

Toward an Egalitarian Theory of Ownership

JOHN CHRISTMAN

New York Oxford
OXFORD UNIVERSITY PRESS
1994

Oxford University Press

Oxford New York Toronto
Delhi Bombay Calcutta Madras Karachi
Kuala Lumpur Singapore Hong Kong Tokyo
Nairobi Dar es Salaam Cape Town
Melbourne Auckland Madrid

and associated companies in

Berlin Ibadan

Published by Oxford University Press, Inc.
200 Madison Avenue, New York, New York 10016

Oxford is a registered trademark of Oxford University Press

Library of Congress Cataloging-in-Publication Data
Christman, John.
The myth of property : toward an egalitarian theory of ownership / John Christman.
p. cm.
Includes bibliographical references and index.
ISBN 0-19-508594-9
1. Property. I. Title.
HB701.C54 1994 330.1'7—dc20 93-31713

2 4 6 8 9 7 5 3 1

Printed in the United States of America
on acid-free paper

To my father,
John P. Christman, Jr.
and to the memory of my mother,
Anna Mae Christman

Preface

This project has a long history, especially if one traces it back to its earliest forms. Indeed, I have been thinking about issues connected with property—and inequalities in the distribution of it—for about as long as I have been thinking about philosophy. Those ideas come to fruition in the present work, which is motivated by a concern for the relation between the prerogatives of property ownership and the goal of distributive equality. At least, this is my *philosophical* concern; my concern (sans phrase) has much to do with the unchecked inequality of life prospects for those in many contemporary societies.

So while the motivations are purely my own, the project's extensive past makes it the case that the contributions of many other people find themselves here. Numerous individuals over the years have generously contributed both to my philosophical development in general and to these ideas in particular by courteously attending to my (often pesky) inquiries. It is, therefore, not at all inappropriate to take this opportunity to thank some of my earliest philosophy teachers. In particular, the members of the Philosophy Department at the University of New Orleans took time away from their extremely taxing teaching responsibilities to give me some measure of special attention. In the end, they provided me with what they give to all of their students, a superb foundation in philosophy. I would like to lend a special note of thanks in this regard to Edward Johnson, Carolyn Morillo, Norton Nelkin, and Deborah Rosen.

Many of the particular ideas here first took form when I did my dissertation some years ago at the University of Illinois at Chicago. At that point, Gerald Dworkin (my advisor), Russell Hardin, John Bogart, and other faculty members and fellow students made comments that in some form survive in the present work. I wish to thank all of these individuals for their support, advice, and suggestions.

More recently, I have benefited greatly from my association with the Philosophy Department at Virginia Tech, which has been tremendously supportive of this and all my other projects. I am grateful to the institution as well as my colleagues and friends in the department. More particularly, Harlan Miller read parts of the manuscript and made very helpful comments. But I would like to extend special thanks to Marjorie Grene. Marjorie read more than half of the manuscript, and although she claimed that her only objective was to make stylistic suggestions, she never failed to offer valuable substantive comments about the arguments themselves.

Most of the book was written during the 1991–92 academic year, during which I was supported by a grant from the National Endowment for the Humanities for which

I am very grateful. I spent that year in Madison, Wisconsin, where the Philosophy Department at the University of Wisconsin was kind enough to grant me the status of Honorary Fellow and allow me to use mail, library, and office facilities. I was invited to read a paper to the department and presented what became part of chapter 8. The comments made by that audience and other faculty and friends there were very helpful. In particular, Andrew Levine and Daniel Hausman read several parts of the manuscript and made many insightful comments. David Weberman also was the source of much stimulating conversation and advice, as were Murry Smith and Miri Song. I thank all of these individuals warmly.

There are others (some of whom I've never met) who were kind enough to look at material and make comments, often in response to my unsolicited requests. These include Stephen Munzer, C. Edwin Baker, G. A. Cohen, Ian Shapiro, and Peter Vallentyne. I am grateful to all of these people for their time and attention.

Parts of this book were read in some form to various audiences, including the Ethics Workshop at the University of Chicago, the Political Theory Workshop at Yale University, the Political Science Department at the University of Virginia, and the Public Choice Society. I very much appreciate the invitations extended to me and the opportunity to share my work in progress. At some of these gatherings, the presentation was commented upon. These commentators included John Marshall, Jonathan Riley, and Sue Martinelly, all of whose ideas contributed to the quality of the finished product.

In addition, some of what follows is based on previous published work. Chapter 3 is an expansion of "Can Ownership Be Justified by Natural Rights?" published in *Philosophy and Public Affairs* 15, no. 2 (Spring 1986), 156–77 (reprinted by permission of Princeton University Press). Chapter 5 makes use of material from "Entrepreneurs, Profits, and Deserving Market Shares," which appeared in *Social Philosophy and Policy* 6, no. 1 (Fall 1988), 1–16 (used by permission). The main line of argument of chapter 8 is from "Self-Ownership, Equality, and the Structure of Property Rights," which appeared in *Political Theory* 19, no. 1 (February 1991), 28–46 (reprinted by permission of Sage Publications, Thousand Oaks, CA). I am very grateful to these journals for permission for use of the material in those articles. Also, in all these cases, many people and audiences contributed to the quality of this earlier work in ways that survive in these chapters. They are named in the journals, but I wish to extend another general note of thanks to them here.

I am grateful to the people at Oxford University Press for their help in bringing the project to completion. In particular, Angela Blackburn was extremely helpful in getting the manuscript together and ready for publication. I would like to extend a special thanks to Juanita Lewis, who vastly improved the manuscript. An anonymous reviewer provided insightful suggestions and criticisms as well, and I thank him or her for this attention.

A project like this also benefits in rather intangible ways from conversation, support, and simple good cheer from a number of close friends. This includes all of my good friends here in Blacksburg as well as others who are now separated from me by time and distance (but whose words and ideas echo in these and any other pages I write). My dear friends Gerald Nosich and Jean Nosich deserve particular mention in this regard. And special thanks are extended to Thomas Christiano, with whom I have discussed virtually every idea in the text (indeed, I'm not sure I have had *any* interesting philosophical ideas that I haven't run past Thomas). His philosophical acumen was especially valuable to me in working through the ideas of chapter 9. No matter how flawed the reader may think these arguments are now, they are extremely improved over the versions first shown to Thomas.

Finally, this project, like any other project I embark upon, could not be completed without the love and support of Mary Beth Oliver. My debt to her for her helpful advice, insightful suggestions, and tireless patience could not adequately be expressed, here or anywhere else.

Blacksburg, Virginia J. C.
June 1993

Contents

THE MYTH OF PROPERTY

Introduction

> *Property is the right of increase.* To us this axiom shall be like the name of the beast in the Apocalypse, a name in which is hidden the complete explanation of the whole mystery of this beast. It was known that he who should solve the mystery of this name would obtain a knowledge of the whole prophecy, and would succeed in mastering the beast. . . . Starting from this eminently characteristic fact . . . we shall pursue the old serpent throughout his coils; we shall count the murderous entwinings of this frightful taenia, whose head, with its thousand suckers, is always hidden from the sword of its most violent enemies, though abandoning to them immense fragments of its body.
>
> P.-J. Proudhon

The word "myth" has two complementary meanings. The first is "a legend," a traditional tale which, while containing various inaccuracies and exaggerations, still powerfully conveys some important moral and social lesson. The second is "a falsehood," an outright untruth which should be revealed as such in order to be abandoned. I shall use both of these meanings in my examinations here. For it will be my contention that "property" in its traditional sense, which I call the liberal conception of ownership, is truly a myth that ought to be exposed and abandoned. But in doing so, I retain the core elements from the traditional understanding of ownership in order to create what I hope is a more useful and constructive model.

In her book on property and American constitutionalism, Jennifer Nedelsky writes: "it may be that every society rests on illusory and contradictory beliefs. And it may be, as I have suggested, that there is something compelling about property and its links to liberty and security that cannot be revealed (or shaken). . . . I do not reject the role of myth in a well-functioning society. But the myth of property is pernicious because it hides a structure of power and insulates it from democratic debate."[1] My project here is to expose the inner structure of this myth in order to separate its pernicious elements from its more compelling parts. In the end, I expose the inadequacies of the traditional view of individual ownership and replace it with an alternative framework through which we can better understand what it means to own something.

I also want to claim inspiration from P.-J. Proudhon, whose inflammatory rhetoric and brash confidence (both of which I hope to do without) might have masked the truly revolutionary insights of his analysis. In particular, it was Proudhon who first drew attention to the aspects of property ownership that by their very nature conflict with the goals of justice and equality. Proudhon's famous claim that "property is theft" is most often understood to mean simply that private property *per se* is inconsistent with justice and must be abandoned.[2] But his arguments were actually more subtle than this. Proudhon's central idea was that what he called the "right of increase"—an integral component of the structure of property on his view—was the real villain in all dramatic struggles for just social relations. His argument went this way: equality of condition was an essential implication of justice; property ownership, in any form that included the right of increase, destroyed equality, so property was unjust (or "impossible"). The right of increase, for Proudhon, was the right to gain income from the ownership of property through either the productive development of the resource or its exchange.[3]

But Proudhon did not reject all forms of ownership, for he later argued against the view of other socialists of his day that all ownership must be abandoned.[4] The explanation of this shift involves a change in his characterization of property, not an abandonment of his principles of justice. The claim of his later work was that *possession* is the essential element of the kind of property constitutive of justice. This shift manifests a conceptual move implicit in Proudhon's work that I want to make the centerpiece of mine, namely, that when one separates the right of increase from rights of possession, one's normative conclusions concerning the right to property in a just society are significantly altered.

The *way* in which a person owns a thing is as central to questions of justice as is the amount of such things that she owns. To see this, imagine that a certain pattern of holdings was stipulated for a society, and goods were all assigned to owners according to some generally accepted distributive scheme. However, it was not stated what rights different people had over those goods: how people could use their holdings, or whether they could sell them and, if so, at what price. Lacking such information would mean, of course, that the real distribution of goods in that society would be wholly undetermined. Distributive justice must concern itself not just with "who has what" but with the nature of "having." The characteristics of having something as one's own—the rights, liberties, and powers that people have in relation to their goods—amount to what I call the "structure" of their ownership. One of the principal aims of this book is to put the question of what is the proper structure of ownership into the forefront of discussions of distributive justice.

Debates over distributive questions take place without an explicit discussion of the nature of ownership often because it is simply presupposed that there are two relevant alternatives: private individual ownership, where owners have "dominion" or "sovereignty" over their goods (capitalism), and state or social ownership of all resources (socialism). But of course, these paradigms are much too simplified to help in sorting out the various alternatives available in the real world. In a basically capitalist society such as the United States, for example, there are any number of restrictions on individuals' prerogatives regarding the way they can use, change, destroy, and charge for the use of their possessions. State agencies and bureaucracies enforce numerous regulations concerning the use and sale of goods, and receipts generated from the rent, sale, or transfer of goods are themselves regulated by taxation. It is not clear how one should describe such cases: is it a question of individuals having diminished control over their property or of the state's having limited rights over *its* property? The notion of private property, then, begins to look rather fuzzy.

But you might quickly say that such cases of state regulation and taxation are just deviations from the *model* or *paradigm* of private property, a model under which owners would have complete control over their goods and complete claim to the sales receipts from trades with willing buyers. It is only for particular social or political goals (which may compete with the goals that private ownership itself embodies) that ownership in capitalist societies has become regulated and circumscribed. After all, the language we are using to describe this phenomenon reveals such a paradigm: the government "restricts," "regulates," and "circumscribes" the full rights of owners.

One of the chief goals of this book is to deny the claim that either historically, conceptually, or (most important) normatively, the paradigm of ownership is the *full* ownership of goods without restriction or regulation. I will argue that although the notion of "sole despotic dominion" is pervasive as a general understanding of property ownership (and hence private property, hence capitalism), such a view, together with the distributive implications of that structure, cannot be defended on grounds of moral or political principle. This implies, as we shall see, that the connection between the state's role in directing a certain distribution of goods and its role in protecting a particular structure of ownership must be more intimate than the individual dominion view of property presupposes.

One could, of course, admit all this, and claim that there is certainly no clear distinction between a private ownership economy and a state-controlled one. There is a continuum, one could say, along which a state might take a greater and greater role in the authority of owners as one moves away from a private property regime. I do not quarrel with this observation except to make three points (each of which will be developed in the chapters to follow). First, the view that there is a clear continuum between full private ownership and state control of property presupposes that the owner of property can always be unambiguously identified. When an "owner" of a factory has rights to the profits from the firm but the workers at the factory have rights to a certain minimum wage (share of the receipts), or rights to certain levels of safety, or to maintenance of machinery and so on, it is not clear whose "private" rights should be considered the locus of ownership (against which state regulation competes). If the state steps in and alters the situation (raising the minimum wage, say), is that a move *away from* private property (the owner's) or *toward* it (the workers')?

Second, it is too often assumed that a private property economy is synonymous with a market economy, that the continuum referred to describes the difference between full state control of an economy and completely free markets. But as I will discuss in detail in chapter 2, the connection between private property and free markets is not so simple.

But, third, even if one does admit that this continuum toward or away from the paradigm of private ownership parallels movement toward or away from capitalist free markets, the central question remains what *grounds* the state has in moving in one direction rather than another. As long as we are not at the extreme of private (liberal) ownership, the state is restricting ownership for some social purpose. What, then, are the proper social purposes or, more contentiously, what is the proper distributive policy that the state should be guided by? By the end of this work I address these questions head on and show that in answering them, one is essentially presenting a theory of property ownership for a society.

I. The Liberal Conception of Ownership

The view of property that says that owners have dominion over their goods in relation to all others is what I will refer to as "private liberal ownership," referring to the classic liberal stance toward individuals' entitlements to their possessions. Although this is a type of ownership and not manifestly a principle of distribution, it is a structure that has close connections with free (or nearly free) market capitalism. I will conduct an extended critical analysis of this paradigm of ownership and conclude that it must be discarded as a model of what it means to own something in a just society.

As I will explain, private liberal ownership amounts to the enforcement of individual rights to use, possess, destroy, transfer, and gain income from goods (or if any of these rights are curtailed, it is not for the purpose of shaping the distribution of wealth in the society at large). That is, liberal ownership is a package of rights that is not regulated or reshaped for distributive purposes. There are many implications for this structure concerning limits on the regulatory powers of central governments, but one of the chief such implications is that any taxation on income (especially that gained through trade of goods in a less than perfectly free market) is ruled out by liberal ownership in that structure's purest form. Indeed, regulations or limitations on any of the rights listed for the purpose of correcting a distributive pattern are just what the paradigm of liberal ownership stands against.

While the idea of liberal ownership per se may not be explicitly defended in many theoretical quarters these days (though it definitely is defended in some), it nevertheless occupies a central place in the general ideology of capitalist market societies. And like any kind of ideological tenet, its details are often not articulated in public discussion, or even in the minds of its adherents. A dominant assumption in capitalist societies is that property owners are in some sense the *sovereigns* of what they own (metaphors about homes and castles reflect this). And even if greater social needs, such as preventing starvation or aiding the disabled, override this sovereignty, they do so only after a fight. Owners of property always see taxation for these types of programs as an encroachment on their private domain, one which even if justified in the end, is an invasion nonetheless.

This kind of thinking is also linked centrally with the public-private distinction crucial to the liberal (and capitalist) legal order. The government's power stops at the threshold of my home (or my car or my suitcase). This presupposes that the more or less full rights that I have over my possessions are part of the sanctum of activity that the state has no business invading, except perhaps for some tremendously weighty social goal. And liberal ownership, in this way of thinking, would afford citizens the greatest possible range of independence, privacy, and personal sovereignty allowable in a social order.

A corollary to this view is the idea that the institutions of *egalitarian* economic policy, traditionally manifested in some manner of socialism, would entail the complete eradication of this sort of private control. Since ownership equals individual sovereignty, an economic policy that sees property as socially owned is then in direct conflict with this sovereignty. And all of the nightmares of central economic planning that were spawned by twentieth-century Eastern European socialism come rushing to mind.

However, I hope to show that this picture of social life is seriously mistaken. Privacy and liberty are certainly important values, but demanding their protection simply does not necessitate or entail the sovereignty model of ownership. Like many related values thought to bear a close relation to private property, such values in no way entail the full package of liberal ownership rights that many accept as the essence of private property systems. I will show further that once the components of ownership are seen in their proper light, the connection between ownership and such individualist values as privacy and liberty will take a new, more subtle, and hopefully more plausible shape.

The primary goal here is to recast, at least partially, questions of distributive justice into a critical analysis of the structure of ownership. This means that this work will tread along some well-travelled paths. There have been several excellent books on the topic of property rights lately, for example, and the material covered here is in some ways similar. But there is a large difference, I think, between this project and other recent works in both orientation and conclusion. Those studies were either surveys of various arguments for whether private property *simpliciter* could be justified or essentially analyses of competing principles of distributive justice. I deviate here on both counts, for I am interested more in the internal *structure* of property (whether, for example, the liberal paradigm should be jettisoned in favor of a more flexible alternative) and in the relation between that structure and distributive justice.[5]

The arguments I survey in support of the sovereignty conception of ownership (liberal ownership) are those that I think provide the greatest support for such a thesis, or at least those that have had the most influence in this regard. These strategies include the argument from natural right, from liberty, from moral desert, and from the principle of utility. In each case I critically analyze the ways that such considerations could be brought forward in support of a liberal property regime and in each case find them flawed. After concluding that liberal ownership cannot be justified on the most powerful grounds traditionally given in support of it, I turn to my central positive argument: in lieu of the failure of the liberal notion, the concept of ownership ought to be recast into an altogether new mold. I argue that such a new understanding of what it means to own something will be relevant to the appraisal of any economic policies, whether they are egalitarian or not.

In particular, I claim that ownership should be seen, not as a monolithic bundle of rights and powers connecting people to goods, but as *two* sets of such rights that must be considered separately in any evaluation of economic policies for a society. The new understanding I will put forward says that ownership can involve a kind of *control* over the thing owned, or it can involve a right to *income* from trade or rent of the thing owned. The interests that these two (sets of) rights protect are different in character and weight and hence the function of the rules underlying such rights is also different. Thus the set of property rules adopted by a society—those rules that principles of justice demand—must be considered as separate packages. The reasons one might give for allowing people to control their property (or for distributing goods so that everyone has property to control) are different from the reasons one might give for allowing people to gain income from it. The former protect what I call "autonomy interests" and the latter "income interests." Correspondingly, control rights serve an autonomy-protecting function, while income rights serve an allocative function. The contrast between each of these pairs is so stark that principles of distributive justice must deal with them as completely separate normative structures.

I intend this work to be a part of a protracted defense of egalitarian economic principles, but as such, this particular study can only serve as a prolegomenon. My strategy is to point out that one of the major reasons for rejecting egalitarian economic principles as unjust or inefficient is that private liberal ownership, which is inconsistent with egalitarianism, is independently justified. Because of arguments such as this, I canvas the reasons people have given for the conclusion that liberal ownership is justified and show them all to be wanting. This negative conclusion is at best a partial victory for egalitarianism, however, since the belief in liberal ownership is certainly not the only reason that people have given for not being egalitarians. But it is my view that the understanding of ownership as a unified and monolithic set of sovereign powers is one of the central elements in the resistance to equality.[6]

I will, however, take a few steps in defense of egalitarian social and economic principles. I shall argue also that egalitarian economic principles must treat control ownership differently from income ownership in specifying the most plausible distributive scheme for a just society. So I want my positive conclusion also to aid in the development of acceptable principles of economic equality.

II. Strategies for Defending Liberal Ownership

It is important to distinguish two types of arguments that will be considered in defense of liberal ownership and treated below. These are direct and indirect arguments. A direct argument, like those appealed to in chapters 3, most of 4, and 5, advance considerations supporting liberal ownership based on its being implied by, or connected with, fundamental moral principles. The strength of such arguments, based on such things as natural rights, liberty, and moral desert, will be independent of the consequences of adopting liberal ownership—independent, that is, of accidental facts about the production levels and distributions that such structures might induce.

Indirect arguments do take these latter things into account, and launch their defense of liberal ownership on the basis of the instrumental value it has in bringing about desired effects. The principal argument of this sort takes utilitarianism as its moral basis and attempts to show a causal link between liberal ownership and efficiency and productivity. This argument is dealt with in chapter 6. It should be noted, however, that indirect arguments are characteristically weaker than direct ones, for the plausibility of the claim that liberal ownership is justified because of its distributive effects depends crucially on one's evaluation of those distributive outcomes. If we have no *other* argument for liberal ownership, we must shift our focus to an evaluation of those outcomes and ask whether they are truly worth pursuing, even if it is true that liberal ownership is most effective in bringing them about. My main conclusion concerning such arguments is that they are hopelessly indeterminate, although I also raise various questions about the attractiveness of the distributive consequences being advanced in them.

This last conclusion may seem like a rather meek one, since the argument over equality versus productivity (or efficiency) is where most discussions of this sort *begin*. But we cannot ignore the serious implications of abandoning direct arguments for liberal ownership. For after this is done, much that is traditionally brought to bear in the defense of free market capitalism is ruled out. For example, it can no longer be claimed that interference with owners' liberal property rights decreases their liberty (in a significant way), or violates their natural rights, or conflicts with what they deserve. What we are left with is a fight over distributions, and this is a fight I am confident that a plausible egalitarian principle can win.

More important, we will see that in the direct arguments for liberal ownership, it is so-called income rights which repeatedly emerge as the culprit blocking traditional attempts to justify that structure. Similar to Proudhon's "right of increase," this aspect of the liberal package will often be left dangling in these justificatory strategies. I will emphasize this further in my attempt to generate a new bifurcated notion of ownership in Part III.

In my positive argument for the reconstruction of ownership, I proceed with reference to interests that people have and to the ways that distributive principles, such as egalitarianism, must take these interests into account. I remain non-committal on the question of the weight that such interests should get in the final analysis (simply because this is not intended to be the final analysis). This is also not to say whether these interests, in the end, ground moral rights. My purpose here is to make important distinctions between kinds of interests rather than to advance final arguments in support of them.

I also make much use of the terminology of rights without supplying a logical analysis of them. That is, I take no stand on the issue of which theory of rights—a will theory, an interest theory, or a benefit theory—is most plausible.[7] I avoid these issues because I do not think their resolution bears on the questions I discuss. For our purposes, rights (claim rights) are enforceable valid claims.[8] Whether the interests I refer to will be weighty enough to secure a claim that must be respected by others and the state—what amounts to a right—will be a question I will attend to when necessary.[9]

Also, I do not throw my lot in with any particular foundational moral theory, such as utilitarianism or Kantianism. However, I do make particular claims about values and interests that do not, it turns out, fit well into the architecture of certain particular moral theories. As I said, I take autonomy interests to be a value that any just society must promote and protect (chapters 7 and 9), and I argue that certain utilitarian attempts to account for this value fail (chapter 9). So I do take stands on substantive value issues, though I do so without adopting a wholesale theory of moral and political principle.

Along the way, other conclusions are defended. For example, I urge that the entire conception of the relation between owners and the state that is usually assumed must be recast. As I said, it is my contention that the received view of this relation is unduly tainted by the influence of the liberal conception of ownership. Under the liberal conception, there exist owners whose rights to fully control and gain income from their holdings can be independently delineated, and in opposition to this set of concerns there is the state, bearing down on these owners and constraining their prerogatives. In such a picture, application of the principles of economic justice are *imposed* by the state upon the individual citizen, tightening the circle that her *prima facie* property rights would have carved out.

I argue that this picture involves several confusions. For example, the rights, liberties, powers, and the like that ownership confers on individuals in a society are not determinable separately from the general principles of distributive justice that apply in that society. If the correct principles of economic justice say that you do not have a certain right (to gain untaxed income from the sale of an asset, say), then there *does not exist* a *prima facie* right that has been ignored, counterbalanced, or outweighed. What one owns is what one owns justly.

Such a revision should throw into sharp relief, for example, public debates over radical revision of tax policy, government control of the economy, or any number of "interventionist" economic policies. Moreover, the usual separation of economies into private property capitalism and public ownership socialism must be rethought. For once the idea of liberal ownership is jettisoned, there is no longer a category of economic organization under which individual citizens maintain full sovereignty over their goods without state structuring of ownership rights.

Although I take on what I consider the most powerful traditional arguments for liberal ownership, I am certainly aware that this group of strategies is by no means complete, and many may suggest different and creative arguments for liberal ownership. For example, one of the most glaring lacunae here is that of contractarian defenses of liberal capitalism and liberal ownership. One could imagine any number of arguments utilizing the model of rational choice and hypothetical contract in support of conclusions I attack.[10] But my opposition to such arguments is too methodological to be of much use in a substantive debate such as this. It is my view that contractarian approaches to these issues can never, by themselves, determine an outcome concerning distributions, for the outcomes of individual negotiations are always a function of the relative bargaining positions of the parties to the contract. Relative bargaining position could not be specified without indicating the holdings of the parties and, more important, the structure of the ownership rights over those holdings (including their own talents). And these are the very conclusions that the arguments are intended to support.

So not all roads to liberal ownership are exhaustively travelled. But in attacking the most powerful and influential of such arguments, I conclude, by a kind of indirect induction, that liberal ownership ought to be rejected as the paradigm of individual property rights in a just society. Upon this criticism I then build the structure that I am most interested in—a new understanding of ownership and of the interests ownership can and does function to protect.

III. Overview and Plan

The argument of parts I and II of this book can be outlined as follows: Under a system of private liberal ownership, the state plays no direct role in structuring ownership so as to promote a certain distributive pattern. It follows that if private liberal ownership can be justified by sound moral arguments, it is *un*justified for the state to directly structure the property rights of individuals for the purpose of directing a distributive pattern. However, the strongest arguments supporting private liberal ownership are all found wanting. I conclude that private liberal ownership should be rejected as the dominant property structure in a society. Therefore, I reject the claim that the state should play no role in structuring property rights for the sake of distributive goals.

These arguments represent the negative portion of my purposes here. I then suggest a new model of ownership. In part III, I argue that ownership must be thought of as two quite different arrays of rights (and liberties and powers): the rights to control (use, manage, destroy, and the like) the thing owned and the right to income flows from the trade, rent, or productive use of the thing. I argue for the necessity of separating these two elements of ownership in the justification of distributive schemes.

Whatever one comes to think is the proper set of economic policies that justice demands of the state, ownership should be thought of as these two different sets of rights. So the question of what package of rights owners ought to have over their goods must be answered in two stages: first, what manner of control owners should enjoy over their goods, and second, what rights to trade and gain income from that property they should have. The interests protected by these two packages of rights, liberties, and powers are so radically different and represent such markedly different social goals that they must be considered as separate kinds of ownership. Although I mean this as a general conclusion, I argue that this bifurcation of the idea of ownership is of special relevance for the development of a plausible egalitarian economic policy. And I lay out some groundwork for such an egalitarian policy—and the use it makes of the bifurcated notion of ownership—in the final chapters.

The procedure is as follows: In the opening two chapters, I discuss the components of ownership and its relation to economic institutions such as free markets and capitalism. I consider the idea, prominent among legal theorists, that ownership is such a variable and indeterminate concept that it ought to be jettisoned altogether from the pages of political theory. And I press the point that although ownership is indeed a highly variable concept, and liberal ownership simply one of its many manifestations, it is not an eliminable notion altogether. In chapter 2 I argue that although liberal ownership and free economic markets are contingently related, liberal ownership is neither necessary nor sufficient for fully competitive markets. Liberal ownership and markets entail one another only when fairly robust assumptions are made about both the economic environment and individual motivations.

In the subsequent chapters, I take on some familiar arguments about economic justice and recast them in terms of a debate over the correct structure of individual ownership. In particular, I critically discuss the following arguments purporting to justify liberal ownership: arguments based on the natural right to property (chapter 3); those based on considerations of liberty (chapter 4); those based on claims of moral desert (chapter 5); and those based on utilitarian arguments (chapter 6). I conclude that although these strategies introduce considerations that must be taken into account by any theory of property, they do not succeed in justifying the proposition that individuals should have liberal ownership rights over their goods.

As I mentioned previously, these arguments are well rehearsed and familiar. But I ask a slightly different question from that which is usually asked, namely, whether the arguments I deal with succeed in justifying a *particular structure* of ownership (liberal ownership). Other theorists who have dealt with this material have not taken seriously enough the variability of the concept of ownership and, in particular, the internal complexity of the concept. By rejecting these traditional attempts to justify *liberal* property rights—as a singular concept but by no means the only possibility—

I invite the question of what would be the correct structure of ownership in a just society. Also, I stress the point that the right to exchange and gain income from one's holdings is repeatedly the most questionable element in the package.

With the rejection of the liberal conception, I then begin the task of proposing an alternative model of ownership that keeps separate the control and income-generating aspects of the package (chapter 7). Included in that discussion are a variety of illustrations of how failure to keep these two notions of owning separate has led to the mistaken conclusion that private property per se is necessary to protect various interests or achieve certain goals. I point out that such interests and goals concern only one of the two kinds of ownership and so do not support the conclusions concerning property that are often reached.

After mounting the case for the bifurcated sense of ownership, I undertake an analysis of the idea of self-ownership (chapter 8) and show that only by virtue of the bifurcated conception can a complete understanding of the essence of self-ownership be achieved. Moreover, I show how the supposed conflict between self-ownership and principles of distributive equality is dissolved by the control ownership–income ownership distinction. I conclude in chapter 9 with a discussion of egalitarian economic policies and the ways that control ownership and income ownership are treated under those directives. In particular, I argue that the notion of individual autonomy must play a prominent role in egalitarian principles, a conclusion that underscores the need to separate the two kinds of ownership I describe. In the end, I hope to make the idea of egalitarian principles of distributive justice more plausible.

So I want to throw out the traditional paradigm of ownership—that owners have a kind of dominion over their goods—and usher in a new view. And the spirit of P.-J. Proudhon will haunt most of these proceedings, by virtue of his insight that property as "right of increase" and property as the right of "possession" are crucially different entities, but also in the abject odium with which he held the deep inequality of status, wealth, and well-being of his society. The abiding, and indeed increasing, inequality in our own society provides the primary philosophical and political motivation of the efforts to follow. Proudhon has taught me, if nothing else, that an understanding of the complex nature of ownership is central to the grasp of the deep injustice of such a condition.

I

THE STRUCTURE OF OWNERSHIP

1

What, If Anything, Is Ownership?

The title of this chapter is meant again to invoke the spirit of Proudhon and his seminal work *What Is Property?*, though my purpose here is more analytical than polemical. I will explicate the various ideas associated with the ownership of property and inquire into whether there is some commonality among those ideas. This will involve taking both a diachronic and a synchronic look at the concept of ownership, and focusing special attention on the concept of liberal ownership in whatever context that appears.

Liberal ownership will be defined later in detail (see chapter 2). As I mentioned in the Introduction, it refers to any property structure where full (or nearly full) rights to possess, use, manage, alienate, transfer, and gain income from property are granted to individuals. Inconsistent with liberal ownership is any legal or social policy that tailors the rights and powers of individuals to use, trade, and profit from their goods in order to implement an overall (in particular, distributive) social goal.[1] The general picture is of an owner with virtually unchecked prerogative and power over his or her goods standing apart from the state as a separate political entity. The rights of such owners are not granted at the behest of the society at large nor shaped or structured in order to serve a social goal. The interests they directly protect, on the liberal view, are those of the owners alone.

But many will balk at this entire way of framing the question. Many thinkers, especially those who might have just come from a law and/or economics classroom, will insist that there is no such thing, strictly speaking, as ownership; there exist only bundles of rights, liberties, powers and such, which have been traditionally associated with property but are so infinitely variable in different contexts that it no longer makes sense to speak of a single concept of ownership at all. To speak of any one conception of ownership, such as liberal ownership, is an exercise in confusion.

I want to resist the total reductionism of this view, and I argue against it later. While ownership is indeed a variable concept, the rights, liberties, powers, immunities, and liabilities[2] associated with it can be fit into a framework whose structure is *not* infinitely invariable. I want to steer a middle course between the liberal conception of ownership and the full disaggregation view of law and economics. (Of course, the rejection of the liberal conception of ownership does not really begin in this chapter, as the full argument against that notion takes place over several chapters by way of normative criticisms).

My plan in this chapter is, first, to clarify the terminology that will be operating in the discussion (section I), as well as to cast a quick glance at the history of the idea of ownership. I next turn to a conceptual analysis of ownership (section II), followed by a discussion of the reductionist view of ownership just mentioned. In the final section, I introduce a framework of analysis for the concept of ownership, which, I think, helps break new ground in clarifying the role that concept plays in our political and legal language.

I. Confusions and Clarifications

Almost any writer who conducts a normative or analytical examination of ownership (especially recently) begins by putting to rest what he or she sees as pervasive confusions in the ordinary understanding of that idea.[3] I will not deviate from this practice. But I also must add that, for many writers who engage in this same clarifying operation, there has been confusion in *describing* the confusions concerning notions associated with property.

Many commentators claim that the "common" (that is, confused) view of property is that property is a thing, identical to the thing owned.[4] There are actually two separable mistakes in such an understanding of ownership. One, which is really just an equivocation, is that the word "property" means *both* the thing owned and the relation of ownership. In the latter usage, the term is shorthand for "property rights" and is interchangeable with the word "ownership." This usage is the focus for us here.

The other point is that it is a mistake to see property as the ownership of a *thing* at all. This is an altogether different misunderstanding, which concerns the variety of entities that can be the object of property rights. Many of the things that are ownable are not tangible objects but abstractions. A company, for example, is not, or certainly not merely, the physical objects located on its grounds. It is a set of complicated legal relations and abstract economic entities, such as equity, capital assets, stocks, and shares. Some writers draw the conclusion that since the entities of ownership are often abstract, the true object of ownership is not a tangible item at all but the *rights* that one has over the things: one simply owns rights (and liberties and powers and such) over goods, not literally the goods themselves.[5] This clarification, however, should be resisted, as it introduces a useless redundancy: owning rights means having (a certain bundle of) rights to rights over or in some relation to some "thing."

The problem of the non-corporeality of the thing owned is certainly not to be overlooked: seeing the paradigm case of ownership as that which one has over one's umbrella can cause confusion when one switches to talk of estates. Nevertheless, it is safe, I think, to conduct the analysis as if material things were the paradigmatic objects of ownership and be careful when one switches to less tangible holdings.[6]

The third confusion often noted is the view that ownership is simply a relation *between* a person and a thing. This view has two components, each of which is inaccurate in some way: the first is the point I just noted, that one of the relata of ownership is, literally, a thing; the second is that this relation holds between a person and the object of ownership. Proper analysis reveals, however, that legal relations hold between *persons*, though perhaps in regard to some thing. The relation in question, then, is not even binary, but triadic: ownership is a relation between a person and all other persons in regard to some (tangible or intangible) thing. The framework I present in section IV should help keep us clear about this.

However, the more detrimental confusion concerns seeing ownership as a *simple* relation between persons regarding some thing, as opposed to seeing it as a complex relation. Even after it is made clear that the relata in question are not simply a person and a thing, it must still be stressed that the nature of this relation is complex and variable, not simple and static.[7] The idea that the relation of ownership is a simple and singular relation stems, I think, from the presumption that the paradigm of ownership is *dominium*, where the owner's prerogatives in regard to his or her property are absolute and unlimited. However, this idea, which amounts to what I call liberal ownership, is what I suggest we abandon as our paradigm of ownership. Not only is it a mistake to think ownership is but a simple relation, it is also wrong to think that it is *that sort* of simple relation (*dominium*).

Lessons from History

The idea that the paradigm notion of ownership is a kind of sovereignty gains credence by virtue of a certain view of the history of property institutions.[8] This tendency to see ownership as a simple relation, and in particular to see this relation expressed as full liberal ownership, rests to some degree on a view of the history of that concept in the Western (European) legal tradition. Most surveys of the history of private property suggest a pattern that might be described this way: the rise, fall, rise, and fall again of full liberal ownership. The suggestion of such a pattern is that liberal ownership had its various heydays but has fallen on hard times of late.

The first rise is thought to have occurred in ancient Rome. In the classical Roman law, where ownership was expressed as *dominium* in the classical Law Codes,[9] an owner was said to have virtually unlimited rights to preside over property without state interference, and legal rules were loathe to allow the disaggregation of the bundle of rights associated with property.[10] But the largely agrarian economy of ancient Rome was not organized to facilitate rent, production, and profit, which many of the components of liberal ownership would be used to protect. Although money lending at interest was certainly practiced, and overseas trade and cash-crop production existed, the foremost aim for most good Romans was to protect the virtue and honor of their families, not increase their holdings.[11]

Individual ownership is not the same as absolute ownership. There *was* taxation in ancient Rome, for example, and at times it was rather heavy in order to support the sometimes overwhelming military establishment needed to protect the provinces.[12] Moreover, there is much to suggest that property owners saw themselves and were seen by their societies as occupiers of a social position heavily burdened with responsibilities and encumbrances, not as the unhindered masters of private estates to which we attach the notion of ownership-as-sovereignty.[13]

When Rome was destroyed by the northern Teutonic societies, a very different system of property built on family estates, one where ownership was fragmented and circumscribed, replaced the notion of the unencumbered individual owner. In what came to dominate English law from the Middle Ages to the eighteenth century, the system of land tenure and estates marked a diametrical shift away from legal recognition of full ownership rights in individuals. In the system of estates, no individual ever was a complete owner of land. The system vested absolute title in no one but the Crown, which granted lesser interests in subjects of various ranks. Though only the Crown could be said to "own" an estate, the landlord could hold a "fee simple absolute" in the land, and thereby rent out lesser parts of it and demand various feudal duties from tenants in return for protection from outsiders. Hence, full individual ownership is thought to have receded during this period.

This feudal concept of ownership is thought to have dominated until the industrial revolution made necessary certain more concentrated ownership structures under which owners could enjoy greater powers of management and development of property. Greater diversification—which in this context meant greater freedom on the part of owners to subdivide estates and vary the utilization of the land—included the agglomeration of ownership rights into the hands of the present generation's owner. This conception of ownership is thought to have found its most unequivocal articulation in the eighteenth century in the *Commentaries* of Sir William Blackstone. Blackstone's view was that the ownership of property was "that sole and despotic dominion which one man claims and exercises over the external things of the world in total exclusion of the right of any other individual in the universe." This view is echoed later by John Austin: "taken in its strict sense, it [property ownership] denotes a right—indefinite in point of user—unrestricted in point of disposition—and unlimited in point of duration—over a determinate thing."[14]

It is at this point in the story that liberal ownership is meant to reappear on the scene. But even in the age of Blackstone, no legal system afforded protection to an unchecked dominion of a resource by an owner. More important, as Patrick Atiyah has argued, the freedom-of-contract model of social relations, which replaced the more status-centered view of the Middle Ages (in England), lasted but a short time and was met with an immediate tide of resistance almost as soon as it was established.[15] Also, the shift from a system of estates to a system of greater power of the present owner can be easily understood as a *conflict* of ownership rights rather than a new centralization. For if I put into my will various instructions as to the disposition of my property by future generations, and those future people ignore my directions and develop the property as they choose, *my* ownership rights have been limited by *their* expanded power.

Then with the development of industry in the late nineteenth century, in particular the diversification of technologies and the economic relations made necessary by this diversification, ownership again became fragmented and divided. Such things as shares, mortgaged holdings, and investment funds introduced such a varied conglomeration of ownership rights that many conclude the concept has lost its usefulness. Whether the disintegration of ownership actually has occurred will depend on the resolution of the conceptual argument we will soon examine: whether the contemporary law of property introduces so much variation in possible ownership arrangements that there is no central notion of "owner" at all. I argue that, despite the variations in history and in contemporary law, the full disaggregation view is not entailed by the rejection of the liberal conception of simple dominion in the ownership of things. The framework of ownership presented later will make this clear.

In any case, however, the picture of ownership that history paints, at this superficial level at least, is much more complex, murky, and varied than defenders of the liberal paradigm of ownership might have us suppose. Seldom (and, arguably, never) was the notion of "sole despotic dominion" by people over their possessions (without state intrusion or social stricture) instantiated to a significant degree in the law. If one wants to defend liberal ownership, it must be for the conclusion that it should be *instituted*, not that it be recovered or retained.

II. The Structure of Ownership

As I have noted, there have been many recent studies of the components of ownership. Virtually any of these analyses focuses on a few central elements of ownership: rights to use, destroy, and transfer items of ownership (*usus*, *abusus*, and *usus fructus*). A. M. A. Honoré has produced a well-known analysis of legal ownership that provides a helpful basis for the present discussion. Honoré suggests that in general the concept "owner" refers to "the person who has the greatest interest in a thing which a mature system of law recognizes."[16] The list of elements of what Honoré calls full liberal ownership has now become familiar, and we need only mention them here: (1) *the right to possess* (the right of exclusive physical control that the nature of the thing admits, coupled with a claim-right to non-interference); (2) *the right to use* (a claim-right to exclusive use of the thing implying a general duty on the part of all others not to use the thing without the owner's permission); (3) *the right to the capital* (the power to make valid disposition of the thing owned as well as the power to transfer title—this element can be separated into the rights of alienation, consumption, and modification);[17] (4) *the right to manage* (a cluster of powers to contract with others concerning control over various uses of the thing); and (5) *the right to the income* (the right to increased benefit from the ownership, where this benefit is derived from others' goods given in trade; this right ranges over the *increased* income or material accrued from a holding by virtue of the productive use of that holding, including, most centrally, trades).

This last element will occupy much of our discussion and so deserves particular attention. The right to the income stands for the combination of the right to transfer (alienate title) and the right to any goods given in return for so doing. The distinction between use and income, in some cases, is easy to make due to the nature of the thing owned and the benefits received, the obvious case being the receipt of money from the sale of a non-monetary holding. Some forms of holdings, trusts and shares, for instance, confer upon the right holder rights *only* to accrued monetary benefits. In an abstract sense, the right to the income derivable from an owned thing includes essentially the right to increased *benefit* from the ownership, where this benefit is derived from others' goods or the net increase in goods or welfare that emanates from having a system of private rights and transfers at all. However, viewing this right only in terms of welfare might make its reference overly broad since virtually any interaction with an owned thing may give one an increase in utility. The scope of this right, therefore, includes principally the *material* goods or income that accrues to an owner by virtue of the productive use or trade of a good. As we will discuss in the next chapter, the income that this right has scope over is different depending on whether or not one is operating in a perfect economic market. If the market does not exhibit the properties of perfect competition, then the income that accrues to an owner by virtue of a trade may well include the "economic rent" available in the area. Economic rent is the surplus income derivable from certain scarcities of goods in the area, where the price of one's goods deviates from the exact cost of bringing them to the market. For now we will define the right to the income as the right to exchange goods and to retain all goods from others in such exchanges.

There are other aspects of ownership that can be mentioned, though the elements listed above are the central rights associated with the ownership of property.[18] But what, exactly, *is* ownership? Is it the *entire* bundle of rights listed here? Are there proper subsets of this list that each would amount to ownership? Several writers have provided answers to these questions,[19] but I want to avoid doing so for now. The principal position on that issue that we will consider is the view that all of the central elements listed above are essential to (private) ownership. This is the liberal view. The opposite extreme, perhaps, is the view that ownership is actually nothing at all. That is, one could claim that the components of ownership should be treated as fully separable rights, where no common characteristics holding them together need be recognized. This position, which I call the "full disaggregation view," will now be considered.

III. The Full Disaggregation View

In many circles these days, it has become a commonplace to treat the notion of ownership with dismissal. That is, while the particular rights associated with property might be mentioned and analyzed separately, it is assumed that there is no sense in looking for some connecting idea that holds them all together, an idea like ownership. The argument for this conclusion proceeds like this: once it is noticed that ownership is not a simple legal relation but a wide variety of legal relationships, and once it is noticed how immeasurably variable these relations can be in different contexts, it ceases to be useful to refer to any one relation as that of ownership.

Thomas Grey has spelled out a particularly perspicuous version of the disaggregation argument that has drawn much comment. He concludes that "the specialists who design and manipulate legal structures of the advanced capitalist economies could easily do without using the term 'property' at all."[20] Therefore, "the substitution of a bundle-of-rights for a thing-ownership conception of property has the ultimate consequence that property ceases to be an important category in legal and political theory."[21]

One of Grey's most powerful lines of argument is what I would call the "no distinct character argument." Specifically, this argument amounts to the claim that there is no consistent way to distinguish property rights from other types of enforceable claims that a person may have against others. The typical distinction made in the law is between property rights and contract-based rights and duties. Since, the argument goes, the array of rights, liberties, and such that a "property" arrangement might be composed of is as various and flexible as one created purely by contract, then there is merely a nominal, and not a substantive, difference between the two. Second, it is argued that property rights cannot be distinguished in an interesting way from personal rights, rights not to be harmed or defrauded or defamed. In both cases, there is merely a variable set of enforceable claims that contains no characteristic marks.

Relevant here are the distinctions among property rules, liability rules, and inalienability rules.[22] These three types of legal norms are used in the protection of rights and liberties. Property rules prohibit all intrusion unless prior permission was given (and if demanded, compensation paid at a rate set by the right holder). Liability rules, by contrast, do not prohibit border crossings at all but require *ex poste* compensation when they occur (at a rate set objectively by the state). Inalienability rules prohibit border crossings regardless of offers of compensation. Grey rejects the claim that ownership is comprised of rights and liberties protected by property rules while personal rights are protected by liability and inalienability rules.

Grey points out that what is usually regarded as the object of ownership rights is not protected *only* by property rules (for example, one's car, a paradigm case of an object of property rights, is not protected uniquely by property rules).[23] One's car cannot be taken without prior compensation (that is, there are prohibitions on such behavior), so a property rule applies; but it is also the case that a person is not, strictly speaking, prohibited from running into your car negligently as long as compensation is paid to you afterward, indicating the use of a liability rule.

But I would insist that there is a difference between the three types of rules that is instructive in picking out the particular character of ownership. Consider, for example, how very much of a difference it makes to me whether my possessions are protected by one or another of these rules. Knowing that violations (border crossings) could occur at any moment—even though I know that I will recover damages that will "make me whole" afterwards—is fundamentally different from knowing that the state will attempt to prevent such violations unless I give prior permission. *Control* of the situation is precisely what is missing in the first case in contrast to the second. No matter what the measure of damages is (and theorists of compensatory damages are quick to point out that anxiety is a real cost that can be covered in the eventual settlement), I will have a fundamentally different attitude toward my situation depending on what kinds of rights I have. The point here is that whatever the final contours of the structure of ownership turn out to be, their being protected by property rules, as opposed to (primarily) liability rules, is based on the real difference in levels of control that owners have of their property compared to the control persons have in other areas of their lives that are not the object of ownership. Even if the protection I enjoy is against only *intentional* violations, and negligent damage to my property merely initiates a liability-rule response, I am nevertheless in a crucially different position than if my rights were protected *only* by liability rules.

The reason that the distinction between liability rules and property rules is often blurred is that theorists see the value of property ownership as a function only of income or at least of consequent preference satisfaction. But this view overlooks the distinction between the components of ownership whereby I can control the thing I own (only *I* get to choose what is done with the thing) and the right to benefit from use and trade of that thing. Liability rules protect my total income bundle (over time) stemming from my holdings, but property rules attach more closely to my control rights. I will make much of this distinction as we go along, especially in chapters 7 and 9 when I discuss the characteristic of individual autonomy. My point is that Grey mistakenly views these sets of rules as located along a single, infinitely variable continuum, and therefore does not see their respective distinct characters.

Moreover, ownership is so embedded in our conceptualization of a society that to simply throw the concept out would be a major revision of our present theories and assumptions. If Grey is right, then a great deal of other important principles and concepts would have to be jettisoned along with the elimination of ownership. Take, for example, the idea of a "distribution of resources": if "holding" or "title" or "ownership" were not a consistent and predictable idea, how could we even speak the way we do about the level of resources held by the various members of a society? Moreover, we could not consistently conceptualize comparisons of different individuals' wealth on Grey's view. Each person would be the subject of such a widely disparate array of legal modalities in relation to various assets that to say one person was wealthier than another would be a gross simplification or even meaningless.[24] But these ideas—distribution and wealth—certainly do have a graspable and consistent meaning, or at least we certainly cannot do without *them* in political theory.[25]

The crux of my response to Grey, then, is that his argument for disaggregation rests on his claim that the rights, liberties, and powers typically associated with ownership have no special character in the panoply of such legal modalities agents enjoy. If one can argue, as my comments just now begin to do, that there is such a family resemblance among the prerogatives of ownership, and that this manifests a moral interest that has a place in political principles and theories, then the full disaggregation view can be discarded. The full response to the Grey thesis, then, will come below, where I will claim that ownership is comprised of *two* clusters of legal prerogatives, one characterized by the "primary functional control" that owners have over goods, and the other by the "primary right to income flows" from trade and development of goods. These organizing ideas show what is characteristic of ownership and what principles of economic justice and policy must take into account when they justify economic relations for a society.

There have been numerous discussions of the disaggregation thesis, and many echo the points I make here (though my conclusions concerning the nature of property are different).[26] Richard Epstein, for example, considers Grey's arguments and replies that the vagueness of a concept does not condemn it to uselessness as long as an overarching general account can be given that captures the central uses and explains why the peripheral ones are peripheral.[27] What Epstein invokes, however, as the general account that can clear up the murkiness is the "sole and despotic dominion" definition of property given by Blackstone (who, as we saw above, represents the pinnacle of the absolute individualist conception of ownership). But the idea that property rights comprise absolute dominion in this sense is not only historically parochial and ideologically contentious, but also obviously false. No legal system comes close to granting such powers to owners, who not only are subject to taxation and zoning restrictions, but who enjoy rights that are intricately tied up with the overall economic policies of the state. To claim that ownership means absolute dominion is to beg several normative questions (which I am concerned to take up) about the relation between individual rights and distributive policy.

The most powerful response to all these arguments, however, is to present an account of the meaning of ownership that is itself plausible. I do this by way of a formal framework, within which important distinctions and clarifications can then be made.

IV. The Framework of Ownership

In providing this framework, I am suggesting that ownership is essentially a relation among variables which find different extensions in different contexts.[28] The relation, however, does not vary in its essential character. Just as the relation "is taller than" is the same whether we are talking about buildings or giraffes, the relation "owns" or "has property rights over" is more or less constant throughout all the changes in its details that can be seen.

We have seen both through historical survey and contemporary analysis just how many different combinations there can be concerning the rights, liberties, power, liabilities, and immunities that owners can enjoy. What is needed then is an organizing picture, a schema for ownership (Figure 1.1).

I divide the categories of the elements of ownership into four cells and have listed background rules necessary for the structuring of property systems.[29] Cell A refers to the class of persons (and person-like legal entities) who are recognized as potential owners in a jurisdiction. There are many variations possible here, of course, since abstract entities (such as corporations) can be owners. As I list below A, however, the major categories of the subject of ownership are private, collective, and common owners. Private property economies recognize (if not encourage) ownership by single individuals or small sets of individuals acting as one. Collective ownership, such as a co-op or worker-owned factory, involves a group of people acting for a single purpose. Common ownership (or public ownership) occurs when the subject of the ownership rights of some asset is the entire community.

In saying this, I disagree with Jeremy Waldron, who argues that "ownership" is a concept that only *private* property systems instantiate. Part of the basis for his argument is his claim that collective property systems decide questions of the use of resources according to "the use which is most conducive to the social interest."[30] However, while individual ownership contains no stipulation as to the interest that is served by the use (though it is usually the interest of the individual owner), it seems inappropriate to introduce the idea of the interests served by use in the case of one kind of control and not in the other. In both cases some entity (the collective, the

Figure 1.1

A → against → C

A	B	C	D
Holder(s) subject	Modalities (rights, liberties, etc.)	Other Persons (rights held against)	"Thing"
private, collective, common, etc.	full, attenuated	in rem, in personum	tangible, intangible

Rules:

1. Fixing title (determining best title) and determining lesser interests.
2. Regulation of transmissibility (intestate rules).
3. Effective enforcement mechanisms (rights to security).

individual) has decisive control over use, and in both cases these decisions will usually be made in order to advance the interests of the owner(s). So the two cannot be distinguished concerning interests. Therefore, the framework of ownership I am describing applies to collective, communal, or private property systems, and these are distinguished according to how the subjects of the modalities (cell A) are systematically organized.

On my view, private ownership obtains when a single person (or person-like thing such as a corporation) stands in such a relation. There is ownership without private ownership when a group larger than a single individual systematically controls certain resources in the manner described by the ownership relation. The word "systematically" in the last sentence brings up a second point. It may not be possible to infer from the extant legal structure of a society what its dominant mode of property is. For example, in the United States it would certainly be *legal* for large groups (even populations of entire states) to pool their resources in a collective ownership scheme. Similarly, the range of resources which are now publicly owned—parks, utilities, the post office—could be expanded to include other industries. Yet the present-day United States is dominated by private ownership. Legal prohibitions and permissions do not stipulate what pattern of ownership actually obtains. So one cannot simply read what the dominant mode of ownership is in the statutory and constitutional provisions of a jurisdiction. One must look at the pattern of ownership structures that is allowed by the law and promoted by the political principles of the society (as well as what actually obtains).[31]

Cell B, the most analyzed component of ownership, is where the various legal modalities that comprise the rights of property belong. The previous analysis of the incidents of ownership is placed here. Cell C contains a description of those against whom the modalities of ownership are held. This is almost always the rest of the community (*in rem*) but sometimes includes the government as a specific element. People have various rights against government action regarding their property holdings (restrictions on eminent domain for example). Components of the ownership relation can be held *in personam*—against particular persons—in cases where particular types of people have certain rights and liberties in regard to a holding (such as a permanent easement). For the most part, however, it will be a distinctive characteristic of ownership rights that they are held not against enumerated individuals but against people in general.

Finally, the thing owned (cell D) will be all the things about which the ownership relation can obtain. I say "about which" since the actual relation is triadic: a relation (in the paradigm case) between a person and all others in relation to the thing. Whatever it is that the law recognizes as ownable belongs here. I am following other writers here in analyzing ownership in terms, first, of *tangible* things, and then assuming that the main elements of the model can be extended to other kinds of property.[32] This method of course raises the question of what counts as ownership, since the state may recognize any number of rights and liberties that are normally *part* of ownership in relation to some things. I will deflect the question of what counts as ownership until I discuss the central relations below.

Although the elements of ownership may vary widely, it still is the crucial *relation*, in particular the relation between A and C characterized by B (in regard to D), that is the core concept of ownership. The relation that an owner or set of owners has with others in the community can be characterized as having two foci or points of emphasis. These two bundles of rights will get extensive treatment below. At this point I merely introduce them in order to characterize the nature of ownership.

The first of these foci is that the relation between owners and the world in regard to their goods is one of *primary functional control.* The use and control of a determinable store of goods are functionally related, at least derivatively, to the desires of the owner. The relation of ownership holds between A and the world in regard to a thing, D, when what happens to D is primarily a function of A's wishes. Other considerations can certainly, *in the end*, determine the fate of D; moreover, A's wishes may be complex and conditional upon the wishes of others. But other considerations that run contrary to A's wishes must *trump* A's prerogative because of special considerations. Now the uses to which D is put are a perhaps derivative extension of A's desires. But if some person other than A can determine the uses of D whenever that person chooses, *completely independent* of A's occurrent or primary desires, then A is likely not the owner of D.

Admittedly, following this analysis, the difference between an owner and a tenant may, in many cases, be difficult to glean. Recall that under the English law of estates, the lord of the manor was technically only the tenant of the Crown, though we would have little trouble labelling him or her the owner in our sense. The difference between a lessee (who enjoys full rights to use, possess, and perhaps sublease) and an owner will be discernible only diachronically. That is, the question must be asked (looking ahead), to whom does the property revert if the present possessors relinquish it without direction? Also (looking to the past), from whom were the present property rights of the possessors granted, and does this person retain any interest in the thing? These directional questions may point to a single person who, since her or his desires can be seen as the ultimate, non-derivative source of the permissions of present use, can be understood as the owner.[33]

This indicates how an owner may, as is often the case, contract away many of the lesser interests of ownership. She may lease the use of her goods for a time, for example. Then the *occurrent* uses of the thing will be a function of the desires of the tenant (T) rather than A. But A is still owner since those occurrent uses can be traced back to A's primary desires to rent the thing to T. As long as the ultimate source of the permission to use the thing as T wants is traceable to A's power to lease (which is an extension of the right to manage), then T's occurrent control does not disturb the determination that A is owner.

The idea of this special relation that is involved in ownership is a point lost, I think, on many economists.[34] Although these writers list the usual elements of ownership—use, transfer, and income rights—it is the *economic* aspect of ownership that is crucial to them. For example, Frederic Pryor defines ownership as a "bundle of rights or set of relations . . . with regard to some . . . 'thing'; such rights must have *economic value* and must be enforced in some societally recognized manner."[35] But the idea that ownership means standing as economic beneficiary of an asset is both too broad and too narrow a model of property rights. It is too broad since there are many "things" from which I derive direct economic benefit but which I certainly do not own (my job, for instance, or the employment positions of those who might work for me).

It is also too narrow because it does not capture the prerogatives of control that we have been discussing. This point, in fact, cuts deeper into the nature of economic models generally. For on a standard economist's view of things, all people in the world are perfectly rational (and are rational in the simple utility-maximization sense). Since this is true, agents' actions are perfectly predictable if one knows their preferences and their opportunities. So their prerogative of choice can be sliced out of the picture since the fact that *I* make a choice adds no new information to the model than is already captured by the assumptions of perfect rationality and full information. This point will be elaborated upon in my discussion of attempts at utilitarian justifications of ownership and in the new theory of ownership I present in Part III.

The discussion of economists' understanding of ownership brings us to the second major family of prerogatives that characterize ownership, namely the right to (at least some of) the income flows from the exchanges of the goods owned. These rights, again, will be examined later, but this set of modalities involves at least some presumption that the owner stands to be a beneficiary of the permutations of the value of the thing owned. This right has been presumed by many to be a *necessary* component of ownership, for example by those who hold that only liberal ownership is the paradigm of property rights structures. This is an idea that I will argue at length is mistaken. My purpose here is to mention those rights and liberties that should be understood as being part of the ownership relation as specified by the framework in Figure 1.1.[36]

As will be seen in what follows, setting out the structure of ownership in this way in no way presupposes that any particular set of rights falling under it is automatically justified. The exact structure of control and income rights will be determined by the distributive principles of the state and hence justified according to normative argument. All that this framework indicates is that ownership is the relative control that individuals or groups legally exercise over things and/or the relative claim to income from those things they have as part of the general economic structure of society.

So the ownership relation can be characterized as whatever combination of rights society recognizes that gives individuals primary control over, and/or claims to the income from, tangible or intangible things. This account implies that more than one owner can attach to a single thing of economic value, one of whom may be the state (or the populace at large) and one an individual. In part III, I present a more complete theory of the organizing ideas of ownership, and I claim that these two notions, control and claims to income, must be completely separated in our understanding of what it means to own something.

As I have said, the framework of ownership I have set out is not peculiar to private property systems, since collectivities might also have rights and liberties to use, manage, and gain income from their holdings. In much of what follows, however, I assume individual ownership. This point will be revisited, though, in the final sections of the book.

So what I have argued here is that the concept of ownership need not be abandoned because of its complexity. In fact, it has a particular though variable structure. I have also suggested, however, that the liberal conception of full ownership is by no means a paradigm manifestation of that structure. The ultimate defense of the liberal conception of ownership is not, of course, conceptual, but normative. This is why it will be necessary to examine the various ways that it has been traditionally defended. This point will be taken up in chapters 3–6. Before continuing to those arguments, however, I must say more about the relation between property rights structures and the economy as a whole.

2

Ownership and the Structure of the Economy

> It is the law of property that controls the distribution of wealth in a society; consequently there must be the most intimate relation between that society's economic and social characteristics and the rules, practices, and institutions of its property law.
>
> J. H. Merryman

I have established that to own something is a complex phenomenon, but not so complex as to be meaningless. I now turn to the economic ramifications of ownership, in particular, the relation between liberal ownership and free economic markets. I will specify more precisely the conditions of liberal ownership, though the general idea was spelled out in the last chapter. Given what was said there, one might think it obvious, as many assume implicitly, that there is a simple and close relation between liberal ownership and competitive markets for goods. But as one begins to consider the analytical conditions of markets—perfectly competitive and otherwise—it becomes clear that this relation is actually quite complex. Indeed, it turns out that liberal ownership is neither necessary nor sufficient for competitive markets, and that they give rise to one another only when fairly robust (and contentious) assumptions are made about both the environment and individual motivations.

In a nutshell, the reason that free markets (and hence capitalism) do not necessitate or entail private liberal ownership is that the definition of markets—whether of fully competitive ideal markets or real-world versions—focuses on the behavior of traders and their motivations concerning the disposition of their goods. Liberal ownership, on the other hand, specifies what rights they have. There are any number of situations where despite having the rights to do so (under liberal ownership), people will *not* be motivated to behave in the way competitive markets demand. Conversely, there are cases where agents *will* behave in competitive ways, despite not having full ownership rights over their goods.

My purpose in this chapter is to explain these notions fairly carefully and, in doing so, to describe how property and markets relate to one another. In section I, I give the notion of private liberal ownership more detailed treatment. In section II, I define markets (both ideal and imperfect ones), and in section III, I discuss how liberal ownership and markets relate to one another. I then move to a more macroeconomic level and discuss, in section IV, capitalism and socialism and their relation to ownership structures.

It is important to explore this relation in order to pave the way for the arguments in chapters 3–6, which include discussions of various attempts to defend the liberal conception of ownership. In particular, those arguments that support liberal ownership directly will in some circumstances imply a justification of capitalist market relations as well, as a probable concomitant to liberal ownership. The connection, however, is most relevant to the indirect arguments for liberal ownership, which rely on its effects, in particular those effects for which market competition is the facilitator. The most important of such strategies is treated in chapter 6.

I. The Specification of Liberal Ownership

In the last chapter the notion of ownership was discussed, but the specification of the idea of liberal ownership was not very exact.[1] What I said there was that liberal ownership is the view that owners have complete dominion over their goods, or absolute use, possession, transfer, and income rights over their property. But the term "absolute" has many connotations: a set of rights can be absolute in scope or absolute in weight, for example. A right is absolute in weight when no other considerations can be brought to bear on the situation that will override the right. This is the strict deontological sense of "right." This is not the sense of "absolute" in liberal ownership, however. For it is possible to claim that liberal ownership contains the full package of use, possession (and so on) rights but that this package of rights has only *prima facie* force. Such a view of these rights implies that ownership may be overridden, though only by weightier moral concerns. The other sense of "absolute," that of being "limitless," also must be avoided or qualified when referring to liberal ownership, for ownership cannot plausibly imply the freedom to do whatever one wishes with one's property. The absolute rights of property will be circumscribed by other aspects of the criminal law. I will return to this point shortly.

Recall the full list of incidents named in chapter 1 that come under the label of ownership: rights to possess, use, alienate, consume, modify, destroy, manage, transfer, and gain income from property. We can simplify the idea of liberal ownership by combining the first seven elements into "use," understood broadly. (In chapter 7, I disaggregate this concept again and introduce the idea of "control" in relation to these incidents.) This implies that liberal ownership amounts to the rights to use, transfer, and gain income without interference from the state.

This account, however, leaves an ambiguity, since the state "interferes" with someone's actions in every case where it enforces rights. So we must understand "interference" in a narrower sense. Clearly, the motivating idea of liberal ownership is that the state does not limit or reshape the rights mentioned for the purposes of *directing the distribution of goods*. This idea leaves room for the imposition of the state's authority to limit the use and transfer of property for other purposes, such as the prevention of harm to others.

The term "private" in private liberal ownership enters when we assume that the owners of goods in the society are, or tend generally to be, individuals or individual-like entities. This does not imply anything about the *motives* of such owners, which can, for example, range from wanting to trade goods competitively to wanting simply to pool them with their compatriots (though of course pooling may involve a change in the ownership structure). So when individuals (I will drop the qualifying phrase "individual-like entities") hold full rights to use, transfer, and gain income from holdings as the general pattern of ownership in a society, and these rights are not interfered with by the state for distributive purposes, then we can say that private liberal ownership holds for that society.

It is tempting to infer from this definition that a distinguishing characteristic of liberal structures is that their enforcement is distribution insensitive, something which can be contrasted with a distribution-sensitive ownership structure of, say, an egalitarian sort. After all, as I just defined it, liberal ownership is inconsistent with state interference with ownership for the purposes of directing the pattern of holdings in the economy. The holdings that result from the use and trades of goods, on this view, are a result of the preferences of the agents, not the regulating institutions (the state). This is what Robert Nozick has in mind in his distinction between patterned principles of distributive justice and non-patterned principles. A patterned distribution is defined as any guided by a principle which "specifies that a distribution is to vary along with some natural dimension, weighted sum of natural dimensions, or lexicographic ordering of natural dimensions."[2] For Nozick, virtually any distribution governed by other than historical principles—principles that refer to the prior holdings of agents and their rights over them—will be patterned.

Unfortunately, however, things are not so simple. Liberal ownership rights will be distribution insensitive only if the people to whom they are granted are not motivated by those very distributive considerations. If we gather up the world's most devoted socialists and give each of them liberal ownership rights over goods, they might immediately proceed to combine and trade goods so as to achieve a particular distribution (an equal and non-exploitive one presumably). So liberal ownership is distribution insensitive only in the sense that the *state* enforces no distributive pattern.

The idea that we can distinguish patterned from historical distributive principles presupposes that we can also distinguish between "natural dimensions" and historical factors. What Nozick has in mind here, I think, is that an entitlement theory is historical if the distribution of goods at any one time depends only on the (private) preferences of the owners of goods (combined and negotiated) and the initial allocation of resources, talents, and technology. If other factors—like the relative needs of members of the society or their moral merit—were to help determine the distribution (aided by state action), then the distribution would be patterned.

The notion of private preferences here bears some emphasis. The assumption is that social preferences, which range over the distribution as a whole, are not to be considered. Now this assumption faces the obvious problem of specifying the *difference* between private and social preferences (someone might, for example, privately prefer just that bundle of goods which her favorite social preference would grant her). But such a specification is necessary to say that liberal ownership is distribution insensitive. So keeping in mind the potentially vague distinction between private and social preferences, we will warily accept the assumption of distribution insensitivity as a characteristic of liberal entitlements.

One of the most important aspects of liberal ownership is the right to the income from all transfers of goods. When trades are made, income from those trades (whether full or partial transfers) may flow to the parties to the transfer, to the state, or to some other party. When such trades are considered in the abstract, the income referred to *is* the goods exchanged (and perhaps the increase in welfare each person receives). (Indeed, in chapter 1, I simply defined the right to the income as the right to the material returns from trades.) But as we will see, under conditions of imperfect competition, the size of those traded bundles is a function of the relative scarcity of various factors—similar goods, other traders, information, or technology. In these cases, the income includes any goods over and above what one would have traded one's goods for under more perfectly competitive conditions.

Therefore, when liberal ownership is fully enforced, there is no taxation of any income that might emerge from economic interactions, from rents to interest to simple profits. So the right in question is not merely the right to trade without distribution-sensitive interference from the state, but also the right to retain income from those transfers. As we will see, this element of liberal ownership is not essentially necessary for free markets unless other assumptions concerning human motivations are made.

One sticky issue sidestepped here concerns the kinds of interference with individual use of property that amount to a denial of liberal ownership (when sanctioned by the state). For on the one hand, people do not have unqualified rights to do with their property what they will (they perhaps may own the gun but they cannot shoot me with it). On the other hand, it is very difficult to specify in advance how one person's use of his or her property may affect others in ways that the state would want to prohibit. But in general, liberal ownership implies as wide a range as possible of unobstructed use and trading rights.[3]

So although I consider any significant and systematic interference in an individual's ability to possess, use, and trade her property inconsistent with liberal ownership, I focus particularly on those interferences that are motivated by economic and distributive goals. The reason for this focus is that the principal aspect of liberal ownership that concerns us here is the way in which such property rights are structured without reference to the distribution of goods generally in the society. So the working definition of liberal ownership is this: private liberal ownership obtains when individuals are granted rights to possess, use, manage, alienate, consume, destroy, transfer, and gain income from holdings without interference, in particular interference initiated for the sake of advancing a distributive pattern.

It must be the case, also, that liberal ownership is the *general* pattern in the society. A structure that selectively or locally enforces this full list of rights cannot be considered a liberal ownership regime. And in adopting this definition, we must be mindful of the simplifications and assumptions that lie behind it, in particular that the distribution insensitivity of this property structure means that only so-called private preferences are assumed to determine the distributive pattern.

II. The Conditions of a Market

A market is any system of social interaction that allows for the exchange of goods. The opposite extreme of a market economy is a command economy, where production and pricing decisions are made by a central entity, like the state. Markets are such that individuals who are trading within the constraints they face decide what rates to accept in the trading of goods.

An "ideal" or "free" or "perfect" market (qualifiers which I will use more or less interchangeably) is a model created artificially by economists. It can be given a canonical specification with the following conditions:

1. Full information. All participants can possess costlessly all relevant information about all available goods, technology, prices, and costs.
2. No transaction costs. All exchanges of goods or information are costless, and all rights and contracts are costlessly enforced.
3. Full rationality. All participants are rational, that is, they always act to maximize their own utility.
4. No monopolies. All participants act independently. No individual or group of individuals can unilaterally affect the prices of goods sold by others. (Everyone is a "price taker.")
5. No externalities. All consumption and exchange affects only the consumer herself or the exchange partners themselves. Non-participants in exchanges are neither positively nor negatively affected.

From these conditions the two basic theorems of welfare economics can be derived: (1) under these conditions, trade will reach an efficient equilibrium; and (2) any equilibrium imaginable could be reached from some initial starting point (allocation of goods and preference set).[4]

Efficiency is an important concept in these contexts and is defined by the notions of Pareto Superiority and Pareto Optimality. An allocation, A, is Pareto Superior to some other allocation, B, when at least one person prefers (her bundle of goods in) A over (hers in) B and no one prefers (her bundle in) B over (hers in) A.[5] Roughly speaking, this means that at least one person is better off in A than in B and no one is worse off. An allocation is Pareto Optimal when there are no allocations that are Pareto Superior to it. Two allocations will be Pareto Non-Comparable when neither is Pareto Superior to the other. This occurs in that wide range of cases where moving from one allocation to another makes at least one person worse off (despite perhaps benefiting some others). Since the use of Pareto measures of efficiency is invoked in order to avoid the problem of comparing utility levels of different people (how *much* better or worse off someone is than someone else), the tests are very narrow in scope. This issue will receive more treatment in chapter 6.

Generally, the theorems of welfare economics have shown that the market, as specified, will allow trades which all manifest discrete Pareto Superior moves: since all trades are voluntary and traders act rationally to better themselves, no one can be made worse off by a binary trade. More important, an equilibrium point will be reached where no pair of individuals want to trade further, and this point is Pareto Optimal.

The so-called indirect theorem of welfare economics is of particular interest here. It states that *any* Pareto Optimal allocation can be reached via market interactions if the proper initial allocation of goods exists and people have the proper preferences (and there are no economies of scale). For example, if from an extra-economic (ethical) point of view it is determined that an equal allocation of goods would be better, such an allocation could be achieved by gathering the preference information about all participants and allocating resources in order that, when the participants express those preferences in their trading behavior, an equal allocation results.

But such a scenario could only be found in the ideal world of economists' modeling. It would be virtually impossible, for example, to gather the information (about preferences, say) necessary to effect an initial allocation in the hope that a particular Pareto Optimal final distribution would result.[6] Moreover, perfectly competitive markets are nowhere to be found. Imperfect markets, of course, are the norm in the real world, and these are modes of exchange where one or more of the conditions listed above are *not* met.[7] And it is here that problems emerge as to the exact specification of markets: how much of a deviation from the ideal will be allowed before the mode of exchange is no longer thought of as a market at all?

Minimal conditions for a market concern the nature of prices and production decisions, in particular whether such decisions are made by the owners of the factors involved or by some other single entity.[8] In a non-market economy, these decisions are made by a central authority. But there cannot be an exact line dividing market economies from non-market ones, since often someone (the government) can do many things that *constrain* the production and pricing of goods. From the minimum wage, to restrictions on child labor, to housing subsidies, to zoning restrictions, and numerous other government interventions into the market, there are any number of ways that individual property rights are circumscribed by government action even in what is generally regarded as a market economy.

At this point, we might be tempted to say that the market determines production and price when the aggregate of individual desires over such things is the determining factor in these decisions, insofar as these decisions are backed by resources. But as we noted before, it is certainly possible that the government's centralized controls on production and price *do* mirror the population's desires in the sense that the system is approved of. This implication brings us back to the notion of private preferences, which must again be assumed to be the only ones operative in economic transactions.

More generally, there are certain other things about the preference structures of individuals that must be assumed for markets to operate. I will trade in a competitive manner only if my preference ordering (of all available goods) is not adjusted in relation to the preferences of those with whom I will be trading. For if I rearrange the substitution schedule of my goods (the sets of combinations of goods that I would be willing to substitute one for the other) according to what my trading partner wants, then I am not setting my price unilaterally. I am no longer strictly a "price taker." If I do this, we will not be able to reach an equilibrium point where markets "clear," where no one wants to make any more trades at current rates. So for competitive markets to operate, my preferences must be non-tuistic; that is, they must not depend on (be adjustable according to) the preferences of those with whom I am trading.

This does not mean that I must be selfish, that I must prefer only things that affect my own condition. Indeed, agents who are, for example, trying to increase the value of their holdings in order to give them all away to charity will be able to trade in a perfectly competitive manner (as long as their preference orderings are all consistent, complete, and continuous). What must *not* be true, however, is that they are trying to advance the welfare of the person(s) with whom they trade. This is what is meant by non-tuistic preferences.

But are these conditions enough to specify when, or the degree to which, human interaction in the non-ideal world can be characterized as a market? Let us consider an attempt by C. B. Macpherson to define a market society (either a "simple" or "possessive" market society) in terms of an "authoritative allocation" of work and reward for work and an "authoritative definition and enforcement of contracts." On Macpherson's model of a "possessive market," the following conditions must hold: (a) there is no authoritative allocation of work or rewards for work; (b) there is authoritative enforcement of contracts; (c) all individuals are rational maximizers of their own utility; (d) they have alienable rights over their labor and holdings; and (e) there are differential endowments of talents and holdings.[9]

First, it must be pointed out that this notion of a market must rely on an implicit distinction between the civil authority and the economic authority of the state. For the state is authoritative no matter what property rights structure it enforces: in all cases, the range of rights, liberties, and powers conferred by ownership (of goods or labor) is authoritatively controlled by the state. However, these points do suggest that a market is a mechanism for facilitating the trade of goods where no central authority intervenes *to direct those trades*. This brings in the familiar feature of markets referred to by the term "competition."

Competition, in its purest form, is a product of less than full information. If all participants in the market know not only all the relevant aspects of technology, goods, and available resources, but also the preferences of potential traders, then the "auction" for goods that market trades are said to resemble would occur instantaneously, and there would not be the dynamic process of buyers and producers positioning themselves that marks competition. On the other hand, *real* owners of goods or services lack such levels of knowledge, so they compete by trying to convince potential buyers that their goods or services are indeed the kind wanted and at the price best suited to the buyers' preferences. So competition is the dynamic revelation of information in the real (imperfect) world. It presupposes more than one producer and/or consumer and the non-tuistic preferences of all. This implies that buyers and sellers will seek each other out (in the absence of full information), set their prices in a way that reflects their preferences but are as attractive as possible to their counterparts, and trade until no one wants to continue. When this occurs, we have reached the competitive equilibrium point of the system.

A very important point about markets that are not perfectly competitive must be made. If certain transaction costs or information and technology shortages prevent some traders from entering a market sector, an artificial scarcity of the factor being traded exists. Were it not for those imperfections, the supply of one or the other of traded goods (we are supposing) would be increased by the absent competitors. This scarcity drives up the rate at which the unencumbered traders can exchange their goods and indeed will push the price up above what it cost the traders to produce and bring to market the good in question. The surplus income that results from such artificial factor scarcities is called "economic rent." Imperfect markets, and only imperfect ones, allow this kind of surplus to be generated in this way, for if competition were perfect, then other competitors would enter and bid the price down to (just above) the price of producing it and bringing it to market.[10]

The question to consider now is whether liberal ownership structures bear a conceptual relation to market mechanisms specified in this way. We will see that the relation is indeed not as intimate as is usually supposed.

III. Markets and Ownership Structure

The conditions that define a market must admit of degrees. To the extent that individuals are allowed to produce, trade, and set prices for goods and services without outside restriction, the market can be said to govern the production and pricing decisions of those individuals. Also, the label "market economy" need not be system-wide in its application. For a society may well allow the market to determine prices of some goods while maintaining strict controls over the trading and production of others.

But what property rights structure must individuals have for these interactions to ensue? One natural answer is that the structure must not be controlled or interfered with by the state. But this response is misleading. For the state's presence will *always* be manifested in any economic organization, because the state is always present as an enforcement mechanism for the property rights that people have over their possessions.[11] And since the structure of the rights and liberties that comprise ownership determines what exchanges take place and under what terms, then the state always, in this sense, helps to direct the distribution.[12]

Market trades in the real world are always constrained to some degree by natural factors, available technology, and in most cases, government restrictions. There is always a certain natural distribution of technology, where that includes natural resources, information, and especially resources needed to overcome natural barriers to trade. A mountain or a river may make it costly for some agents to gain access to others or to sources of goods (like mines, fish in oceans and lakes, oil, and the like). The accidents of natural placement of human beings relative to other humans and to resources place differential constraints on the workings of market transactions.

Moreover, and this is the crucial point, property structures enforced by the state must always, in part, be a response to this *de facto* distribution. Liberal ownership structures "leave the situation alone" in that they allow this natural distribution to have whatever effect it will in determining differential endowments (both initial and subsequent endowments) and hence the inequalities resulting from trade. Alternative ownership structures might try to correct for this distribution in any number of ways. The state may construct various right-of-way patterns to ensure larger access to areas or resources. It may use tax revenues (from income from trades) for redistribution to those who face greater costs. It may also restructure use and consumption rights that are sensitive to these differential costs.

A typical assumption in economic models is that rational maximizing individuals face an environment and a set of technologies that are (exogenously) given and unalterable, as are the individuals. These all combine to form the "possibility frontier" that constrains the rational maximizing decisions of the agents. But it is an open question whether the *property rights structure* recognized in the area should be considered part of the environment (and hence merely another fixed parameter within which market competition can take place), or whether that structure is endogenous (and hence part of the decision matrix of the actors in the economy). The latter possibility would imply that ownership structure is part of what is negotiated and bargained about in market interactions. But the simple assumption that liberal ownership is the norm, and that any alternative arrangement is an interference into the workings of the competitive economy, is to beg the question of how property rights should be treated in such models.

Recall that liberal ownership is defined as that set of enforced property rights to use, transfer, and retain income from trades of holdings. If these rights are protected in an economy, will free markets obtain? That depends. Free markets are trivially equivalent to liberal ownership if the "right to the income" is *defined* as the right to retain income from prices set by free market mechanisms.[13] This definition makes it appear that liberal ownership is a sufficient condition for the existence of free markets, since the provision of full income rights implies market prices. But that is to ignore the variety of other conditions that must obtain for market trades to occur in the first place.

It does seem, at first glance, that whenever there is liberal ownership and the owners are rational and the economy is in disequilibrium, there will be incentives to trade goods in a way that follows the dictates of market mechanisms. Since rational agents will want to increase their store of goods by trading with others for their store, and liberal ownership gives them the right to do so, then it appears that market interaction must ensue. However, since liberal ownership does not *itself* indicate anything concerning the surrounding environment, the distribution of technology or information, or the preferences and motivations of the actors, this property structure itself does not guarantee that market interactions will occur. Only if other conditions are assumed to obtain—conditions stipulated in the definitions of perfect markets (such as zero or low transaction costs)—will interactions between owners manifest competitive markets and be efficient. There is nothing about private ownership structures themselves that would prevent one person (or one group), for example, from owning all of a particular resource and hence setting its price unilaterally (that is, there might be a stable monopoly present). So for liberal ownership to give rise to markets, things such as monopolies, monopsonies, and cartels would have to be absent or be unstable in the area.

Also, for liberal ownership to imply markets, agents in the area must face relatively low transaction costs. Private owners of goods may well be such that they would trade if they could find each other, but the costs of doing so are prohibitively high. Imagine that two willing traders existed but were separated by a huge mountain range and lacked the resources to cross it. Then despite all the rights and motivations in the world to do so, no market interactions would ensue there.

But these other conditions are, of course, specified in the conditions of markets themselves, so it is no great revelation that liberal ownership alone is not sufficient for market interaction. More interestingly, however, is that even if liberal ownership holds in an area *and* the other conditions of markets obtain, competitive trading will still not occur unless, to put it simply, people *want* to trade.[14] I discussed above the necessity of non-tuistic and private preferences on the part of individuals in the market, and that is relevant here also. For giving individuals the right to retain income from trades will not ensure that they will trade competitively (even if the surrounding environment gives them the opportunity) unless they are motivated specifically to maximize their income. If motives such as camaraderie or communal solidarity or simply a penchant for sharing (none of which is in a straightforward sense irrational) were included in the desire sets of the agents, liberal ownership would not ensure markets.

Perhaps the more interesting question, however, is whether liberal ownership is in fact *necessary* for market competition. After all, condition 4 of the definition of a competitive market implies that no one has dictatorial control over the pricing of goods. This condition would rule out the possibility of the state's limiting the rights bundles of owners (in effect, fixing prices).

This observation seems to indicate that liberal ownership is one of the necessary conditions of competitive markets. The belief that such an ownership structure is necessary rests on the thinking that only when owners have unrestricted rights to all income from sales of goods (and they are self-interested) are the incentives in place for them to produce in accordance with market forces. Owners will, under certain conditions, be motivated to possess or produce goods that will fetch the highest price in a trade, and it seems that these rights are necessary for such trades.

But the presence of perfectly competitive pricing does not imply that those trading have full rights over their goods, for some kinds of taxation, restrictions on use or possession, or other deviation from liberal structures will not prevent a perfectly competitive market from emerging. In particular, perfect competition does not presuppose liberal ownership whenever the agents in the market are motivated to trade by factors *other than the income flows from their assets*. An example might be trustees who invest and trade goods owned by others. Consider also a case where the Leviathan dictator of the society simply *commands* people to trade competitively and backs the command with effective threats. Or imagine that people get *moral satisfaction* from engaging in market clearing transactions,[15] or any number of other possibilities. All of these will be cases where markets emerge without the services of liberal ownership.

In other words, people could rank all available goods and trade at the margin in accordance with these rankings, even if the resulting holdings were taxed or partially confiscated. (The rankings would be hypothetical in such a case.) When prices are set by a currency, this scenario is not so difficult to imagine, since one simply sets prices as high as possible whether or not one will keep the income from those trades. In other cases, the imagined trades are like proxy bargains where a person trades according to how much she thinks the items are worth (to her or to others), even if she will not enjoy the whole of those very goods.

Another major reason that private property structures are not equivalent to market interactions is that markets can be set up where the traders of goods are other than individuals.[16] As the framework for ownership (Figure 1.1) makes clear, the distinction between private and collective ownership has to do with the kinds of entities in whom the modalities that comprise ownership are vested. These can be individuals, individual-like entities such as corporations, or collectives. And since collectives can compete among themselves and trade goods for prices set by that competition, the existence of market interactions does not entail private property structures. The example of the economy of what once was Yugoslavia comes to mind, where worker-owned factories competed among themselves.

A point to which we keep returning is that for liberal ownership to be necessary (and indeed sufficient) for market mechanisms, certain assumptions need to be made concerning the motivational structure of agents. Only if the prime motivating factor of agents is the maximization of their income will having the right to income from trades be necessary for them to trade competitively. This point brings into sharp relief the relation between traditional (neoclassical) economic models and the theory of rational choice. Therefore, it is necessary to take a brief side trip onto that terrain, since the motivations of individuals are the crucial contingency that determines the relation between ownership structure and markets.

For liberal ownership to be necessary for competitive markets, it must be the case that individuals are motivated to trade only by the opportunities specified by that property structure. This is usually assumed to be the case, since economic theory utilizes a model of rationality that seems to make such motives inevitable. That is, the models assume that individuals are rationally self-interested maximizers of their own utility, and income functions directly to achieve this maximization. Therefore, everyone will set prices for her goods—will have substitution schedules—that reflect her preference ordering for goods and income (and only for goods and income). So trades occur only on terms that are strategically set (that is, set without cooperative negotiation that affects the preferences of the traders). In turn, prices reflect the maximum possible return for each actor.

This assumption amounts to the claim that agents must be rationally self-interested maximizers of their own income. I will examine the components of this postulate in turn. To say that a person must be self-interested is ambiguous in a number of ways. It could mean that a person's welfare is a function of only her experience or consumption, or that a person *aims* only at her own welfare, or that she aims only at her own *goals.*[17] In all cases, moreover, it is ambiguous whether the person's preferences concern the welfare of other people or of things other than the person's own economic interests. Someone may most prefer to benefit another person, as in gift giving (even if a predictable side effect is self-satisfaction), or she may benefit from the mere act of choice, or in any number of ways that would stretch the concept of narrow self-interested behavior.

What is relevant here is specifying the subset of these possibilities that are necessary for the economic behavior in question. For a person to set prices in a way that reflects a market structure, she must order her preferences (over tradable goods or services) independently of her trading partner's preferences and independently of any factor that cannot be evaluated in economic terms (such as the trade setting). This last point will rule out wanting to trade just for the fun of it, or as a means of getting to know people, or to test one's talents at trading, or because one was asked or commanded to do so, or any number of other possibilities. The after-trade distribution must reflect an increase in utility solely on the basis of the bundles traded and their value to the agent.

The third component of the economic model of rationality is that only economic value is considered by a rational, competitive actor in the market. Such a person wants only to maximize her income and will not trade optimally if she cannot. This is a substantive and contingent assumption about agent motivation that goes beyond the purely formal notion of rationality as choosing the best means to given ends. (An ascetic may, for example, be rational and even engage in trades but would not be motivated by economic gains or by the prospect of increasing holdings.) But such a substantive claim is necessary for the characteristics of market interaction to follow from the assumptions of individual rationality. Additionally, these components of rationally self-interested choice must all be assumed in order for liberal ownership to be necessary for markets. As we will see in chapter 6, there is much reason to believe that many things *other* than rational economic self-interest might be effective in motivating people to trade their goods, in which case the rights delineated by liberal ownership will not be necessary for market mechanisms in the allocation of goods.

If the rationally self-interested economic maximizer model of behavior is *assumed* in models of economic organization (as it usually is), it will look as if liberal ownership is a conceptual necessity for efficient competitive markets. But as should be clear from these brief observations about rationality, whether people will be moved to act only in the way that narrow rationality says they will is a highly contingent (and, I think, highly implausible) general proposition. So despite the seemingly necessary connection buried in the usual assumptions, liberal ownership is in fact only contingently connected to the operation of competitive markets.[18]

Also, as I said earlier, that property structure is only contingently *sufficient* for markets as well, and this connection holds when similar motivational and environmental assumptions are made. Only if we already assume that people want to trade competitively and that the other characteristics of market operation hold (low transaction costs, high information, etc.), will the granting of full ownership rights entail market behavior.

In fact, protecting the liberal ownership rights of owners when certain distributive conditions hold—for instance, when a stable monopoly or cartel operates—actually *conflicts* with the workings of a market. And the decentralized operations of the price-setting mechanisms of markets can be restored (in many cases) only if the liberal ownership of present holders of goods is *curtailed*. Illustrative of this conflict are cases of anti-trust legislation and any number of other government limitations of property rights instituted for the sake of allegedly freeing up the wheels of trade. In order to protect the competitiveness of the market, the state often restricts the ownership rights of owners of goods.

This entire discussion suggests an important point, namely, that there is a crucial difference between what individuals have a *right* to do and what they have an *incentive* to do. Recall that the rationality that is assumed for economic agents merely directs agents to maximize their utility function. This in no way entails that the person will maximize productivity and profit. That empirical assumption must be added to the model for this conclusion to follow. But such an assumption is questionable, for people have many goals and purposes, including ideological, religious, and patriotic goals, which they might pursue in addition to their economic interests. Arguments that lunch counters in the South, for example, would have been more profitable if opened to all races would have had no weight with the racist owners of some of those establishments who supported the restrictions for their own social reasons. We will see below how this observation is important in "invisible hand" arguments, which rely on the contingent connection between liberal ownership and free markets.

The relevance of these points reemerge in the chapters to follow, especially in chapter 6, where utilitarian arguments for liberal ownership are discussed. At that point I explicate more fully the claims I have made about the plausibility of assumptions about human motivation and preferences that underlie the connection between liberal ownership and markets.

IV. Property, Capitalism, and Socialism

In an idealized sense, "capitalism" can be defined straightforwardly: it is a regime of private ownership of the means of production. More generally, it is an economic system in which the productive resources available in the society are owned by individuals (or individual-like entities) and used to maximize the profit of those owners; and labor (or labor power) is owned by individual laborers. In this way, capitalism can be equated with a private property economy. We have seen, however, that the latter idea is subject to variations that make this definition complex. If liberal ownership were the sense of private property referred to here, this idealized definition would have few if any referents in the real world. For as we noted in the last chapter, seldom, if ever, has a regime of liberal ownership been put fully into place.

For the economy to be called capitalist, it is at least necessary that the rights to transfer and gain income from holdings (to some degree) are included in the structure of ownership that individuals have over productive goods. But as is the case with market economies, whether an economic arrangement is capitalist is a matter of degree.

Traditionally, theorists have connected the idea of capitalist economic relations with a class-structured society of wage laborers and capitalists. The brief definition of capitalism I just gave will imply such class divisions whenever certain minimal distributive conditions are met: the distribution of productive resources is unequal and there is a class of individuals who own no (non-personal) productive goods. So if there are those in the area who own productive resources and many more individuals who do not, the latter will have an incentive to provide services (labor) to those owners in exchange for remuneration. These conditions are what connect the property structure of capitalism (private ownership) with a system of wage labor and class division.

Let us return to the relation between liberal ownership and capitalism. It will be the case that if all resources (including labor) are owned in the liberal sense by individuals who are motivated to pursue their own economic self-interest in a rational manner, then capitalism obtains. Since the means of production are a subset of the total resources in an economy, our definition of capitalism implies the traditional Marxist view that capitalism is the private ownership of the means of production.

In the framework for ownership set out in the last chapter, I was quite vague about the kinds of things that might be put into the D cell, the kinds of things that are owned or are ownable. There are two kinds of things that are often distinguished in the context of defining capitalism. These are capital goods, which are any factors in a production process specified by their functional role in production, and non-capital goods, which is everything else. The ownership of capital, which is equivalent to ownership of the means of production (under most definitions),[19] issues in the use of the resource in the production process in order to gain income for the owner from the produced asset. Since by definition the major function of capital is production and profit, use fades into both transfer and income rights in the case of capital assets.

As I said, however, liberal ownership regimes have been few and far between in economic history. Yet we seem to know a capitalist economy when we see one. A capitalist economy seems to be compatible with a variety of restrictions on owners' use and transfer of their goods: the Occupational Safety and Health Administration restricts the techniques of production and the use of labor; there are zoning laws prohibiting many uses of property in certain areas; there are any number of income, sales, and user taxes, all of which restructure the ownership rights that people have over their goods. The list of such restrictions is endless, and this in a country (the United States) that is thought to be capitalist.

There also seems to be room, in economies otherwise considered to be capitalist, for many redistributive or welfare measures that involve the restructuring of private ownership (in a way that deviates from liberal ownership). In a welfare state, taxation limits the income rights of individuals, and other fees and charges serve to fund a general assistance pool that is used to guarantee an economic minimum (or to fund particular services) for the poor. I discuss such arrangements in chapter 9. What is relevant to our purposes here is that property rights under such systems deviate from liberal ownership. Goods are owned by individuals, but the ownership structures involved include limitations on full income rights (as well as, possibly, use restrictions) that constitute a revenue-gathering tax policy.

Socialism is also difficult to characterize since it admits of so many variations (and is in such flux). The traditional account of socialism is that it is the public ownership of the means of production. But as we saw with private ownership, the range of possible construals of "public ownership" is quite wide. There are innumerable ways that the public can stand in the A cell of figure 1.1—that is, be the entity in which the modalities of ownership vest. There can be *control* of the goods in question by the public, where the entire population can or does make decisions about use, management, and the like. However, there can also be public income rights, in that revenue from the property flows into the general budget of the state. The first of these is very seldom manifested (indeed for most goods and most populations it is impossible), for management decisions concerning publicly owned assets are usually made by some formally designated subset of the public, such as a city council. For complete occurrent control of an asset by the full public to manifest itself, a host of coordination and collective action problems would have to be overcome. Still, insofar as democratically elected bodies can be said to express the control rights of the public, the public controls the goods through such bodies.[20]

Public income rights are somewhat different, in that rent, taxes, tolls, and other fees collected from the use of some resource can be directed into the public coffers. Similarly sales of government holdings can return to the state, and in this way the public commands rights to the income from property. Public ownership in this sense, it must be pointed out, is also a matter of degree, in that even in private economies some income flows are inevitably returned to the state through taxation of income and assets, assets which are not at all considered public property. Moreover, the structure of the modern public corporation in capitalist societies gives a subset of the general population some claim to the income flows from its productive enterprises.

But even in socialist economies, complete public control of goods is eschewed. In the former Soviet Union, for example, individual ownership of goods possessed for private consumption was constitutionally recognized. What was illegal was the ownership of "private" property, by which was meant capital goods owned for the purposes of profit. In other words, use rights were held by individuals, but income rights (from productive resources, or capital) were held by the state. Under socialism, I should add, the primary goal of distributions is, ostensibly, to preserve basic equality and prevent exploitation of one citizen by another.

So we see again, and this is not surprising, that the difference between capitalism and socialism is not a difference in kind (private versus public ownership schemes), but a difference in degree. The degree to which the individual ownership of goods, especially productive goods (capital), is structured by the state for some distributive purpose is the degree to which that economy deviates from capitalism. And to the extent to which the structuring of this ownership serves the purpose of ensuring public control of the distribution of goods, in particular the equal distribution of resources, power, and well-being, to that degree the economy is socialist.

This approach to capitalism and socialism may suggest, however, that a difference in *kind* between these two extremes can be constructed out of the continuum just described. In one case (socialism) there is a direct distributive policy that guides the structuring of ownership, while in capitalist economies, the shape of ownership is not fashioned, in a systematic way, for some distributive purpose. So capitalist property rights are those where the *de facto* distribution of resources, information, technology, and talents, and the private, non-tuistic preferences of individuals, are allowed to determine the resulting distribution of goods through (market) trades. This is not to say that capitalist states have *no* distributive policy, for when the *de facto* placement of environmental factors (resources, information, etc.) is known, and their effect on the resulting (unequal) distribution can be determined, the capitalist ownership regime will be structured so as to let this process ensue. So while we still may want to call market capitalism a distribution-insensitive economic system, it can be claimed that in a negative manner (by not correcting for the unequal distribution of environmental factors) capitalist regimes have a kind of distributive policy nonetheless.

So socialism is a system that structures use and income rights for the central purpose of equalizing the distribution of goods and power in the society. Such a system certainly involves deviations from private liberal ownership. Nevertheless, as we saw in the preceding sections, this in no way rules out the possibility of markets, since liberal ownership is not necessary, in all circumstances, for competitive markets. This account leaves conceptual space for the idea of market socialism. If it is determined, for example, that prices for goods set by competitive markets are a more effective mechanism for the equalization of the goods and well-being of citizens, then such retail markets can be instituted under the description "socialist." All these points are reprised in chapter 9 when I discuss an egalitarian theory of ownership that is in general conformity with some forms of democratic, market socialism.

The general point of this section is that although liberal ownership is the most common paradigm of capitalist economies, in the real world capitalism cannot simply be equated with a private property economy. For even in so-called capitalist economies, ownership is restricted in countless ways. The difference between capitalism and socialism, then, is the extent of these restrictions and, more important, their purposes. In capitalism, there is no systematic structuring of ownership for the purpose of directing the overall distribution of goods, while under socialism there is such a structuring for the general purpose of equalizing power and resources. This account preserves the characteristic of liberal ownership being distribution insensitive. This is so even if there exist tax schemes that are meant to supply some in the society with basic needs. So since liberal ownership is diametrically opposed to egalitarian distributive structures, if liberal ownership turns out to be recommended by unassailable moral argument, then unassailable moral argument *against* economic egalitarianism has thereby been provided.

V. Strategies of Justification

The complications of much of the foregoing will, perforce, be glossed over in many of the discussions to follow. In the next four chapters I consider the possible justifications of private liberal ownership. It will be relevant to point out occasionally the conclusion I have just reached, that liberal ownership and competitive markets do not entail or necessitate each other. The contingencies that must obtain for these to be connected may not hold. However, when nothing about such contingencies is mentioned, the connection can be assumed. This assumption implies that in most cases, arguing for liberal ownership will involve trying to justify the capitalist market relations that come with it.

So far, I have tried to show how concepts have a certain structure, how mechanisms are related, and how historical developments shed light on these things. However, my major focus in this work will not be conceptual or historical analysis, but rather normative argument. In the end, I provide a framework for egalitarian property structures. As part of those arguments, I also argue *against* the traditional understanding of liberal ownership which is the structural basis of market capitalism. We must begin that process now.

The strategies of argument that I want to keep distinct are what I am calling direct arguments and indirect ones. A direct argument for liberal ownership is one where certain basic moral considerations are said to entail or generally necessitate liberal ownership (and this may include the complex array of economic details of a liberal ownership regime). An indirect strategy justifies liberal ownership because it always or often *brings about* some desired end (such as greater productivity or greater liberty). This distinction may sound a bit like the division between consequentialist and non-consequentialist moral arguments, but that need not be the case. For the kinds of direct arguments I will appeal to (natural rights, the right to liberty, moral desert) rest on moral considerations that could, in the end, be justified on consequentialist grounds (though I admit that traditionally they are not). The difference lies in the role that liberal ownership plays in the overall argumentative strategy.

I have said a great deal about what liberal ownership entails and is connected with. The most important implication is that liberal ownership is insensitive to, and indeed will inevitably produce, inequalities in wealth in the society. Recall that liberal ownership is (weakly) distribution insensitive. So since I am concerned to defend economic egalitarianism, I must reject in the end any defense of liberal ownership and free market capitalism.

A number of arguments are mounted for the traditional idea of liberal ownership. The arguments to be considered are based on natural rights (to one's body and labor), liberty, moral desert, and utility. The first three are, for the most part, direct. Their claim is that individuals should have liberal ownership over their goods, and this conclusion is independent of the value of other goals worth pursuing that such ownership may bring about. Indirect arguments, the most famous of which are the utilitarian arguments considered in chapter 6, use as a premise the proposition that liberal ownership is necessary for the advancement of some separate moral goal and is thereby justified. Although some of these arguments rely on claims of moral principle that I will not abandon (I consider them in the positive view I advance later), I conclude that all these attempts to justify liberal ownership are flawed.

II

ATTEMPTS TO JUSTIFY LIBERAL OWNERSHIP

3

Can Liberal Ownership Be Justified by Natural Rights?

> I cant repudiate it. It was never mine to repudiate. It was never Father's and Uncle Buddy's to bequeath me to repudiate because it was never Grandfather's to bequeath them to bequeath me to repudiate because it was never old Ikkemotubbe's to sell to Grandfather for bequeathment and repudiation. Because it was never Ikkemotubbe's fathers' fathers' to bequeath Ikkemotubbe to sell to Grandfather or any man because on the instant when Ikkemotubbe discovered, realised, that he could sell it for money, on that instant it ceased ever to have been his forever, father to father to father, and the man who bought it bought nothing.
>
> William Faulkner,
> *Go Down, Moses*

In the next several chapters I will be examining arguments for the ownership of property that have been much commented upon, especially in recent decades, and some may question whether another treatment of them will be fruitful. But first of all, I hope that the manner in which I examine these arguments will reorient the questions being asked, from the traditional question of what criterion should be used to distribute resources in a just society to the question of what property rights structures should be recognized in a just society. Traditional treatments of the proper grounding of the right to property consider that ownership is basically a simple idea (despite the fact that commentators almost always begin their discussion of these arguments with an analysis of the various components of ownership) and that ownership cannot be disaggregated to any extent into its component parts. I, on the other hand, will keep squarely in mind the complex nature of ownership. In particular, I ask whether the specific understanding of ownership I have labelled "liberal ownership" can be justified by these familiar arguments. I conclude that it cannot, and this conclusion is not exactly equivalent to the claim made by others that private property cannot be justified when that notion is considered as a simple and monolithic idea. It is the claim that *particular* aspects of private property (liberal ownership) cannot be justified by these traditional arguments that is of special interest here. Indeed, I put these negative arguments to a different use, namely, as a partial motivation for the new model of ownership that I present in part III. Moreover, even if these arguments have been much discussed of late, I believe that new insights might be gained by another treatment.

The first of these traditional arguments is the argument based on natural rights.

* * *

It is a commanding moral intuition—some would say an undeniable one—that there are certain things that it is wrong for others to do to me, such as torture, kill, or abuse me, which are wrong completely independently of the existence and nature of governments. This intuition, stated here in its barest and least sophisticated form, finds its articulation in the idea of natural or human rights. These rights are traditionally thought to be expressed by the rights I have over myself—my self-ownership—and grounded in the dignity and independence that self-ownership guarantees. Moreover, the intuition also states that my self-ownership is not founded upon the contingent consequences of respecting these rights. In particular, it seems not to matter to the status of these rights that others around me have certain goods or enjoy minimum levels of welfare.

Now if the rights that owners have over their property could be shown to have *this* kind of status, or if they can be derived from rights of this sort, then that would provide a powerful justification for them indeed. While I do not intend to endorse any of the intuitions that form the basis of natural rights,[1] I do want to examine the attempt to treat the rights of ownership as having this status, or as deriving their status from such basic rights. I hope to show in what follows that the traditional ways of trying to establish that sort of claim all fail. Even if we might regard the rights one has over one's body and one's labor as having the status of natural rights, the typical arguments that attempt to extend that status to the ownership of material things are all found wanting.

What I am particularly concerned to show here, though, is that natural rights arguments are insufficient to justify *liberal* ownership, ownership structures that include rights to use, possess, and (especially) gain income from property. I point out how glossing over the complexity of ownership structures has given these arguments more initial plausibility than they merit. In particular, I show that what is at issue in such arguments is whether owners can secure full rights to transfer, rent (and so on) their belongings and to claim the income from so doing without external interference, and whether such rights have the status of natural rights.

What will also emerge is that attempts to ground property ownership in natural rights seem to fall into two categories, which turn on differing views about the nature and value of labor. For one kind of argument, associated with Locke, the central idea is that the act of laboring has such unique and special status that performing labor that involves other objects vests in those objects a similarly unique status, of which ownership is the proper expression. In the other sort of strategy—which Robert Nozick relies on in his work—the nature of labor itself is not as important as the surrounding distribution of goods that imposes a constraint on the acquisitive activities of agents; natural rights to property vest, in this approach, whenever those constraints are not violated, irrespective of the intrinsic character of the laboring process utilized in making the acquisitions.

There are at least two senses of "natural rights" that ought to be explicitly distinguished. A traditional sense of a natural right is one such as the following:

> (SON) A right is a natural right if and only if persons would have this right in a state of nature, prior to, and independently of, the establishment of any civil or political institution.

This is the sense of natural right that Locke and the rest of the natural law tradition of political philosophy made famous. One major problem with this conception, however, is that it is not clear what, exactly, things would be *like* in the state of nature, a question which gives rise to the differing conceptions of that state in, for example, Hobbes, Locke, and Rousseau.[2]

But there is a different sense of "natural right" that has been influential, at least since H.L.A. Hart's discussion of the matter.[3] He puts it this way: "This right is one which all men have if they are capable of choice; they have it *qua* men and not only if they are members of some society or stand in some special relation to each other." He adds to this a second reason for calling some supposed right a natural right: (S) "A right is natural if it is not created or conferred by men's voluntary action," that is, it is not a right derived from positive law or social institutions.[4] As Hillel Steiner puts it, natural rights are non-contractual and non-conventional.[5]

Note that Hart's phrase that the right cannot be "created or conferred by men's voluntary action" seems to limit, by definition, the realm of natural rights to liberty or freedom, *ex ante*. Steiner also invites this implication in the inference that if a right is a natural right it "cannot accrue to [its] possessor by virtue of some action that he or another has previously performed."[6] This implication will be relevant in the arguments to follow, for it shows the line of demarcation between rights that everyone has no matter what the conventions of his or her society and rights that have been created by positive institutions and actions taken by individuals.

So with all this we can adopt the following definition:

> (R) A right is a natural right if its possession is justified only with reference to a certain set of natural attributes of persons, that is, without reference to social conventions, legal institutions or other institutional relationships within or among groups of persons.[7]

The question then is, could there be property rights in the sense of liberal ownership that meet the conditions in (R)? Can non-institutional, non-conventional property rights that amount to liberal ownership be derived and justified?

It is presumed for the purposes of this chapter that natural rights are not nonsense (in particular the natural right to one's body and labor), though just what kind of sense they make is left open. I discuss Locke's view, but I argue that, contrary to the understanding of many, Locke did not succeed in justifying liberal ownership as a set of natural rights (section I).[8] This exegetical point becomes relevant as I consider other arguments in the Lockean spirit that *do* attempt to justify liberal property rights by virtue of natural rights (sections II–III). I then step back and divide the strategies of natural rights argument for property in the ways just described, and show why all of them are hopeless in their attempts to justify liberal ownership structures (sections IV–VI).

I. Locke

In this section I explicate the argument in the well-known section of Locke's *Second Treatise of Government* called "Of Property,"[9] in order to show that, contrary to traditional understandings of Locke,[10] he does not justify liberal ownership of property based on natural rights. The familiar problem with which Locke begins his argument consists of a conflict between two precepts, both of which he claims are grounded in natural law as well as Scripture. These are that (a) "God . . . hath given to men the world in common" (26); that is, each person in the state of nature has a common right to all things; and (b) persons can "come to have a property in [things]" (25)—in principle, people could have individual, exclusive, property rights in things. The question that Locke tries to answer is, how can a person gain a property right in natural objects without the consent of others when God gave all the fruits of the earth to humanity to enjoy in common?[11]

After pointing out that in a state of nature private appropriation of some sort is necessary to make natural resources "of any use or at all beneficial to any particular man" (26), Locke states his famous argument: (a) "every man has a property in his own person" (27); and thereby (b) has also a property right in "the labor of his body and the work of his hands" (27); so (c) if he removes some object out of its natural state by mixing his labor with it, and (d) there is "enough and as good left in common for others" (27); and (e) the object or objects do not exceed "[a]s much as anyone can make use of . . . before it spoils" (31); then (f) the object has "something annexed to it that excludes the common right of other men" (27). That is, a person has thereby "fixed [a] property in them" [the objects] (28).

So Locke argues from the claim that every person owns (has a property in) her or his labor to the establishment of a property right in the unowned thing with which that labor is mixed, subject to the two provisos expressed by (d) and (e). But notice, all that has been established by the quoted argument is that something has been "annexed" to the thing "that *excludes the common right of other men.*" I take that to mean that the "property in" the object amounts to rights against expropriation and, therefore, rights to use and possess (and security in the possession of) the object. But this kind of ownership is not what I have been calling liberal ownership, which would include the right to accumulate and gain income from property (among other things). This point is developed later.

The unique character of Locke's argument, as many have noticed, is the emphasis on labor in the grounding of a title. One way to see this point is to understand Locke as needing to show that there is a method of establishing a title which does not require universal consent but which also can be distinguished from mere declaration. It must be the case that the actions that one takes to establish ownership have greater moral weight than *mere* acquisition and labelling "this is mine." In this regard, Locke has much to say about the special nature of the act of laboring. In particular, he bolsters the claim concerning the status of labor by describing the tremendous contribution that labor makes to the value of resultant commodities. He repeats in many places that the value of things owes almost all (from nine-tenths to ninety-nine hundredths) of their value to the contributions of labor.

Many have taken this line of argument—the added value argument—as separable from the more non-consequentialist argument quoted above.[12] The added value argument is understood to rely more on the value of the consequences *for others* of the original appropriator's act of acquisition.[13] But I think this way of reading it may seriously misinterpret Locke's text. Locke first mentions the idea of the value contributions of labor as an *aside* ("To which let me add, that he who appropriates land to himself by his labor does not lessen but increase the common stock of mankind"

[37]), and adds the longer explanation of just how much value laboring adds to commodities as a defense of the labor-mixing premise of his original argument. He says, almost defensively, "Nor is it so strange, as perhaps before consideration it may appear, that the Property of labor should be able to over-balance the Community of Land. For 'tis Labor indeed that *puts the difference of value* on everything" (40). He then goes into great detail about just how extensive is the difference that labor makes in the value of things: "I think it will be but a very modest Computation to say, that of the Products of the Earth useful to the Life of Man 9/10 are the *effects of labour*" (40). (He immediately increases this estimate to ninety-nine hundredths.) From here, Locke drives home the point that most of the value of manufactured commodities can be traced to the labor inputs in the production process, and as an illustration he describes the process of making bread, cloth, and the like.

But these passages occur as a way of supporting the contested premise that it is the special status of labor that makes the difference in securing title. For after Locke concludes his various illustrations of his point about this status, he returns to the main line of argument: "*From which all is evident*, that though the things of Nature are given in common, yet Man (by being Master of himself, and Proprietor of his own person, and the actions or Labor of it) had still in himself the great foundation of property" (44). In other words, the claim Locke makes about how much value labor adds to commodities is a *subsidiary* argument intended to support the premise of the labor-mixing conception of appropriation.

Now on this reading of Locke's text, the crucial premise is that labor mixing is fundamentally different from simple first occupation. The latter view, which would not have been convincing to Locke, is a separate and much weaker line of argument than one based on labor.[14] But even granted the great value that labor adds to the quality of things, it certainly does not *follow* that since I labored on something (increasing its value a hundredfold), I thereby own it. It is at best an impressionistic argument. What is the difference, we might ask, between such an act and any other proclamation of title that we would consider arbitrary and empty: the friars of Saint Francis, for example, upon arriving in what is now Santa Fe, declared all the land from the Pacific Coast up to Saint Louis to be the property of the king of Spain. We can hardly, in retrospect, take such claims seriously. Locke's reply is that labor (unlike a mere declaration) adds value to the thing appropriated. But how is laboring any more relevant than planting a flag? Certainly if I am a bystander (or a Pueblo Indian), I would need more convincing than this, since *I* have certainly lost something by the act in question, namely, the right to appropriate that piece of land. This is a crucial point, which, as we shall see, plays an important role in this line of argument. This is essentially the line of criticism that Proudhon levels against Locke.[15]

Lawrence Becker reproduces a slightly different version of Locke's argument, which he extracts from that same chapter of the *Second Treatise*.[16] Becker takes seriously Locke's reiterated claim that labor and the mixing of labor with natural resources account for ninety-nine hundredths of the resulting value of the developed resource. The argument Becker constructs resembles the one above through premise (e), but includes the following extra premises (paraphrased): (f') the mixing of labor adds value to the resource (in fact, it is responsible for perhaps ninety-nine hundredths of the value of the products of the earth); (g') "since things are of no use until appropriated" (Locke: 28), and appropriation in most cases involves labor that would not be undertaken except for the expected benefits, to let others have "the benefits of another's pains" (34) would be clearly unjust; so it follows that (h') one is entitled to the whole of the benefits of the developed property.[17]

But notice how radically (h') differs from (f) above, which is a quotation from Locke. The question here is whether Locke intended his argument to justify ownership that includes rights to *the whole of the benefits* of the property: whether the resulting rights include the right to the transferability of, and income from, holdings (as well as the other incidents of liberal ownership). Becker admits that the right to transmissibility (bequest) has not been established by this argument.[18] It is my view, however, that the right to the income has not been grounded either. All that Locke intends, even in a version of the argument that stresses the added value of labor, is to establish rights to exclusive use, possession, and management in a world where the enjoyment of such rights is necessary for the "advantage of life and convenience" and where others are not made worse off by such appropriation.

A second reason for thinking that Locke did not supply a justification for liberal ownership has to do with money. The crucial link in Locke's argument between gathering small amounts of resources for use and consumption and the accumulation of stores of goods beyond what one needs is, of course, the invention of money. I have argued elsewhere, however, that this link makes the rights to such accumulated stores of goods *essentially conventional*, even on Locke's own terms.[19]

For Locke, the particular rights and privileges within civil society are not themselves natural rights, since their source is consent. Crucially for us, the implicit conventions that underlie the use of a currency *also* remove the web of rights to goods from the purview of natural rights. The invention of money was instituted and justified by tacit consent, according to Locke. In a money-based economy, accumulation of goods (wealth) without the spoilage of those goods is possible. But Locke is explicit in his claim that the *justification* of such accumulation, made possible by the use of money as a trading voucher, is not a natural right based on labor investment, but is a right based on the conventional consent that justifies the use of money and the other particular aspects of a developed economy.

Locke did not regard the natural right to one's labor as justifying more than the rights to use and manage the property labored on (in a state of nature), and this does not amount to liberal ownership. "Right and convenience went together" (51), but "right" in the sense of a natural right does not extend to the accumulated possessions made possible by money. Whenever Locke refers to the ability, incentive, or right to "enlarge [one's] possessions" (especially paragraphs 45–51)—a right that would be included in the liberal ownership of property—he is referring to rights made possible by the convention of money and hence a conventional right. As Locke writes:

> since gold and silver . . . [have their] value only from the consent of men . . . , it is plain that men have agreed to a disproportionate and unequal possession of the earth, they having, by a tacit and voluntary consent, found out a way how a man may possess more land than he himself can use the product of. . . . (50)

And it must be remembered that conventional rights are always, for Locke, subject to the limitations, revisions, and the like necessary for securing and promoting the common good.

A third reason for not attributing liberal ownership to Locke is that Locke stresses that the second proviso, the non-spoilage condition, is justified by divine command and natural law: "God, when He gave the world in common to all mankind, commanded men also to labor" (32). Thus, if goods that a person had acquired through laboring "perished in his possession without their due use . . . [the person] offended against the common law of nature and *invaded his neighbor's share*, for he had no right farther than his use called for any of them, and they might serve to afford him the conveniences of life."[20] So accumulation of income from property, through trade or rent, which is not necessary for the conveniences of life, is not justified by natural right, according to Locke.

This brings us back, of course, to the question of the role that money plays in the relation between natural and conventional rights on Locke's view. The key passages for this question occur in paragraphs 46–49 where Locke traces the history of the accumulation of possessions and the adoption of gold and silver as legal tender. He argues there that unless money had been invented, it would have made no sense to accumulate more than one needs since such an amount of goods would go to waste. But money solves this problem, and so since the provisos can be respected despite large accumulation, such accumulation can be grounded in natural rights.

But although these passages indicate that the development of money was an inevitable and predictable development for human society, Locke makes repeated references to the tacit *agreement* concerning the value of money, which grounds any claims to goods based on it. Never in this chapter does Locke mention the use of money without also qualifying his description with a reference to the conventional nature of the value of the currency. And although this convention, based on tacit consent, could well have occurred outside the bounds of civil society (before the social compact), it is nevertheless not a natural right in the sense specified above. For rights gained through the trading of goods in a market setting, which necessitate and depend on the use of money, are not grounded "without reference to social conventions, legal institutions or other special relationships within or among groups of persons," as the provisions of (R) demand.

Interpretation of Locke is not, of course, the principal subject of this chapter. It is relevant, however, since it aids in the understanding of various permutations of natural rights arguments. Pursuing the interpretive question one more step, then, we can observe how that question turns, most likely, on whom one understands Locke to be directing his arguments *against*. One obvious answer is that the arguments of the *Second Treatise*, like those of the first, were directed at the work of Sir Robert Filmer. Filmer, the author of *Patriarcha*, argued that all ownership claims, as well as all political power, derive from God's original gift to Adam and proceed through the fathers of all families (who own their children) as well as through the kings (and queens) ordained by God and the Church with temporal power. One of Filmer's lines of argument is to repudiate the only reasonable alternative theory of ownership around at the time, which is the view that ownership claims are based on general consent.[21] Such a defense of property is absurd, he argued, since it would demand the virtually unmeetable condition of universal consent for the approval of every ownership claim.

One of Locke's strategies of criticism of this line is that the correct paths of lineage could never be drawn tracing such claims from Adam to the present king of England (or any other monarch).[22] So any view that necessitated such an unbroken chain of possession and right could not be used to sustain contemporary claims of right. Furthermore, on this conception of Locke's strategy, Locke was attempting to show how property rights could indeed be established in the state of nature without universal consent. The labor-mixing model, then, provides such an account, and hence Filmer was wrong to think that the rejection of the absurd Adamite view entails the alternative of unwieldy universal agreement.

The other view about Locke's adversaries holds that he was directing his arguments at various egalitarian theorists—the Levellers, for example—and attempting to ground the property claims of the wealthy middle classes in the firm soil of natural rights.[23] On this reading, it would be implausible for Locke to see the unequal holdings of contemporary owners as based on compact (convention), for this would make them revisable according to the needs and desires of the community (and hence subject to egalitarian "levelling").

While I cannot argue for one side or the other in this dispute, my sympathies are with the former reading. The relevance for the arguments of this book, however, is that one can read Locke as a source for the very argument I want to make concerning the irrelevance of natural rights claims. For that argument, expressed in the epigraph from Faulkner, rests on the claim that since all contemporary ownership claims are due to transfers from others, they therefore depend for their legitimacy on the justice of those prior claims. This argument is taken up in section VI.

So on my reading of the *Second Treatise*, Locke did not succeed in justifying a natural right of ownership in the liberal sense. In particular, the rights to transfer and gain income from property are not supported by Locke's premises except when the convention of money is introduced. Now this hardly settles the matter in general of course, since Locke himself is not the only Lockean. So before casting a wider glance at the general strategy of natural rights arguments, I want to consider two other arguments which, making use of Lockean premises, try to justify such rights.

II. Variations on Locke

One of the ways that Locke's arguments fail to supply a natural rights basis for liberal ownership is, I have argued, that the labor-mixing model supports, at best, use and possession rights to acquired goods. (This is hardly a new conclusion.) Let us look more squarely, then, at the question of whether transfer rights could be vested with the status of natural rights. And in doing so, we will stay within the labor-mixing model, but allow ourselves to depart from what Locke actually said on such matters. This query arises when we see that transfers are not themselves instruments of labor, nor is it obvious without further argument that a person's labor extends into the future to include sales of the object. One could proceed by claiming that Locke's view does indeed provide a ground for title from transfers (transfer and income rights), in that when Locke speaks of having property in one's labor, he thinks of this right as including the power to give one's labor away. The idea is that Locke's conception of property in labor assumed liberal ownership of that labor, which includes the right to the income from its transfer. And it follows that since a person has a right to transfer or alienate her labor, she also has the right to transfer or alienate the products she mixes her labor with, namely appropriated and developed property.

I show later in this chapter (and again from a different angle in chapter 8) that the idea of ownership of labor is more limited than the above argument presumes. Indeed, Locke did not think that rights to life, liberty, *or* labor were fully alienable (see his comments on suicide and slavery, for example, at 22).[24] Here I wish to point out that the argument described in the above paragraph is not strictly valid.[25] First, even if I have liberal ownership rights over my labor, and I mix my labor, in a Lockean sense, with an unowned, abundant bit of nature, and thereby add value to that bit (even by a hundredfold, as Locke supposes), it would only be a violation of my ownership of my labor if the new object were *fully* expropriated from me without compensation. For it then would seem that my labor had been stolen from me. This inference appears to provide the core idea for the Lockean argument. But it does not follow from these considerations that I have acquired liberal ownership rights to the new object. If, for instance, a tax were levied where I was compelled to pay one-hundredth of the value of the new object (we are supposing that my labor increased its value by a factor of 100), this tax would disturb my *liberal* ownership over the new object but would not violate my rights to my labor or its equivalent value; for the latter accounts for ninety-nine hundredths of the value of the new object, which is left to me after the tax.

Also, as I argue in more detail in chapter 7, persons who gain entitlements through embedded labor may enter into a market, the very existence of which will serve to lower the costs of trade (due to economies of scale, increased coordination, and the like); this process, in turn, serves to increase the net social product produced from those entitlements without demanding extra labor from individual traders (these savings automatically result from having any system of property at all). Thus, taxation which redistributes that extra product would not amount to a limitation of the ownership rights of the traders over the commodities in question, since they would *not* constitute an encroachment on the rights anyone has to her or his labor (since the product redistributed can come from the increased efficiencies of the market mechanism, not increased labor).[26]

This point underscores a major lacuna in the labor-mixing picture presented by Locke and Lockeans. For the value of my labor at time t_1 is fixed by virtue of the surrounding social structure, which determines the precise demand for that commodity. This complex and multifaceted relation may be altered radically by the time I mix that labor with an object at t_2 and enter that new commodity into the surrounding market. The new value of my embedded labor may be only distantly related to the original value it had at the pre-mixing stage. Values, if they exist at all apart from concurrent prices, vary over time, and hence ownership rights based on labor values would be highly unstable and variable.

Furthermore, if laws existed placing severe restrictions on transfers of developed resources, for instance, taxes on rents from such objects, but no restrictions on what persons could do with their real, unembedded labor (except where direct harm is or might be produced), such laws would not amount to limitations on the ownership of a person's labor, though they would amount to attenuations of ownership structures over alienable resources. So in these ways limited property rights over alienable resources is *consistent* with liberal ownership of labor even when the latter is the basis for the justification of the former.

III. Rights to Property from Rights to One's Body

These comments indicate the difficulty of grounding property rights in the allegedly special status of labor, and doing so in a manner which preserves the particularly non-consequentialist nature of the rights in question. To make these difficulties more apparent, I want now to examine another attempt at a natural rights justification of ownership where the specifics concerning the mode of appropriation—the moral metaphysics of the appropriation, we might say—purportedly provide a set of sufficient conditions for the legitimacy of the right so grounded. That is, it is sometimes thought that what is special about labor is that, as a matter of psychological fact, "labor *is* psychological appropriation—appropriation in the sense of a 'felt incorporation' of the thing labored on 'into one's person'"—that "I am what I have made."[27] In a spirit similar to this, Sam Wheeler has argued that a derivation of the (natural) right to property in objects is possible from the ownership of one's *body*.[28] Wheeler argues that the rights we have over our bodies are not contingent on our particular talents, or whether the parts of our bodies are attached (in the usual manner of agent-type control), or whether the parts are essential for staying alive. When one acquires an external piece of property, however, there is no important distinction between that new instrument of our agency and our body parts. Since we have natural rights to the latter, and there is no morally relevant distinction between those items and body parts, then we have natural rights to the former (appropriated resources).

This is an interesting line of argument, since it puts such direct emphasis on the extension of one's self onto material objects, in a way analogous to labor mixing. However, the most that such a strategy could ever justify is the right to use and possess such items. For the intuition that we all have absolute rights to our body parts is applicable (arises out of) a world where people precisely do *not* try to incorporate body parts in the way that they accumulate a fortune. We would not hold firmly to the idea that everyone has absolute exclusive rights over her or his body if people went around accumulating parts of their bodies in order to buy and sell them, hire people to buy and sell them, amass wealth, and so on. Happily, our world is not like that, and so the intuition that everyone has absolute exclusive rights over her or his body parts is uncontroversial. But the extension of those rights to the use, transfer, and income rights of ownership structures would be quite controversial.

Also, it is quite vague in an argument such as this what would count as proper appropriation of the new body parts. The way we "appropriate" our original bodily equipment is hardly analogous to the accumulation of other goods. The problem is a fundamental one. For we cannot extend the rights we have over our bodies over all kinds of objects which we happen to move or use unless there is a moral argument to the effect that those things become like a person's body in the *relevant way*. So this argument merely leads us back to where we started, searching for an adequate theory of original acquisition.

Although I do not consider Hegel's work on these topics in any detail,[29] the present discussion may bring to mind his claims about the importance of the acquisition of property. Although Hegel was an outright critic of Locke, Hegel's view that property can function as the externalization of the will of the subject—turning an "oppositional," objective thing into a component of the agent's subjectivity—could be used in support of labor-mixing models. But for two reasons connected with the arguments I develop here, I think such a line of argument would not succeed. First, the idea of extending subjectivity over material things is, while highly suggestive, at best merely metaphorical. For as we have seen in Wheeler's arguments, it is mere assertion without argument to claim that the objects over which I gain ownership rights are the same kind of thing as the parts of my body or mind over which my will can be said to operate. The branch that I might break off a tree to use as a crutch is different from my actual leg in as many uncountable ways as it is similar to it. To say that since my will comes to govern the operation of both then the crutch is as much my own as my leg is to beg all of the controversial questions. Second, the use of Hegelian models here gives no special support to a natural rights argument based on the mixing of *labor* with unowned things. For I can extend my will to a physical object by simply (and effortlessly) grabbing it as I can by changing its value and characteristics by working on it.

Finally, to repeat a crucial point, arguments attempting to ground rights to external property in our connection with, or our rights over, our bodies and personalities suffer most from the attempt to cover not only use and possessory rights but transfer and income rights as well. Such (income) rights depend on such things as interactions with others, the existence of a market, stable social relations, and the contingencies of others' desires for one's goods (prices). Such complexities and contingencies make it generally quite difficult to extend the relatively non-contingent rights we have to use our bodies to such economic interactions. As will be increasingly obvious as we go on, the considerations that might be brought to bear on the justification of use and possession rights just won't do the job when it comes to trying to justify transfer and income rights. And as I point out in part III, a very important lesson emerges from this fact.

So the strategy of grounding ownership rights to rights we have over our bodies also comes up short. In the arguments so far, we have seen an attempt to describe the relevant aspects of appropriation whereby ownership of property is justified without reference to the distribution of goods generally. This is what I meant above by a thoroughly non-consequentialist grounding to ownership. It is such in the way that desert claims and rights to our body parts are often understood as non-consequentialist: they can be accepted as justified when no mention of the resultant distribution of those things is made. That these arguments turn out to have no force leads us to consider the natural rights approach more generally.

IV. The General Failure of Natural Rights Arguments: Labor

As we have seen, many natural rights arguments attempt to extend the status of labor or one's body to the external goods that the person has acquired. The Lockean arguments we considered construed labor as having so special a status that, it was claimed, external goods embedded with that labor have attached to them something of equally special status, something that grounds ownership. Let us now take this kind of argument and break it down into its crucial components. As we will see for all these kinds of arguments, either the rights over body and labor are described so pervasively that they justify too much, and are thus implausible, or these rights are described within more plausible limits but then do not justify anything close to liberal ownership (based on natural rights).

To illustrate, let us return to the abstract principles from which all of these arguments begin. The right to one's body is often described, at least implicitly, as "owning one's body." So the first premise could be something like the following:

(1) Everyone has liberal ownership rights to his or her body.

This means that each person may use, destroy, sell, and gain income from her own body and body parts. It was pointed out above that Locke explicitly denies this premise since he did not think that suicide or complete voluntary slavery was morally permissible. For Locke, God had partial rights in the bodies of individuals since God figured in their creation.[30] But the other Lockeans we have discussed do have the view that persons have liberal ownership rights over their bodies. And while this premise might be brought into question, I prefer to turn to the more crucial question of what this premise entails:

(2) Every person owns his or her labor.

This indeed is the most natural suggestion, and the most common, but what does this mean, and is it really entailed by (1)?

Concerning the first question, the most obvious reading of (2) might be the following:

(2') Every person has the right to do any act, gain income from any act, prevent him- or herself from doing any act (by whatever means), under any conditions he or she chooses.

All of (2') is obviously qualified by the stipulation that none of these acts can violate the rights of any other person, or more strongly, they cannot negatively affect other persons (all these rights propositions should be read as similarly qualified). This is a highly artificial caveat, of course, for whether one's rights over one's body entail rights to act however one wants depends tremendously on what one plans to do. If the rights and liberties of others must be defined prior to the specification of one's self-ownership, then the latter postulate does little independent work and simply follows from the general idea that what one is not prohibited to do, one is permitted to do. Self-ownership isn't needed to establish that.

But this is not the strategy that Lockeans want to push. For their view is that the rights one has over one's body produce a unique set of moral rights and permissions that serve to constrain the legitimate actions of others. So we can accept (2') (and adopt a narrower no-harm constraint) and then proceed to investigate what follows when we describe some of the acts in question as labor. Much ambiguity remains, however, in the notion of labor itself, so it is necessary to examine that idea a bit more fully.

Laboring has gotten much attention in the history of Western political philosophy (not to mention classical economics).[31] At one end of the spectrum, it is understood as the natural expression of the true human spirit, one's "species being," to use the Marxian phrase. In this light, one might see labor as a purely creative act that expresses the pure will of the agent and embodies the natural creative impulse. At the other extreme, labor is toil—effort made necessary by the constraints of a post-paradisiacal state—which humans must engage in to survive and meet their basic needs. If there is satisfaction in the activity, then all the better, but ideally one would prefer a life of leisure and hedonic freedom from labor. Clearly the first picture is espoused in some form by those influenced by romantic expressivist views of the self, a tradition that finds its apex in the early Marx, while the latter view is more straightforwardly utilitarian (or at least based on an instrumental view of the value of labor).

Now it is interesting to observe that the closer one gets to viewing the labor process as pure creative expression, the less one is inclined to think that such activity could ever ground a set of rights—such as ownership rights—that in turn limit the opportunities and choices of others. For why should I step out of the way of your romantic creativity and adapt my choices and life plan to what is left after you're done? After all, insofar as this is freely creative activity, it is something that you could have easily chosen not to do, and it is something that should most likely be constrained by the needs and relative positions of others.

Now the more instrumentalist view, that labor is necessarily toilsome and is necessary for meeting our need to survive, certainly does seem to motivate the intuition that others must have some respect for an individual's activity of this sort. But then it is not the special status of *labor* that motivates this intuition but the necessity of what it produces for the agent. And patterned theories of justice, which fix entitlements according to some natural attribute or characteristic present in the population (like need), will satisfy this intuition more directly than the granting of a natural property right to the laboring individual. Such rights, we are supposing, are distribution *in*sensitive, after all.

But let us look more closely at the way labor might be described. It may be suggested that the notion of labor involves, not merely free action, but activity involving effort that is purposive or goal directed. The condition that labor necessarily involves effort might be too strong, however, since the phrase "she labored effortlessly" is not a contradiction *in adjecto*. It will be insisted by many, nevertheless, that labor must be understood as costly to the agent, though I think even this should be questioned.[32] All this aside, if one wished to add a separate premise to the effect that labor usually does involve effort, and continue an argument from there, nothing I say here prevents such a claim. But we shall leave the concept itself explicated as in (2').

But a more interesting claim is that labor is necessarily a goal-directed activity. But this addition comes out as either trivial, false, or question-begging. If by "goal-directed" one merely means "intentional," then its being included in the definition of labor is trivial since the idea of intentional action is already implicit in (2'): the acts in question are ones that the person *chooses* to perform. If, on the other hand, one claims that labor, contra (2'), is always goal directed in the sense of involving expected returns, then the claim is false. For certainly people sometimes labor without expecting any benefits for doing so (besides those emanating from the performance of the labor itself). Third, one might claim that labor, in that it is purposive and (usually) goal directed, is such that one *could* or *ought to* expect benefits in return for the labor. But this understanding of the term begs the question of whether laboring activity does in fact supply a sufficient ground for the receipt of a benefit. We will see in chapter 5 how an argument from desert of this form fails, and it does no good to collapse the whole of such an argument into the concept of labor itself.

Now is (2'), as we have it, entailed by (1)? It is, but only by virtue of the fact that ownership includes use rights; so (1) entails (1'):

(1') Everyone has a natural right to use any part of her or his body.

And (1') entails (2') when "using one's body" is taken to mean or include "acting intentionally." But notice that all (2') says is what is usually captured in the claim that persons have a natural right to *liberty*. That is, when "ownership of labor" is explicated, it amounts to nothing more than the natural right of persons to act freely (within the scope of the rights of others). This explains why it is not plausible to go from claims like (2'), which amount to the postulation of natural liberty, to claims of ownership of property. Acting freely, or refraining from so acting, does not necessarily involve affecting the choices of others, if persons are sufficiently separated, while the appropriation of objects that other people, even future generations, may come to want (because of eventual scarcity or just changing preferences) certainly does. There is always a gap, a missing step in the justification, between the right to act freely and the entitlements to (perhaps) a disproportionate amount of benefits in a certain distribution of goods. The failure of the arguments above provides good reason to believe that such a gap is not likely to be filled, in particular because, as I argued, there is nothing special about labor per se that will bear the brunt of the justification.

But of course the view of liberty here assumed and that of natural rights to one's body remain plausible only in the state-of-nature scenarios typically imagined. A natural right to non-interference with free actions is well grounded when there are not appreciable disparities among the abilities of people to freely move and use their bodies. If the world were different—if, say, in the state of nature most people were helplessly crippled and dependent on the healthy minority to make wheelchairs and such in order that they could survive—the intuition that all people have natural rights to act or to refrain from acting however they choose would be strained, I think.[33]

But our purpose here is to see the relation between (2') and some proposition concerning the ownership of non-human property. In the argument of section III above, and in some traditional interpretations of Locke, we saw an attempt to spell out how a right to one's body is directly transferred to the use, possession, and accumulation of non-human objects. But notice that, as I have explicated that argument, there was no reference made to a proviso concerning how much was left in common for others, and it is instructive to note why this is so. For, just as our rights to our bodies and free actions are secured without reference to the general distribution of bodies and people's abilities to act freely (in an environment of generally healthy people), so would rights to property be justified without such reference. That is, if criteria could be set out that would justify a natural right to property, and this right had the status of the natural right to one's body and labor, then the former would not have to make reference to the resulting distribution, since the latter does not. But no one believes that the acquisition of property could take place *without* such reference to the present distribution; appropriation in the state of nature couldn't plausibly be *simply* a first-come first-served arrangement with no restriction. What this shows is that property rights are not natural rights in any sense analogous to the rights to one's body.

V. General Failure II: Surrounding Conditions of Acquisition

So attention to laboring and the special status of that activity does not succeed in justifications of ownership. Let us take a different tack, then. Maybe we should take seriously the implication drawn out above that the right to one's labor reduces to a right to liberty and see if this could be used as a ground for the natural right to property. (I consider the relation between liberty and property more generally in the next chapter.) One might claim, for example, that specification of the conditions at the time of appropriation are sufficient to justify the natural right to property, without special attention to the status of labor as such. I think that Robert Nozick puts forth such a view.[34] Since for him the relevant starting point is that all persons have an equal right to non-human, unowned objects, premises about exactly how rights to one's body and labor transfer to rights over property through certain actions are unnecessary.

Nozick's views have been well discussed and their particular failures well documented. Here I summarize my own arguments for their failure in a way which connects with other themes that will concern us in various places.

Nozick views appropriations—whatever acts comprise appropriations—to be just if they do not violate the Lockean proviso of leaving enough and as good in common for others. For Nozick, the rights of surrounding individuals, whatever their specification and scope, amount to "absolute side constraints" on the actions of all others. In the acquisition of goods, the Lockean proviso of leaving enough and as good acts as a measure of the scope of those surrounding rights. It must be the case that none of my actions, whether these include acquisition of goods or not, can render the life prospects of those around me significantly worse than if I did not exist at all. If they do, then I can be rightly accused of violating their Lockean rights to be left alone.

But where acquisition is concerned, we must find a threshold, a baseline, that helps define the scope of those surrounding rights. However, Nozick claims that in order for my action to comprise a rights violation, the way in which someone is made worse off (by my appropriating some unowned object X) is not that he is no longer at liberty to appropriate *that X* (this would be too stringent), but rather that he may have "lost the opportunity to *improve his situation* by a particular appropriation *or any one*" (emphasis mine).[35] So if the X here is a bushel of peaches, say, and Clara (a passerby in the state of nature) cannot appropriate the bushel of peaches that I have put into my basket (since I did), she may be able to pick some apples nearby (which are just as good) and thereby would *not* be rendered significantly worse off by my appropriation of the peaches, in Nozick's version of the "weak" Lockean proviso. He asks, if all the unowned objects have been appropriated through a system of private property, are people better or worse off *with that system* than they would have been without such a system, as in the state of nature before the appropriations? If they are at least no worse off, then the appropriations that began the system of private ownership are legitimate, and therefore the resulting distribution of rights is just.

But why is it that your owning all the oil wells on earth (and thus living in indescribable luxury) and my making a subsistence wage at your factory are justified because private ownership (the specific structure that allowed you to own all those wells) makes us both better off than we were when still eating fruit from trees in the state of nature? Nozick does not consider, in the counterfactual calculation that goes into the proviso, the *alternative* systems of property rights (socialism, redistributive capitalism, and so on) that would make certain persons better off than under a system of private liberal ownership. That is, I cannot complain that a system of liberal ownership has made me worse off than I would have been with *no* system of appropriation, but I can complain of being worse off than I would have been under *another system of property* (like socialism). So what makes the present (unequal) distribution just? It can't be that I have no grounds for legitimate complaint, for I do.

This is how a central intuition behind this argument's strategy is undercut, namely, the intuition that a person can only *insist* on the level of welfare and opportunity that would have resulted had she been simply left alone. However, that sequence of events (what would have happened had one been left alone) is indeterminate. For if the property owner had never existed, our factory worker might have developed *her own* property to an extent that would have rendered her much better off than the level afforded her in the original scenario. Thus, of the several counterfactual sequences of events subsequent to original appropriation, none is unique in being all that the property owner could insist upon.[36] Therefore, the strategy of considering only the conditions at the time of appropriation is also unsuccessful in justifying liberal ownership on the basis of natural rights.

Furthermore, seeing the strategy this way indicates how these kinds of arguments simply collapse into "first occupation" views, or at least "first occupation with constraints" views. I have not bothered to take on these specific kinds of arguments, ones based on what Murray Rothbard calls the "homesteading principle," for it seems quite obvious that merely being the first to declare "this is mine," without others around who are simple enough to believe it, will not be sufficient ground for liberal property rights.[37]

Our discussion of the proper interpretation of Locke again enters here. For one of my interpretive points was that all of Locke's claims about how much labor adds to the value of goods were subsidiary supportive premises for his crucial labor-mixing argument. Whether that reading is correct is what will determine where Locke belongs in the particular divisions of argument that I provide here. For if what Locke says about the contribution that labor makes to the value of goods is taken as a separate line of argument in support of liberal ownership rights, then Locke should be understood as a proto-Nozickean, as arguing that no one could ever complain about the actions of initial appropriators since the world is so much more valuable as a result of their efforts. This, then, would run afoul of the objections just made, namely, that complaint is indeed legitimate since how valuable things turned out to be is variable and in that way arbitrary.

But my view of the interpretive question placed Locke more squarely in that category of thoroughly non-consequentialist theorists of initial appropriation. For while the provisos are meant as constraints on initial property rights, they are merely ancillary to the major thrust of the argument, which is that there is something special about the laboring process that is sufficient to ground a title. Therefore, Locke's views are prey to my skepticism about whether labor has this important character.

VI. General Failure III: The Inapplicability of Natural Rights Arguments

In the arguments so far I have taken seriously the possibility that successful natural rights defenses of liberal ownership would be applicable to contemporary political policy and principle. The assumption has been that if natural rights arguments were successful, the ownership claims of present owners would be *violated*—indeed their natural human rights would be violated—by any sort of redistributive policy inconsistent with liberal ownership. This view relies on the unstated premise, however, that the philosophical counterfactual models within which this debate has been conducted have relevance to these contemporary claims. But it does not take much reflection and investigation to see how faulty such a view is.

Present-day libertarians often write this way, claiming that somehow egalitarianism or redistributive economic policies actually violate natural rights. But such policies can only be counted as rights violations if the pedigree to these present-day claims is not tainted with illegitimate transfers. Nozick, after all, adds a principle of rectification to the principles of just acquisition and transfer in his tripartite theory of distributive justice.[38] He understands the necessity of correcting the legacy of past violations in order to claim that the present distribution accords with individual right.

For contemporary ownership claims to be justified by virtue of natural rights, the following cluster of assumptions must be accepted: (a) the abstract strategy of justifying ownership based on natural rights is sound; (b) someone somewhere actually acted so as to meet the conditions set out in that abstract strategy; and (c) the present owners of goods are either the people referred to in (b) or are people whose claims can be traced to such people by way of justified trades and transfers.

I have argued through the bulk of this chapter against (a). But a quick glance at the way that land and other resources actually *were* appropriated in, say, the period of the settlement of the United States by Europeans shows that (b), probably, and (c), almost certainly, could not be met in a way that would justify *any* contemporary claims of ownership.

It may take a moment to see the obviousness of this claim. For many see the original settlement of the United States by Europeans the way that Locke himself did, as individual homesteading by labor in an area of unclaimed and abundant resources. It is an accepted component of the American mythos that the struggles and competition envisioned in natural rights arguments were an actual part of our political heritage, and that, since such activity would ground an unassailable claim in goods and territory (contra my view), then the claims made under those conditions attained a sacrosanct status. Events like the settling of the western plains (by Europeans), the Oklahoma land rush, and the great mineral discoveries are thought to fit this mold.

But things certainly did not happen this way.[39] Many of the claims of land appropriation of the United States are made after the forcible (and certainly unjustified!) slaughter of the native American inhabitants who first occupied the area.

Moreover, it is only because the central government *declared* various areas free for settlement that the original claims (by U.S. citizens) could be made and respected. Such a declaration presupposes that the government is itself the holder of titles which it then transferred by decree to individual (white, male) citizens. But this means that the system of opportunities was neither universally applied nor fair. The fact that in some instances (the Oklahoma land rush, for example) government policy chose to *mimic* a state-of-nature scenario, where the equivalent of labor mixing could fix a title, does little to upset the conclusion that the actual course of events hardly conforms to the general conditions of a natural rights theory.

Here is another place where my gloss of the correct interpretation of Locke can have more than an exegetical purpose. On my reading of Locke, for example, the rights that one has over one's property in a developed market economy are not natural ones since those rights stem from the use of money whose value is set by convention. This argument cashes in, so to speak, on one of the points I made earlier about the nature of natural rights. I urged that rights can be considered natural only if they are *independent* of the conventions and institutions of society. So insofar as the legal institutions of a market economy, in particular conventions concerning currency values, are not the pure expressions of natural attributes of persons, then rights that are based on them are not natural.

This point serves as support for the irrelevancy argument I am now making, that even if natural rights could, counterfactually, extend to the rights of ownership, that point would have no importance in the actual world of felonious acquisition and transfers. This is doubly so, given that in the actual world the rights that ownership affords me are intertwined with the past and present workings of a thoroughly *conventional* market economy, in which my particular rights and privileges are a contingent aspect of my society. The particular packages of property rights over goods recognized by societies over the generations have varied enormously as well. So since virtually none of the ownership rights persons now enjoy—even in economic systems that approach free market capitalism—can be understood independently of the myriad conventional relationships that have been adopted over the millennia, then these legal modalities are bereft of their natural status.

It is puzzling that this line of criticism against natural rights defenses of ownership is not given more attention. It is true that Nozick includes a principle of rectification of past injustices in his theory, and in response to the possibility that past injustices make the present distribution diverge from legitimate natural rights claims, he argues that one must adopt a probabilistic matrix according to which goods are distributed to those who would most likely own them if there had been no injustice. He even expresses sympathy for a Rawlsian maximin strategy as a best approximation of such a rectification in a given society (since those who now have the least are probably in this situation as a result of injustice, and *mutus mutandis* for the rich).[40] But there are two glaring problems with this stance. First, our information about what the distribution of goods would have been in a world of no injustices is reduced virtually to zero. For one would have to factor in not only the *holdings* of the would-be owners, but the variations in *what would have been produced*. For different owners have different aspirations, creative capacities, and opportunities, and hence a thoroughly different line of production and use of resources could be expected if the goods were in different hands. (Recall also the variability in the kind of ownership bundles that have been recognized by different generations and governments.) Second, directing a distribution according to the probable rightful owners of goods, based on the scant information alluded to just now, ceases to bear any resemblance to a rights-based theory. For to claim that "I have a right to X because the probabilities that I would have had a right to it in a perfect world are higher than the probabilities that anyone else would have" is a deeply different claim from "I have a right to X." In addition, these probabilities are so close to zero that anyone's claim on a particular item *must* be outweighed by considerations other than rights-based ones, such as the surrounding needs of the comparatively worse-off.

Murray Rothbard is one of the few libertarian thinkers to address this problem in any detail. On his view, the present holders of property retain a natural right to it unless (a) someone can be located who was the victim of injustice regarding that property, and/or (b) the legitimate, would-be heirs of those harmed by a past injustice can be located, and (c) the value of the present holdings was not completely created by non-detachable improvements of the present possessors. If such conditions cannot be met, then the present possessor remains the rightful owner (by virtue of natural rights), even when there is irrefutable evidence that injustice has taken place along the line of transfer leading to the present holder.[41]

But this conclusion implies that the ground of title is *mere* occupation, for occupation is all that the present possessor can claim against the rest of the community. No untainted labor mixing and transfer had taken place leading up to the present holding, nor did the possessor take any steps (other than occupation) to secure the rightful title (since we are imagining that she simply got the property from a transfer from someone whose title to it was lacking in historical grounding). But this approach reduces the basis of property rights to a paper-thin first occupation theory.[42] On this view I could simply kill the rightful owner of a piece of property, and if she had no legitimate heirs, and after I paid retribution for the crime of homicide (which by no means must include giving up property), and if I could guard my possession while paying for my crime, then I would be the owner of the property by natural right. But mere occupation is hardly sufficient to ground title when there are others around who also desire (not to mention desperately need) the good in question.

The cruel facts of history, then, should be enough to put to rest the various labor-mixing strategies of justifying liberal ownership. Failure to see that this difficulty derails the applicability of the whole apparatus is quite puzzling. As Blackstone put it,

> [p]leased as we are with the possession, we seem afraid to look back to the means by which it was acquired, as if fearful of some defect in our title; . . . not caring to reflect that . . . there is no foundation in nature or in natural law, why a set of words upon parchment should convey the dominion of land: . . . or why the occupier of a particular field or a jewel, when lying on his death-bed, and no longer able to maintain possession, should be entitled to tell the rest of the world which of them should enjoy it after him.[43]

Conclusion

This chapter was intended to show why a number of proposed justifications for liberal ownership based on natural rights fail, and to explain how all these arguments are likely to fail. In my discussion of Locke, I urged a different interpretation of his views which I think is instructive in the following way: when it is seen that Locke took seriously the limitations on what natural rights to property amount to (use and management rights), it is clear how taking into account the equal right of all people to shares of natural resources blocks an argument for liberal ownership based on such natural rights claims.

I then generalized from these conclusions and argued that natural rights strategies for defending liberal ownership run aground in three general ways. (1) Labor does not, as a morally relevant concept, have the kind of weight necessary to justify liberal ownership (which does not take into account ongoing distributive concerns): for while it may connect significantly with potential rights to use and possess goods, it fails to ground the transfer and income rights that are central components of liberal ownership. (2) When distributive considerations are introduced as constraints on the initial acts of acquisition, there are no good arguments against *extending* such considerations to all subsequent distributions or against the claim that they dominate the picture. (Thus, the two strategies of natural rights arguments mentioned at the outset—one emphasizing the moral status of labor, the other the conditions at the time of appropriation—lead nowhere.) (3) Natural rights arguments are hopeless because the history of our own world has been so unkind as to fail to live up to the stringent conditions such arguments demand if they are to legitimize contemporary property claims.

One of the chief lessons I want to draw from these arguments about liberal ownership, however, is that being sensitive to the internal complexity of the structure of ownership casts a new and particularly skeptical light on attempts to justify private property of the sort we are considering. More particularly, the move from rights to one's labor to rights over external things is most shaky when those rights include the right to the income that I have said is a central component of liberal ownership. This element is the least possible to justify in its pure form, and this claim will be a large part of the motivation for a new model of ownership that treats income rights as totally separate from the other rights in the package.

This discussion of the natural rights that individuals have over themselves and their labor leads naturally to a discussion of the connection between rights to property and the right to, or general value of, individual liberty. I now turn to attempts to justify liberal ownership, and the capitalist free markets built upon them, on the basis of considerations of liberty.

4

Liberty and Liberal Ownership

> [I]t has been driven by the manifest teaching of experience that liberty without equality is a name of noble sound and squalid result.
>
> L. T. Hobhouse

This chapter concerns various arguments that might be constructed for liberal ownership based on considerations of liberty. This subject follows neatly from the discussion of the last chapter, since one of the conclusions reached there was that traditional natural rights defenses of liberal ownership in many cases collapse into arguments from liberty, in particular the natural right to liberty. The present discussion takes up that point and, eventually, rejects it as a plausible basis for justifying private liberal ownership.

Questions concerning the nature of freedom and its relation to the distribution of resources have, of course, been analyzed and debated by many others before. What redundancy there is in the present discussion will, perhaps, be alleviated by the somewhat different tack I take on the issue. As is the case all along, I ask the particular question of what the proper structure of property should be in light of considerations of freedom. The particular structure examined here is liberal ownership, which, I argue, is not supported on the basis of liberty. Moreover, this conclusion will begin to pave the way for the replacement model of ownership to be presented in part III, a model where autonomy, a key component of individual liberty, plays a central role.

One of the problems with discussing strategies of this sort is that there is such an endless array of possible versions of the arguments, as endless as are the versions of the key concepts involved.[1] Specifically, the concept of liberty (or freedom) has itself been the focus of centuries of discussion and debate. For that reason, I combine analyses of the central concepts with evaluations of arguments based upon them. I construct and evaluate what I take to be the most powerful versions of such arguments, based on what we hopefully can agree is at or near the core of the tradition that prizes private property largely because of its relation to freedom. The main thrust of my argument here is that what I call direct arguments that a particular property arrangement will promote or protect liberty are irreparably indeterminate. This means that defenders of liberal ownership must rely on indirect arguments, which, I claim, are also inadequate.

There will be much stage setting and conceptual digression, but the general plan of the chapter is this: I first discuss the concept of liberty itself and, in particular, explain a crucial distinction between normative concepts of liberty and non-normative concepts. In section II, I consider an argument for liberal ownership based on normative liberty (this will be akin to the argument from the right to liberty mentioned in the last chapter). I next discuss non-normative liberty and consider the variety of ways that reference to this concept might be used to launch a defense of liberal ownership. I thus bring into question some of the assumptions that any such argument must make: the claim that liberty (construed non-normatively) itself has value, that amounts of freedom can be compared interpersonally, and that either liberal ownership guarantees equal liberty or it allows for maximum liberty (which, it must be claimed, is a good thing). I raise objections to all of these presuppositions in turn and so try to derail the general range of liberty-based arguments for liberal ownership.

For the purposes of this chapter, I assume that liberal ownership implies (in most instances) the presence of relatively free markets which produce inequality in distributions of goods. I also assume that some agents will not own any external property and will have an incentive to trade their labor in that market for a wage (by "have an incentive" I mean they will be moved to, which for some may mean that they will have to do so to avoid starvation). The arguments to follow do not rely on assumptions that the class of those who must sell their labor (to earn an income) is overwhelmingly large, only that the liberal ownership structures involved ensure that the income and wealth in the economy will be unequally distributed.

I. The Concept of Liberty

The arguments defending liberal ownership on the basis of liberty discussed below virtually all turn on controversial interpretations of the key concept "liberty." Therefore, a fairly thorough, though albeit not really ground-breaking, analysis of that notion is called for before we start.

The most widely discussed distinction between rival conceptions of liberty is that between negative and positive freedom.[2] The negative concept is, roughly, that individuals are free relative to the number (or kinds) of restraints they face in acting on their desires. The positive conception has it that people are free only when they are able to effectively carry out their (true, authentic, and so on) desires. This account suggests a range of possibilities for what is meant by the "authentic" self. At one extreme, positive liberty means being able to effectively act on desires critically appraised by the agent; at another, freedom means acting on desires that are in line with nature, virtue, justice, or the like. Often, the idea of positive liberty is understood to be synonymous with individual autonomy.

For ease of reference, let me list the gradation of concepts of liberty stretching between the pure negative notion and a full-blown positive one:[3]

L1. Liberty is the relative absence of external physical restraints that prevent agents from acting on their actual desires.

L2. Liberty is the relative absence of restraints (L1) and the presence of resources enabling agents to carry out their actual desires.

L3. Liberty is the relative absence of restraints (L1) and the presence of resources (L2) enabling agents to carry out their *critically appraised* desires.

L4. Liberty is the relative absence of restraints (L1) and the presence of resources

(L2) enabling agents to carry out critically appraised (L3) desires that conform to the standards of nature, justice, or virtue.

Many subsidiary categories could be created from this list. For example, one could combine L1 with the clause in L3 concerning critical appraisal of desires but not include enabling conditions (L2) as relevant to freedom. Also, L4 admits of many variations and subgroups itself, in that "correct standards" can range from "those standards that would direct the deliberations of a rational autonomous will" to "those standards specified by the social and moral conventions of one's society." Most theorists draw a line between L1 and L2, and call L1 "negative freedom" and any of the rest some variant of positive liberty. I follow this usage generally, and it is negative liberty that concerns us most here. After all, it is the negative concept that is virtually always at work in attempts to justify capitalism, free markets, or related systems involving liberal ownership.

For any of these conceptions of the predicate "is free," however, a full accounting of the idea would have to specify the kinds of persons who are eligible for free action (does one count non-humans? children?), the kinds of things that will be counted as restraints to freedom, and the nature of acts (or character development, or whatever) that one is free to do when one is free. Rendering the possibilities this way makes use of what has been called the triadic view of freedom: any particular conception of freedom is an interpretation of the three variables which are the relata of the relation "is free."[4] What one takes as the true notion of freedom will necessarily involve an interpretation of one or more of these variables. This framework helps to organize the sundry dimensions in which the concept of freedom could be varied.[5]

The most complex set of difficulties in defining the notion of freedom surrounds the question of what is supposed to count as a restraint. The usual breakdown distinguishes positive from negative, and internal from external restraints.[6] A more crucial question, in my view, is whether it must be the case that *human action* caused the placement of the purported restraint for it to count as such. I call this last point the question of a humanity condition. Such a condition amounts to the claim that a person is made less free only if the obstruction she faces in the carrying out of her desires is present by virtue of some human act, whether voluntary or accidental. And the humanity condition can also vary by degrees: at one extreme, one could claim that only obstacles (or threats) *intentionally* placed in the way of someone count as restraints to action (call this the "strict" humanity condition); at the other, one could hold that whenever the obstruction that faces a person could *in principle be removed* by some human act, the person is unfree vis-à-vis that obstacle (call this the "weak" condition).[7]

Debate about this humanity condition is central to our present concern because it will in part determine the relation between freedom, on the one hand, and the distribution of resources and/or the actions of surrounding individuals on the other. If I am unable to do something because of some restraint, but there is a person nearby who could remove the restraint (in particular use some of her resources to do so), a weak humanity condition implies that I am *unfree* by virtue of that person's inaction. Under a strict condition, however, I am only unfree if the nearby person (intentionally or accidentally) *put* the constraint in my path. Therefore, under some concepts of freedom, the structure of the property rights in an area—

and the inequalities that such rights may induce—directly connects with the freedom one finds there.

Another conceptual debate that bears on the question of property rights is whether we should include the lack of enabling conditions as a constraint on freedom (that is, construing L2–L4 as conceptions of freedom). Doing so would mean that a person's freedom is in part a function of her material wealth. (Let us assume that wealth is a sort of universal enabling condition: the more one has, the more one is able to do.)

This is an important point of contention, since the liberty-based defenders of liberal ownership must take a firm position on this issue in order to keep the property of being free separate from the ownership of goods. We will see why they want to do this in section III. For now I want to introduce a different but crucial distinction between conceptions of freedom relevant to arguments about property.

There are two importantly different ways of understanding what it means to say a person is or is not free to do something.[8] On one view, the concept of freedom describes a property of only morally permissible actions or morally impermissible restrictions, while another sort considers *any* kind of acts (or obstruction to such acts) as comprising the extension of freedom. So normative freedom (N-freedom) refers to those conceptions of freedom or liberty that define the ranges of the variables discussed above using normative concepts, while non-normative freedom does not.[9]

A clear example of a moralized notion of liberty has been attributed to Robert Nozick[10] by virtue of his view that a person's choice among a number of unpalatable alternatives "is not rendered non-voluntary [i.e., unfree] by the fact that others voluntarily chose and acted *within their rights* in a way that did not provide him with a more palatable alternative."[11] On this view, free actions are only those morally permissible actions available to an agent, and hence freedom is limited only by morally unjustified restraints.

Some, for example, might define freedom morally by the use of a moralized conception of a constraint, so that on their view only *coercion* can count as a limitation of freedom. And when these theorists make clear what they mean by "coercion," they utilize normative concepts: they might define coercion as an action that violates the rights of the coerced, for example.[12]

Non-normative freedom, on the other hand, is any conception which, in the specification of the extensions of the variables of the concept's relata, does not make reference to norms of behavior. Only under this conception would questions such as "how much freedom should be allowed by moral norms?" make sense. Of course, someone could well claim that, as a contingent matter, liberty construed this way always has some sort of value, either to the agent who is the object of freedom or to society in general. I discuss such claims below. At this point, though, it is necessary to keep clear which sort of concept is at work in the arguments that make reference to human freedom.

II. Liberal Ownership and Normative Freedom

If one understands freedom in the normative sense—the freedom to do morally justified acts (or, conversely, freedom from unjustified interference)—and one expresses the idea of moral permissibility in terms of rights, then one can claim that people have, by definition, a general right to freedom.[13] This is true because "freedom" means being unobstructed in the doing of morally permissible acts; so insofar as one has a right to do morally permissible things, one has a right to freedom.

The argument supporting the right to own property in the liberal sense based on the right to liberty could take one of two forms. In one version, it could be assumed that there are already owners of property in the population, and what is being defended is that such owners should enjoy the full set of liberal ownership rights over their property. Otherwise, the claim goes, their right to liberty would be violated. The other strategy is to attempt to justify the *acquisition* of property by virtue of the right to liberty and to claim that it is liberal ownership structures that are so acquired.

The first strategy is this: any limitation of liberal ownership rights on the part of *de facto* possessors of property is a violation of liberty; such violations of liberty (construed normatively) are always at least *prima facie* wrong (by definition); so granting any but liberal ownership structures is always *prima facie* wrong.

But such a strategy is obviously circular. For the question of just *what* one is at liberty to do (just what the scope is to one's right to freedom) must be determined by an independent argument that establishes the proposed action as morally permissible. Only after it is known what acts are permissible, or what interferences are unjustified, can it be determined which interferences amount to liberty-limiting coercion and which are merely enforcing the law. So one cannot use the right to liberty as a basis for anything until one has established independently what scope the right has.

Recall that taxation of income is inconsistent with the liberal conception of ownership, so arguments based on liberty that purport to show that taxation is impermissible can be understood as partial defenses of liberal ownership structures. In this light, let us consider Robert Nozick's claim that redistribution of resources unjustifiably restricts liberty. Nozick's view is that if the state were to prevent individuals from trading their goods in a market and keeping the proceeds from those transactions—an activity that liberal ownership structures permit—this would involve unjustifiable coercion; indeed, it would amount to "forced labor."[14] (We can assume for now that the *de facto* possessors established this possession by moral means.) Nozick supports his contention that denying these people full liberal ownership rights is a violation of their liberty with his use of the famous Wilt Chamberlain example.

The example is meant to show that given a legitimate distribution D, allowing persons to act freely will necessarily upset the pattern of D, and thus maintaining D could only be effected at the cost of limiting liberty. The example, very briefly, is this: assuming that some just distribution of goods exists (that is, assuming our justly established *de facto* possessors), we are to imagine that many of the possessors would like to pay a certain basketball player, Wilt, an extra amount of money for playing basketball, an amount which across the population adds up, say, to $250,000. Assume that a million people choose to put an extra quarter into a separate box for Wilt as they walk into the games. They do this voluntarily and are happy with the deal. After any one game, the wealth distribution that results will alter the original pattern (which is, *ex hypothesi*, just), but it will do so through the free voluntary acts of individuals. Preventing people from acting in this way in order to preserve the distribution, Nozick argues, severely restricts their liberty. Underlying this case is a principle, articulated elsewhere by Nozick, that "whatever arises from a just situation by just steps [i.e., fully voluntary transactions on the part of all legitimately concerned persons] is itself just."[15]

First, for it to be the case that the fans in the example are *free* to give their quarter to Wilt, Nozick must assume that they act within their rights in doing so. We are, after all, attributing to Nozick a normative conception of liberty. But the way Nozick supports this assumption (that the fans act within their rights) is to *assume* that entitlements have the structure of liberal ownership. He says "the central core of the notion of a property right in X . . . is the right to determine what shall be done with X; the right to choose which of the constrained set of options concerning X shall be realized or attempted."[16] Now such an account does not state the entire parameter of liberal ownership, but it is enough to support the view that the fans have a right to act as they do. But as is clear from our various discussions, it certainly cannot be automatically assumed that entitlements must contain full rights to transfer and income.

Moreover, why should the property rights of the basketball fans in Nozick's case necessarily include having a say over *where* that extra quarter goes—that they can demand that *Wilt* gets the whole quarter (as opposed to only some of it while the rest is redistributed to preserve the just distribution)? Certainly they have a *desire* that Wilt get it, but that is because (let us imagine) he is holding out for just that much and won't play for less. But this desire clearly does not give them a *right* that he get the quarter, for that would mean that they have a right that Wilt get whatever it would take to get him to play, and that is absurd.

But my central point is that the claim that the *de facto* possessors must have liberal ownership rights over their goods is *necessary* to establish the claim that denying such rights to them is an interference with their liberty. For otherwise, whether or not they had a right to do that thing—and hence whether restricting them is a restraint of liberty in the normative sense—is an open question. And after all, we are imagining that the pattern that the state is trying to protect here has at least a *prima facie* grounding in a principle of justice. And we are asking if there is a consideration on the other side that weighs against this. But this is not a balance at all, for the liberty to upset the just distribution is not a liberty at all unless it is otherwise justified by moral argument. Utilizing considerations of liberty to establish liberal ownership rights for *de facto* possessors simply begs the question or is dizzyingly circular.

But what about the other strategy just mentioned which utilizes a normative understanding of liberty? Can it be claimed that when the *de facto* possessors first acquired the goods in question, the rights structure that they acquired over those goods was liberal ownership?[17] Many have supplied strong reason to deny this,[18] and we saw in the last chapter that arguments based on the natural right to one's labor were similarly deficient in this regard. Can a natural right to liberty (in the normative sense) do any better?

I don't think so, and for reasons that the arguments in the last chapter make clear. For such a strategy would reduce to an argument for the right to property based on first occupation. And as many critics of that argument throughout history have shown, a person's right to accumulate goods is not self-evident or unassailable when so doing makes other people comparatively worse off (independent of whether they fall below some baseline set by a proviso). Invoking a general right to (moralized) liberty does nothing to change that, since again the determination of the scope of that right—and hence the question of whether it includes a right to acquire and accumulate goods—is left open. The right must be established by other means before it can meaningfully be said that a person's liberty includes such action. And consequently, when the state determines that whatever possessory rights a person might have established do not amount to liberal ownership, this cannot be said to violate the person's liberty.[19]

III. The Argument from Non-Normative Liberty

I now turn to arguments attempting to defend liberal ownership by virtue of reference to liberty in the sense that is not qualified by moral predicates. The kind of argument I have in mind here would be constructed around a premise that claims some *prima facie* value for liberty in the non-normative sense. Added to this are premises claiming that only under liberal ownership structures is this valuable phenomenon protected or maximized, despite severe inequalities of well-being that such ownership structures allow and encourage. These arguments, then, will involve at least the following claims: (1) liberty has serious *prima facie* value; (2) liberty should be protected, equalized, and/or maximized; (3) (presupposed by [2]), we can compare levels of liberty across states of affairs (that is, amounts of liberty can meaningfully be quantified); and (4) liberal ownership uniquely supports the value specified in (1). The procedure for this section is to advance considerations that weigh against each one of these assertions by focusing on three pervasive difficulties with the foregoing argument: the problems of determining how liberty is to be valued, how it is quantified, and how it could be maximized.

One question that will be crucial in all these arguments is whether a person's freedom can properly be understood as being a function of her level of material well-being. The liberty-based defenders of liberal ownership want to avoid this implication; at least most of them do. (Below I consider those who accept this implication but argue that liberal ownership allows for the maximization of *both* liberty and material well-being.) For it is accepted on all sides that the world of liberal ownership is manifestly *unequal* in terms of material wealth. And libertarian defenders of that structure want, in most cases, to rest their defense of it on the claim that liberal ownership will equally protect people's liberty. Therefore, any connection between liberty and wealth is anathema to this argument.

This is why the exact contours of the property of being free will necessarily occupy us here. In particular, it will matter very much what exactly will count as a constraint on freedom. Remember also that throughout this discussion we are considering freedom in its non-normative guise, a characteristic of persons the value of which is not given by the concept of freedom itself. This leads us to the first of the problematic premises noted just now.

The Problem of Value

Freedom construed in the non-normative sense is defined as the absence of restraints in the carrying out of a person's desires, and none of those key terms—"restraints," "person," or "desires"—is understood as a moral notion. It is simply the absence of physical barriers to action. Hence, since non-normative freedom refers to *any* acts by persons free of restraints, the concept of freedom itself does not distinguish between being free to hit others with baseball bats and being free to make political speeches in a public park. Even if we allow qualifiers of rationality into the notion (and still are willing to call it a non-normative conception), nothing in the specification of this kind of freedom narrows the range to only morally permissible acts. So the moral evaluation of allowing such freedom to flourish is not provided by the concept itself. Also, defining freedom with the use of a subjective value qualifier does not avoid difficulties, for a person may well value the act of hitting people with baseball bats a great deal, and for such a person a great deal of freedom is denied her by restraining such actions.[20]

But recall that a separate premise—that liberty of this sort (construed non-normatively) has intrinsic value—will be included in arguments linking negative liberty (L1) and liberal ownership. This value, moreover, must be intrinsic, since it would not do to say that liberal ownership protects liberty but the value of liberty is merely instrumental (in bringing about some other valued end, say). For we would then have to look more closely at the kinds of things that L1 is valuable for bringing about (L2, for example) and ask if property structures *other* than liberal ownership would more directly and effectively bring about or foster this goal.[21] It is clear, for example, that material wealth enhances L2 *directly* (since wealth is uncontroversially a general enabling resource). So if it is L2 that L1 is valuable for bringing about, and property is distributed unequally under liberal ownership, then the goal of equal liberty prized by defenders of that structure is quite elusive.

So what *intrinsic* value can negative liberty, by itself, turn out to have? Imagine cases where people have L1, freedom from restraints, but lack the enabling conditions to do what they want to do. Certainly the "freedom" to do the act, intrinsically and by itself, has no value whatsoever to the agent. For unless the absence of external physical restraints facing the agent in some way enhances the possibility that she will achieve something she wants to achieve, such an absence can have no value for the person. That is, L1 has no value except for its power to allow or bring about other things, such as L2, L3, or some other good for the agent (like desire-satisfaction generally). This point has relevance for us in that property structures like liberal ownership may equalize only L1 and, in fact, reduce (or distribute unequally) the enjoyment of L2 or L3.

The exact relation between property structures and quantities of liberty will be taken up below. For now let us simply draw the following cautionary conclusion: if liberal ownership maximizes or equalizes L1, but L1 gets its value only in its connection with L2–L4, and departures from liberal ownership promote L2–L4 directly, then the argument for liberal ownership based on liberty is on shaky ground.

The Problem of Quantification

In order to mount a defense of an economic system or property structure on the basis of liberty, one must set out exactly what it is about liberty that such systems or structures make possible. One could argue either that such systems *protect* liberty best, or that they *maximize* liberty, or that they *equalize* it, depending on which goal one thinks is worth pursuing. I will ask whether liberal ownership accomplishes these things later. Now I raise the question of whether such goals are truly worth pursuing or even whether they can be coherently described.

The protection of liberty per se (with no qualifying phrases) cannot be a plausible goal for a society, since we would then be referring to all acts of any sort (given that we are considering *non-normative* freedom here). Clearly, though, what gives the goal "protection of liberty" its intuitive pull is the protection of *particular* freedoms. Specifically, the protection of civil or political liberty, or what John Rawls calls the basic liberties,[22] is what is being described in this argument.

A famous argument for the view that liberal ownership (and free markets) protect such basic freedom was provided by Milton Friedman, who argued that only those economic systems that disseminate wealth and power *away* from the state could effectively protect political freedom. Only when the motives of profit maximization are allowed their full fruition is it possible for individuals to gain the economic power to outweigh the political control that governments wield.[23] This argument, however, presupposes that the political agenda of the corporate world will be sufficiently diverse, and sufficiently independent of the state's, for this balancing act to take place. But if the political views that one wants the freedom to express, for example, run directly counter to the interests of *both* the state and the corporate structure, there is little basis for faith in the protection of these rights. (And if such views amount to the desire to restructure the entire economic system for more egalitarian ends, this message will hardly fall on sympathetic ears in the corporate boardrooms across the country.) One need only look at how little the supposedly "free" press in the United States actually opposes the basic structural policies of the government—and remind oneself that these news organizations are owned by huge corporate entities—to realize how little economic markets ensure such freedoms. At least the incentive structure in these institutions makes no such assurances concerning general protection of these kinds of liberties.[24]

Let us now turn to arguments that defend economic structures on the basis of *promoting* liberty. This strategy involves answering the very difficult question of when, and to what extent, liberty has been increased. This question could be recast as the question of when, and to what extent, restraints have been minimized. But what, exactly, is a restraint? Presumably it is some physical barrier that makes a certain desired action or set of actions impossible for an agent. But must the actions be made *impossible* by the obstacle? It is not totally impossible for me to overcome a robber who has a gun to my head (saying "your money or your life"), but this certainly can't mean that I am really free to keep my money. This raises the sticky problem of the extent to which threats can be counted as restraints.[25] And we can skip around it as long as we maintain consistency; for example, it must be remembered that if effective threats count as restraints, then laws enforcing property structures count, *pro tanto*, as restraints on those whose actions they prohibit, and hence such laws limit their freedom.

But apart from the question of threats and coercion, how are we to determine just how much freedom different agents (with differing desires, plans, and outlooks) enjoy? For virtually any conception of a restraint, reference will necessarily be made to the desire set of the agents.[26] That is, restraints are those things that make what an agent *desires* (at a time) impossible or too costly. And once such reference is included in the concept of a restraint, the number and kind of restraints an agent faces will be as variable as the desires she has. For example, the books on my shelf apparently are not a restraint to my free action. However, if I decide to walk in a line that crosses through where they are (say a fire starts and they block what becomes my only escape route), then they are. And, on the other hand, if objects are counted as restraints only if they frustrate *actual* desires, the status of objects as possible constraints changes according to alterations in desires of the agent. (And this is not to mention the obvious problem of enumerating desires: imagine that a new law makes it impermissible for me to go out after nine o'clock. My desire to go out of my house is thereby frustrated, but so is my desire to walk down Main Street, or Jennifer Street, or Spaight Street, and so on.)

Now we could, obviously, enumerate restraints by specifying *types* of acts. But, in doing this, one must be careful not to beg crucial questions. For example, the question remains whether the quantity of non-normative freedom can be specified in this way without making contentious value judgments about the types of acts being allowed or restricted. Does X's freedom to play golf count as more or less a bit of freedom than Y's liberty to eat?

Nevertheless, for any measure of freedom where the possible or actual actions of an agent must be calculated or aggregated, the virtually intractable problem of enumerating actions will arise. For whether one counts act types or act tokens, the number of act descriptions under which a (so-called) single act may fall can be infinite, or at least only arbitrarily delineated. Also, many acts that persons desire to be free to do are better described as omissions; for example, the freedom to live in a certain place can be described as not being forced to move (being free to not move). But how many actions does living in one place over time count as? The conclusion I want to draw from these points is that it is not at all clear that the aim of increasing freedom per se is an identifiable and measurable goal at all.

Let us now consider the goal of equal liberty (or maximal equal liberty) as part of the argument for liberal ownership.[27] Such a move will not vitiate the problem of counting restraints, of course, since it must remain possible to compare the relative freedom of individuals in order to specify when they have achieved equal freedom. But I want to focus on what most see as the central bone of contention in this debate: whether to adopt a strict or a broad conception of restraints in one's calculation of freedom. This question brings us back to the issue of what I called the "humanity condition"—whether restraints are defined as those barriers to action placed (intentionally, accidentally) by human action, or more broadly, as *all* barriers to action, no matter what their genesis.

The connection between this question and liberal ownership is this: defenders of liberal ownership who base their argument on the goal of providing equal liberty must assume a "strict humanity condition" in their definition of a restraint. This is because, on their view, only effectively enforced laws count as restraints on their accounting of freedom.[28] And since, they argue, the laws that protect property apply equally to all—everyone has the same rights and opportunities with respect to her property—then the liberty that such restrictions demarcate is equally distributed. The crucial steps in that argument, of course, are these: only laws protecting property already held or protecting the opportunity to acquire (unowned) property count in the calculus of restraints, not laws that might guarantee a certain minimum level of property or income; also, only intentionally placed restraints—barriers put in place for the purpose of constraining action—matter in the quantification of liberty. The latter step is what concerns us here. For if this view is not accepted—if *any* obstruction counts in the calculus of liberty (whether placed there by the intentional actions of the state or merely by accident but in principle removable by human action)—then relative *wealth* matters in the determination of liberty. This last possibility is problematic for defenders of liberal ownership since unequal wealth is an inevitable consequence of that structure.

One position along these lines that many liberty-based defenders of capitalism take on this issue is to define restraints in terms (only) of coercion. Many versions of this kind of theory, however, utilize a moralized conception of "coercion," which will be subject to the criticisms of section II. There are, of course, versions of the coercion conception of restraints that do not imply a normative view of freedom. Such arguments are essentially the same as those defending a (strict) humanity condition, since the only thing unique about coercion relative to other obstacles is that its source is intentional human action.

What is at issue, then, is whether the strict humanity condition crucial to the argument for liberal ownership is plausible. Let us consider three attempts to defend it. A first move in this defense is to stress that the discussion of these issues must be reserved to "social freedom" and not other kinds of freedom (like freedom of the will). As Jan Narveson puts it, "Liberty in general [liberty in the sense broader than social freedom], I believe, is absence of impediment to one's actions, and it is beyond question that many such impediments are not put there—certainly not intentionally or even knowingly, at any rate—by one's fellows. . . . But our specific question in this investigation concerns the class of impediments posed by the actions of one's fellow persons, and in particular those posed knowingly (intentionally or otherwise) by them, and those whose impedimentary character, even if not known or intended, is establishable and preventable by methods of social control."[29]

But it certainly will not do just to claim that it is social liberty that we are concerned with, and since social liberty is restricted to (the absence of) humanly placed restraints, we must restrict our attention to those. For the question then arises, *why* restrict ourselves to social liberty? That very restriction is what is in question. Narveson, in the passage just quoted, does not seem to see that once we start to articulate our reasons for focusing only on intentionally (or knowingly) placed restraints, we begin to commit ourselves to a wider scope. Those restrictions on actions "whose impedimentary character . . . is establishable and preventable by methods of social control" is certainly a much wider arena of restrictions than impediments "posed by the actions of one's fellow persons." As I argue below, property rules that make it probable that some people are comparatively less able to do as they wish (because they are poorer) are certainly "established and preventable by methods of social control." Moreover, we can apply the social and material resources that might be used, say, to free spelunkers who are accidentally trapped in a cave in the same way that we can mobilize those resources to prevent someone from intentionally trapping them. If what matters to us is whether the presence of the obstacle is amenable to political or social alteration, then surely the net must be cast wider than the strong humanity condition allows.

A second reason that could be given for the requirement that only human action can (conceptually speaking) cause restraints is that unfreedom must be something which someone can, in principle, do something about. This consideration, however, will not support the strict humanity condition, since under the weak humanity condition (that something counts as a restraint if there is some person[s] who is merely *causally* responsible for the obstruction), it will *ipso facto* be possible for a person to alter the situation. This means that if a person gets accidentally locked in a closet but I happen to have the key, I am part of her lack of freedom (the obstruction she faces) when I knowingly fail to open the door. More broadly, natural barriers, such as mountains and lakes, could be included in the calculus of freedom if in principle (or even just realistically) these things could be altered by people in a way that allows some previously prevented actions.

Third, one could claim in the defense of the humanity condition that unless liberty is construed solely as L1 with a strict humanity condition in the definition of a restraint, then the property of "being free" collapses into the property of "being able to do." The latter condition (power) cannot be meaningfully quantified at all, they argue, and hence the inclusion of such a condition makes arguments from liberty useless.[30]

This last point is bolstered by the argument that a recognizable distinction must be preserved between acts and omissions.[31] That is, if mere "potential for human alteration" is the understanding of the humanity condition in defining a restraint, then the mere presence of a person (walking onto the scene, say) becomes a restraint: for example, with the weak condition, my being accidentally stuck at the bottom of a well suddenly becomes a situation of unfreedom as soon as a passerby comes upon the scene, and this result implausibly implies that that unwitting person (if she fails for any amount of time to save me) becomes part of that restraint.

The relevance of examples like this to questions of economic justice is that owners of property could always give away some of their resources to the less well-off and afford them opportunities to do things they would like to do. If a weak humanity condition is what defines a restraint, then these better-off people would contribute to restraining the freedom of the poor. This would have the unpleasant implication that liberal ownership (with unequal holdings) does not amount to equal freedom. For this reason, defenders of liberal ownership using this line of argument must insist on a strict humanity condition.

However, the acts-omissions distinction is not as relevant to this issue as defenders of liberal ownership make it sound. The analogy between the passerby in the well example and the property owner in an unequal economy is, I think, a false and misleading one. For there is not simply an omission in the case of property owners who enjoy property structures that do not include provisions for redistribution to the less well-off. As with all ownership structures, there is very much an *active* part played by the enforcement mechanisms of the state to keep resources in one set of hands instead of another. Imagine two cases. In one there are liberal ownership and unequal holdings, where the state's enforcement mechanisms keep the poor from treading on the land of the rich (say the poor are homeless squatters who need a place to live and try to camp out on the rich person's field). In a contrasting case, imagine that the state protects a different property structure, which uses some of the land in question for state-subsidized public housing for the poorer person (who merely failed to settle the land first). In *both* cases there is an active agency setting up restraints that limit one person's choices and expand those of another. If one includes those intentional acts of state agencies as possible sources of restraints, then there is no reason to call the redistribution an *introduction* of a restraint or to say that the protection of the rich person's land is simply leaving things alone.

But the major thrust of the line of argument defending a strong humanity condition is that the weaker condition will count as restraints all those obstacles that it is physically possible for people to alter, which has the effect of shrinking the category of "mere inability" almost to a vanishing point. "[F]or who can say what impediments to individual action might not be removed by the concerted efforts of [people]? For instance, all those who wished to fly to the moon might be able to do so, if human resources were devoted entirely to this end, at the expense of all the other projects on which we are now engaged."[32]

One response here would be to try to qualify the weak humanity condition by saying that obstacles must be easily or feasibly removable for them to count as restraints.[33] (This move obviously introduces an indeterminacy in the concept since feasibility varies with circumstance.) But a bolder tack would be to claim that broadening the concept of freedom in this way, and hence acknowledging the implications just mentioned, is not so very implausible after all. Take, for example, a clear case of mere inability that seems to turn into a case of unfreedom under the weaker condition: someone wants to fly without an airplane, and she claims that if enough research and technology were devoted to that end, she indeed could do so. But if she actually claims that the only reason she cannot fly is that the resources that would make it possible are being used elsewhere, and they *could* be used to allow her to fly, and there are people who could act in a way that delivers them to her, and she is correct in these claims, then what is conceptually implausible about saying that her claim involves a question of freedom? After all, the *structure* of her claim is the same as the case where a prison guard is in a position to unlock a cell door but chooses not to do so and therefore contributes to the unfreedom of the prisoners. Now certainly the claim of unfreedom by the erstwhile flyer would get virtually no *weight* in political discussions, for what is necessary to remove her constraint is too costly. But this does not entail that the case is not one of freedom.

This response amounts to shifting the intuitive burden. On the strict view, for some obstacle to count as a restraint on freedom, some individual must have put it there (or be responsible for its removal). But such a position simply avoids, through conceptual sleight of hand, the very focus that certain critics of free markets and capitalism want us to consider: that even though no individual ever intended to limit the choices and opportunities of the poor and working class, and even though no individual did some act X which, by itself, had this effect, it is nevertheless the case that the *structural* organization of capitalism (in particular the unequal access to capital resources) makes it *inevitable* that those classes suffer those limitations of their opportunities. And to say that this cannot be spoken of in terms of freedom—especially given that the experience of limited choices for those people is as real and painful as it would be if some dictator planned it all out—is to commit a sort of conceptual kidnapping.

An example may make this point more convincing. Imagine a community of people who live in a valley that has only one route of access. Say that some other group, the homesteaders, start building houses on the side of one of the mountains.

The collective effect of this home building causes a rockslide on another part of the mountain that blocks the route of access to the valley. Now assume that the homesteaders had gotten permission to build (that is, except for the rockslide, there would be no complaint), and assume that no *one* house contributed enough erosion of the soil to cause the slide (not even the last one—say that all of the houses are built simultaneously but that after some time, the soil weakens and the slide occurs).

It seems clear that the valley residents are straightforwardly unfree to leave because of the rockslide. And to say that since no homesteader *intended* their state or knowingly caused the rockslide is merely to introduce what to all concerned will be a gross irrelevancy. The valley people simply can't leave because the homesteaders built their homes, and this seems as clear a case of unfreedom as we are likely to get.[34] So if this is the right conclusion in this case, it shows that *individual* responsibility is not necessary for restraint of freedom. Neither is it necessary that the presence of the obstacle be intended. What one is left with, then, is the weak version of the humanity condition.

Now this, as we have seen, is exactly the conclusion that defenders of liberal ownership do not want. For if a person's lack of opportunity to do something is due merely to factors which others could (feasibly) alter, then a person's liberty becomes partly a function of material resources. And since liberal ownership will, *ex hypothesi*, result in the unequal distribution of resources, then liberty also will be unequally enjoyed by people in that economy. The enforcement of liberal ownership by the state actively puts into place a nexus of constraints and opportunities that are differentially and unequally distributed in the society. Hence, one cannot argue with these premises that liberal ownership protects equal liberty.

Does Liberal Ownership Maximize Liberty?

There may seem to be an initial attraction to the claim that only liberal ownership allows for or promotes *maximal* freedom. After all, liberal ownership ostensibly includes the fullest package of rights associated with property. The claim is that there are things one can do under a regime of liberal ownership that cannot be done in the relevant egalitarian alternatives. An owner of property under liberal ownership can possess, use, or trade a thing in a way that no one else can possess, use, or trade that thing (without her permission). If A has liberal ownership rights to a piece of land, say, all the uses that the land could be put to, all the free acts that are performable vis-à-vis that land, are things that only A can do or allow to be done.

But how does this increase liberty overall? How are there more kinds of performable free acts under this system than under a system of more limited rights? Under the latter sort of system, *other* individuals might be able to do some of the things with the land that only A (the property owner) could do under a system of liberal ownership. Under a system of communal ownership, for instance, the same number of free acts could be performed with a single piece of property, but things would be done by different people.

An argument defending liberal ownership along these lines would have to claim that liberal ownership requires fewer restraints on the actions of persons generally than would alternative, say more egalitarian, sets of property rights. However, as long as all threats and sanctions are viewed as on a par, then the freedom of the property owner is but one side of the coin; the other is the restraints faced by the non-owners to do those same things. If the alternative to liberal ownership is structured in order to redistribute property, then no increase in restraints is necessarily put into place by these kinds of property rights. All property structures are bound by the sanctions of law regardless of who enjoys the rights, so if A is denied the right to accumulate a greater fortune so that a sum of money can be transferred to B, no new restraints are necessary to bring this about.

To make this point more obvious, just imagine that all transactions between individuals had to go through a central clearinghouse. The differences between liberal ownership—where all the proceeds to trades flow to only the explicitly contracting parties—and a redistributive property system would not involve any new restraints facing actors. It is merely a question of routing income flows in a different direction.

Although we assumed it for the purposes of this chapter, it is important to state here that liberal ownership structures are not necessarily equivalent to free market mechanisms. As I argued in chapter 2, under a system of liberal ownership monopolies are not ruled out. If they were (based on concern for the distribution of scarce goods), that would amount to a limitation of ownership rights because of distributive considerations and therefore not liberal ownership. Under the terms of liberal ownership, when a monopoly is formed on some commodity (even labor), the person who owns the monopolized product sets the terms of sale of the good (if sales are intended—they needn't be). The price of the good, as set by the owner, determines that a set of people who otherwise would have bought the product in question may not be able to do so because of the enforcement mechanism of prices and sales. And as long as the monopoly holders are not forced to sell their products at prices most can afford, the freedom of many (to use the products) is dependent on the monopolists, whose interest is not to increase freedom but to increase their own profits. The inevitable result is a significant loss of freedom. The point here is not whether the owner in question might be induced to sell (out of self-interest), for we are asking about the amount of freedom allowed under a set of laws, and here maximum use of the products is guaranteed only through *limitations* on the property rights of owners.[35]

But of course many defenders of private property would never accept the assumption that the total store of goods produced in the economy remains constant no matter what property structure is adopted. The major thrust of their argument, in fact, will be that the greater *productivity* of private ownership regimes makes for larger stores of goods and hence more freedom to use them overall. We will examine this claim shortly, but notice that such a move crucially alters the strategy of justification of liberal ownership from a *direct* to an *indirect* justification. What is being argued here is that a state should adopt that property structure that best achieves its distributive and productivity goals; liberal ownership does this; so one should adopt liberal ownership. I will strongly question, as many have, the second premise in the argument, but it must be stressed that the value of liberty in this line of reasoning has been thrust into the shadows.[36]

Many libertarians and conservative political theorists justify institutions of private property with reference to the instrumental role played by such structures in increasing productivity, and thus maximizing freedom overall in the economy. Any justification of liberal ownership along these lines must suppose not only that the economic system for which private property is a necessary component is a more productive economy, but that the larger stock of commodities produced is then *distributed* in a way that increases overall liberty.

But even if it were admitted for the sake of argument that total productivity is maximized under liberal ownership, the system of wage labor and class division that it inevitably engenders must be considered in light of its effect on freedom. For wage laborers (who may far outnumber the owners of capital goods) have no say in the organization and production decisions that directly affect their lives. Ownership of the productive facilities permits the owners to make a wide variety of decisions—such as to open or close a plant—which may cause employees to move or change work hours or shift their skill development, decisions that directly enhance their freedom and control of their own lives. And this level of freedom and control is exactly denied to those hired under contractual arrangements, notwithstanding the leverage that collective bargaining might afford to a limited number of workers who can utilize that tool effectively.[37]

Finally, since the value of non-normative liberty of the sort we are considering is only *prima facie* value, the disvalue of the inequalities themselves produced by liberal ownership structures in a market economy have an independent and perhaps overriding moral weight in directing the distribution of liberty, especially if the total amount of liberty is not significantly lessened by a more egalitarian distribution. Since liberal ownership in a market economy will inevitably result in great inequalities of income and wealth that result in great inequalities in freedom, then the disvalue of these inequalities would justify favoring an alternative distribution (based on a different ownership structure that serves to reduce such inequalities).

To sum up, I have argued that in order to mount a plausible defense of liberal ownership based on considerations of non-normative liberty, one has to make an array of claims concerning certain aspects of liberty construed in the sense of L1. These claims were that liberty so construed had *prima facie* intrinsic value, that its presence could be quantified (which included the claim that restraints could be neutrally counted), that a strong humanity condition must be included in its definition, and that liberal ownership would be effective in bringing about the laudable goals of protecting, equalizing, and/or maximizing individual liberty. What I have done in the foregoing discussions in section III was to raise serious questions about the cogency of each one of these claims. I conclude that although considerations of liberty should enter into justifications of property structures at some point, these considerations do not support liberal structures in any systematic way.

The idea of being free from external, physical restraints but lacking the enabling resources to carry out one's wishes hardly qualifies as a political notion that inspires devotion or obligation. This is all the more true if the person in question lacks the basic capacity for autonomous choice—if the values and desires she finds herself with are so ill-formed or fractured that she would not think of herself as leading an authentic and independent life. If liberal ownership is the framework for the economic policies of the state, there are no guarantees that economic patterns will ensure that citizens can achieve such autonomy. This conclusion provides even more reason to reject that notion when considerations of freedom are before us.

So far, the arguments I have assembled here, many of which have been made by others in different form, have centered on the distributive characteristics of liberal ownership and of the detrimental effects these have on freedom. It is worth repeating that the reason liberal ownership conflicts with all citizens enjoying equal freedoms is that when owners have rights to trade goods and keep income from those trades (in a world of unequally talented people and differential access to new goods), people will enjoy different amounts of freedom. This is not (necessarily) the case if only possession and use rights (alone) were granted with restricted rights to income. We will make use of this conclusion in Part III below, where I will present a model of ownership that I will claim more faithfully captures the basic components of freedom (autonomy), a model that makes much more explicit the true relation between the ownership of property and political liberty.

5

Ownership, Markets, and Moral Desert

I was driving in La Jolla, California, once and noticed on the new, gold Rolls Royce in front of me the following personalized license plate: EARND. The ideas contained in this chapter were probably first galvanized at that moment.

What could it *mean* to say that such a bit of luxury was earned? How many times greater effort did that person put into her paid activity, or how many times more valuable was that activity, than was the case with the person in the next lane whose car cost approximately one-sixth the cost of the Rolls? Or, more amazingly, did that person think that she was to that degree more *virtuous* than those of us around her who received such relatively paltry rewards from our society?

Turning these thoughts in the direction of property rights, we should now ask whether, when the state restructures the liberal ownership rights of individuals, or when it refuses to recognize such rights that individuals might claim to have over their legitimately acquired property, does it thereby give insufficient respect to what those individuals legitimately deserve? And do the free markets that liberal ownership allows and fosters in fact succeed in giving this respect to people? In particular, doesn't the market reward participants exactly in accordance with their contribution to the welfare of other willing participants, and isn't such contribution grounds for moral desert?

I construct arguments in this chapter that answer all these questions in the negative. I proceed by dividing the claims into two categories: those contending that when individuals acquire goods through labor investment, they are given what they truly deserve *only* when the rights they acquire over those goods amount to liberal ownership; and those claiming that the markets that are facilitated by liberal ownership in fact deliver goods to individuals in a way that accords with their just deserts. My major concern in this chapter is with the latter claim, for the right to retain goods from market interaction and competition—the right to the income—is a key component of liberal ownership. Since, as I argue, individuals do not deserve the income flows from imperfect markets (profits or, more specifically, economic rents), then they do not deserve the rights to those flows. Therefore, liberal ownership is not justified in this way. Before attending to that argument strategy, let us consider again the question of initial acquisition.

I. A Lockean Desert Argument

Lawrence Becker constructs what he believes is a Lockean argument for the ownership of property in which emphasis is placed on the merit of adding value to undeveloped resources and on desert claims that could be made on the basis of such merit.[1] For Becker, "desert" is a moral concept that is essential to moral discourse itself; that is, a coherent moral system could not be constructed without the use of a notion of deserving. The basis for this claim is this: moral systems must include moral requirements of agents; these requirements entail, according to Becker, moral *sanctions* (blame, for instance) for those who violate the requirements; and since these sanctions, which are constitutive of moral systems must be, by definition, deserved (that is, the persons to whom the sanctions apply must be blameworthy or deserve blame) then "to ask whether desert is an intelligible concept is to call into question the whole enterprise of moral judgment."[2] So morality per se includes and makes intelligible the notion of an agent's deserving something.

With this notion in place, Becker constructs the following argument for property ownership.

1. When it is beyond what morality requires them to do for others, people deserve some benefit for the value their (morally permissible) labor produces, and conversely, they deserve some penalty for the disvalue their labor produces.
2. These benefits and penalties should be proportional to, and fitting for, the types of labor done.
3. When, and only when, nothing but property rights in the things produced are a fitting benefit for the labor, and the benefit of property rights is proportional to the value produced by the labor, the property rights are deserved.
4. Any diminution of value by labor is assessed against the laborer as a penalty deserved for the loss produced.[3]

In short, developing resources through labor makes the resources more valuable, and since making a thing more valuable can be considered a service, the laborer deserves some benefit for that service. And when *owning* the resource is a fitting and proportional benefit, then the laborer deserves to own it.

I do not think, however, that this strategy succeeds in grounding *liberal* ownership rights in acquired resources. First, Becker puts much more weight on the notion of desert than is justified by the argument cited above. For all that is shown there is that deserving *blame* or *praise* is essential to the notion of a system of moral requirements.[4] Second, it is not at all clear just how the community is benefited by the development of a resource by a laborer (which is what Becker thinks grounds the desert claim). Certainly if the laborer develops the resource and then sells it to individuals in the community for a price they are happy to pay, then we might say that the latter are benefited by the development. But this transaction is in no way *required* by the laborer-owner since the right to transfer or alienate the resource is hers alone. If the transaction in question *were* required, the laborer would not have liberal ownership rights over the resource (that is, the right to alienate would not be fully hers). But a requirement that an owner sell at an advantageous price is the only way that everyone in the community benefits from the development of the resource. And if the community does not benefit (potentially), then why does the laborer deserve anything for adding value to the resource?

Recall that for this argument to stand up, it must be the case that the community benefits *maximally* from the act of appropriation and the liberal ownership of the appropriator. That is to say that the combination of act (of appropriation) and ownership structure benefited the community more than some available alternative (for instance, the combination of the act and a redistributive property structure). The claim that granting liberal ownership would provide such a benefit is, of course, highly contentious and gets us into questions of maximal productivity and overall benefit, which are treated in detail in the next chapter. But like the indirect argument based on liberty at the close of chapter 4, the strategy of defending liberal ownership based on maximal productivity of the economy it engenders, is an exceedingly unstable defense.

This brings our attention to the requirement of proportionality (this criticism is not made fully clear until the close of the next section). To say that I deserve my property ownership because I benefited the community with my labor is to say that the value of that benefit is proportional to the enjoyment of the ownership of my property. But these values are exceedingly hard to measure meaningfully. More important, it is inevitable that the patterns of supply and demand that at one time fix the general value of my laboring activity will not remain constant. So what I deserve will be a fluctuating and ill-defined entity. An argument such as Becker's can only support at best a synchronic and fleeting entitlement. And what I say in the following section casts even more doubt on the plausibility of making the kinds of value comparisons that are necessary for arguments like this one to fly at all.

So Becker's argument fails as a desert-based defense of liberal ownership. Even if the argument were successful in the abstract, however, its conclusions would have little applicability to real-world economies for reasons discussed at the close of chapter 3. Namely, history did not occur in the way that the desert-based arguments require if they are to be used to bolster the claims of contemporary property owners. So the desert argument concerning first acquisition remains purely hypothetical.[5]

II. Markets and Moral Desert

Now let us take a look at desert arguments from a slightly different angle. Imagine that all the appropriating in the economy has been done. The question, then, is what structure of ownership rights these individuals should have over their goods. The particular aspect of liberal ownership that we will focus on here is rights to transfer and gain income from property, for these are the rights that connect property rights with free markets (along with other complex assumptions). We must ask whether free markets (which, let us assume, liberal ownership ensures) operate so that goods are distributed to those who most deserve them. If they do, this provides a powerful argument for liberal ownership, and, conversely, it provides a powerful criticism against alternative, distribution-sensitive property structures based on their alleged conflict with the deservingness of the participants in the economy.

I argue, however, that in general people do not in fact deserve what they get from market interactions when "what they get" is determined by the competitive forces coming to bear on the market (the laws of supply and demand). This more general claim is meant to apply to all participants in the market (workers and their wages as well as capitalists and their profits). However, my strategy here is to focus on the particular question of whether owners of firms (entrepreneurs) deserve income rights (the profits they reap in a competitive capitalist market). In particular, I argue that it is not plausible to claim that entrepreneurs deserve their profits, and hence it is not plausible that they deserve the income rights that grant them these profits. Therefore, liberal ownership is not fully justified by considerations of desert. Generalizing from this claim, I suggest how moral desert is inappropriate as a justification of market shares whenever competition determines the magnitude of those shares.

I deviate significantly here from the usual strategies for denying the relevance of desert claims to principles of distributive justice. These strategies include either a challenge of the moral value of the benefit provided by entrepreneurs and capitalists upon which claims of desert are based (the provision of goods to consumers),[6] or an argument, like that made by John Rawls, that the winning of profits in the end emanates from the possession of talents and dispositions that are not themselves deserved.[7] Although I am not unsympathetic to these lines of criticism, my argument does not depend on either of them. In fact, I assume that selling goods via market mechanisms can provide some benefit to willing purchasers,[8] and whatever talents entrepreneurs utilize are themselves deserved. Despite these assumptions, I claim that entrepreneurial profits are not deserved.

I begin by defining the relevant terms and then explicating the structure of desert claims. In section IV, I consider an argument that entrepreneurs in fact do deserve their profits, and I raise several objections to it. I then set out the argument that owners do not deserve the income flows from trades in a market. I use the example of entrepreneurs and their profits as a test case, though I close by showing how this case can be generalized to all participants in a competitive market. And, in particular, it is the income rights component of the ownership package that is brought into question by these arguments.

III. Entrepreneurs and Profits

The term "entrepreneur" has been used variously to refer to anyone from a robber baron to a small shop owner to a moneylender. There seem to emerge from these usages, however, two general ideas that also fit with some of the standard economic definitions of an entrepreneur:[9] the entrepreneur is the primary organizer of production and is the person who holds primary title to the capital assets of the firm. Both of these notions can be summarized by calling the entrepreneur, simply, the person who owns the productive factors of a firm.

This definition obviously collapses the familiar notions of an entrepreneur considered as the creator of a new business who seeks investors to back the venture, and the capitalist, considered as the investor of his or her own capital in anticipation of positive returns. Combining these roles in this way helps to clarify the question of whether profits are deserved by imagining a single person who both organizes production and collects the profits of the firm. This broad characterization lends the most plausibility to the claim I am denying, for I am thereby considering a wider range of activities and characteristics that could serve as the basis for a claim of moral desert.

An entrepreneur who owns the capital assets of a firm will have final say over how those assets are utilized. The entrepreneur is the *primary* organizer of production in that she holds ultimate organizational control even if she chooses to delegate managerial functions to representatives—that is, she could hire consultants and managers. But in such a case, the entrepreneur still has the primary organizational control insofar as whomever she hires she can also *fire*, if not tell what to do. So in this sense, the entrepreneur is the primary organizer of production. In short, the entrepreneur is the person who perceives a certain malallocation of resources, information, or technology, and exploits this situation by starting a firm.[10] Even if all the start-up capital was borrowed, and even if managers and consultants were hired to carry out the organizational tasks, it is the entrepreneur who begins the process and thus is responsible for its operations.

Turning now to profits. This notion has also been variously rendered in the literature, with meanings ranging from merely "interest on investment capital" to (the morally question-begging) "reward for innovations and risk taking."[11] Generally speaking, however, profit is the difference between the market price for a good and the total cost of its production. Hence, in imperfect markets, the price of production (where that includes wages, rents, interest on borrowed capital, and the like) may differ from the price of the good that the market yields. Pure profit is this difference, whether it is positive or negative (though here I simplify and speak only of positive profits).[12] This understanding of profit makes it equivalent to what I have defined in earlier chapters as "economic rent."

It is important to remember that production costs (the aggregate price of all input factors) include the wage bill, interest payments, resource costs, and depreciation costs. An input factor is any component of production that makes a marginal contribution to the monetary revenue of the firm. An entrepreneur's contribution here is not, strictly speaking, an input factor, since payment for whatever services she renders is (by definition) not part of the wage bill. Her income (profits) is whatever is left after the complete bill is paid for all inputs after a cycle of production and sale.

As I discussed in chapter 2, under conditions of perfect competition—ideal markets—an equilibrium will be reached, and at this equilibrium, profits for all firms will be zero. This falling rate of profit results from constantly emerging competitors' entering any market sector where firms are enjoying positive profit, thus driving prices down until they do not exceed the costs of production. But in real-world markets positive profits emerge when there is not completely free and costless shifting of resources. This malallocation of resources (where that includes information, technology, or even credit) allows the market price of a commodity to stabilize above the marginal costs of the production of that commodity. An entrepreneur exploits the opportunity to produce such a good at a cost lower than the price the market will yield and to do so before others do.

So profits arise only when there is a sufficient lack of competition from other potential producers of the good. What *determines* the margin of profit is the presence of effective barriers to the entrance into the market of other producers. Such restrictions on entrance could be caused in any number of ways: monopolies of various kinds (on resources or technology), high transaction costs, lack of credit for start-up capital, and lack of information about consumer demand are examples. None of these factors are things an entrepreneur brings about herself (or so we are supposing), but they are nevertheless crucial in the determination of the quantity of profit returned to the firm (and thus to the entrepreneur). This is not to deny the importance of consumer demand for the economic success of a firm. But entrepreneurial profits are the result of *both* consumer demand and the presence or absence of competing firms. This point, as we shall see, is crucial.

We come now to the concept of moral desert. This notion has been given a much recognized structural analysis by Joel Feinberg along the following lines: "S deserves X in virtue of F, where S is a person, X some mode of treatment, and F some fact about S, [and] the value of F (the desert bases) are determined in part by the nature of the various X's in question."[13] So a person deserves some benefit or loss when there is some fact about her that is generally accepted as providing a reason grounding such a claim. And the response in question is both appropriate for, and proportional to, the relevant characteristics of the desert bases.

In addition, the concept of desert is an essentially non-consequentialist notion. The justification of a particular claim to deserve something cannot, by the logic of the term, make reference to the results or consequences of the person's getting the reward or punishment in question. This is not to say that consequences are barred from consideration at the level of evaluating the bases of the desert claim. We do say, for example, that the criminal *caused* harm and therefore deserves punishment. But it is inappropriate to justify the reward or punishment itself with regard to *its* consequences. We will see in section IV the relevance of this fact. Also, for the purposes of this chapter, I view desert claims as *prima facie* moral claims, which provide a defeasible moral reason that the deserving person(s) should receive the thing or mode of treatment deserved. This is not to say that denying the appropriateness of a desert claim rules out various alternative justifications for the receipt of some treatment, but the desert claim can be separated out of the justification and tested for its independent plausibility.

The condition of proportionality necessitates further attention, as it will be crucial in the arguments to follow. For a person to deserve, for example, a favorable mode of treatment like praise, there must be some fact about her that provides a basis for that praise. If she performed some difficult and noble act, for example, we would say the praise was deserved. But what must also be true for it to hold that she deserves the particular bit of praise offered, is both that praise is an appropriate response to the behavior in question and that the amount of praise given is proportional to the goodness or nobility of the act. If the condition of proportionality is violated—when the response is too much or too little—we say that the person in question does not deserve *that*.[14]

Another way to put the proportionality condition is this: it must be the case that the factors upon which the desert claim is based are the determining ground of the magnitude of the benefit or harm deserved. Proportionality does not mean merely an accidental correlation of one with the other, but a relation between the two where the person receives a certain mode of treatment *because* of the characteristics calling for that treatment. That is, S deserves X in virtue of F only when the nature of X—its magnitude and quality—is determined in strict accordance with the value or disvalue of F. As we will see, the details of these concepts are crucial for evaluating the arguments that rest upon them.

IV. Why Entrepreneurs Do Not Deserve Their Profits

Upon what basis, then, might it be claimed that entrepreneurs deserve their profits? What is it that entrepreneurs do, in the course of their roles as primary organizers of production and owners of productive factors, that might ground the claim that they deserve the economic surplus after the production and sale of their goods? Later in this section, I consider two answers to these questions: one is that the entrepreneur takes the relevant risks with the initial capital investments and so deserves the resulting profit; the second, which is my main point of concern, is that the effort and skill that entrepreneurs display in spotting the relevant demand for a product, and then meeting that demand, result in the provision of a benefit to the consumers of the product, and for this they deserve the resulting profit.

Before considering these issues, however, I would like to consider a desert-based argument for entrepreneurial profits that travels a different path and that I also think is mistaken. One could argue, for example, that allowing owners or entrepreneurs to keep the profits returned to them by the market provides valuable incentives both for themselves to continue their production practice and for others to join in. This observation could motivate a kind of institution-relative desert claim. Such desert claims are structured so that those who engage in activities that contribute to the smooth operation of an established institution whose rules indicate that the receipt of certain reward is appropriate for such activity deserve that reward.[15] If one of the essential goals of baseball, for example, is that the best team should win, and my playing contributes to my team's being the best, then I (in part) deserve the victory.

Applied to entrepreneurs and profits, the argument would depend on the claim that the market is an institution with well-defined goals and reward systems. The goals of the market surely include directing the distribution of scarce resources in an efficient manner. Profits, then, provide the appropriate incentives in relation to those institutional goals. This incentive mechanism operates because profits emerge from an initial malallocation of resources, and signals sent by prices (and carried on by profits) serve to correct that allocation and put items into the hands of those who most value them, so those profits serve the essential goals of the market (efficient distribution of scarce resources).

But such a defense of the claim that profits are deserved fails in several interesting ways. First, the institution-relative desert claim must be only as powerful as (and indeed is derivative from) a separate moral evaluation of the goals of the institution. If the institution had *evil* goals, its rules awarding goods to its constituents would hardly qualify as meeting the conditions of moral desert. Consider an institution such as the Mafia, for example, whose institutional achievement rules might demand that a person kill another person in order to avenge a minor insult made against the godfather. Imagine also that the effective carrying out of this action successfully contributes to the institutional goals of the syndicate. Certainly one could not say that the henchman who does this job well deserves a reward, in the morally relevant sense of that term. For no one would thereby have a moral reason to respond to the claim and grant the reward. This point applies even if one views institution-relative desert claims as having only *prima facie* force but subject to being outweighed by other moral considerations. In cases such as these, I would contend, it has no moral force *at all*. To say that there is an institution-relative sense in which the person deserves the reward is merely to use the word "desert" in a non-moral manner.

More importantly, when one breaks down this strategy of defending entrepreneurial profits, it turns out to be a *consequentialist* defense of a claim of desert. If one bases the desert claim on the entrepreneurial functions of changing production strategies and on the incentives for continued investment by herself and by others that the receipt of profits induces, and one also refers to the beneficial effects of this incentive pattern, one is focusing on the beneficial effects of *awarding the benefit deserved*. And such a desert basis is inappropriate, for, as we have said, desert is an "essentially backward looking concept."[16] (We might say, for example, that if we gave in to the demands of a terrorist organization, it would, given the constrained choices we face, have the good result of initiating the freeing of the hostages being held. But this would not by any means entail that the terrorist deserved the ransom.)

So the argument grounding the receipt of profits in a claim of desert cannot point to the beneficial *effects* of that process. Rather it must depend only on the past actions of the deserving person (or her abiding character traits). It is therefore crucial to avoid turning a purportedly desert-based argument into a result-oriented, incentive argument for owners' profits.

With this point in mind, let us now focus squarely on the activities engaged in by entrepreneurs which, apart from the results of their receiving profits, provides a benefit. In particular, we will look at the supposed benefit that the entrepreneur delivers in developing and producing a new product (or an old one in a different way) as that which would provide the direct basis for a claim of desert.

Within the parameters to which we now turn, there are two separate strategies for arguing that entrepreneurial profits are deserved. The first is to claim that in winning profits, an entrepreneur displays superior traits of character that can themselves be the basis for a claim of desert. This is a position that Rawls attacks. He argues that such traits of character, while they may be noteworthy and valuable, are, in part at least, the inevitable results of natural talents and inborn capacities that are not themselves deserved, and thus cannot be the basis for a claim of moral desert. "[A person's] character depends in large part upon fortunate family and social circumstances for which he can claim no credit. The notion of desert seems not to apply to these cases."[17]

Rawls has been variously criticized for this line of argument.[18] One type of response is to say that our natural talents are in fact deserved if anything is, for eventually all our actions and dispositions can be traced back to either natural capacities or conditions of our upbringing. So if we do not deserve things based on these, how can anything be deserved at all?[19] Second, it can be argued that Rawls is too narrow in his focus on moral *character* in evaluating the status of moral desert. For a claim that entrepreneurs deserve their profits could be based on the moral worth of *actions* taken by these individuals that are voluntary and cannot be said to be necessarily the result of natural endowments or upbringing. If anything is the basis for desert claims, it is the free actions of agents. Penal systems are designed according to this very idea. So I now want to consider this line, namely, that the actions of entrepreneurs are such that they ground desert of the profits granted by their income rights.

The first suggestion I consider is that entrepreneurs deserve their profits because they have borne an undue burden of risk in developing productive factors and starting a firm. That is, the entrepreneur takes a less risk-averse stance toward capital (and time and even reputation) in facing the possibility that the goods he or she produces will not be met by sufficient demand from consumers. Hence, it is claimed that the bearing of this risk is the basis for the desert of profits that arise if the venture is indeed successful.

However, the objections to this line of argument are straightforward.[20] First, taking a risk, by itself, would not qualify as grounds for a desert claim unless the point of the risk taking is in some independent way praiseworthy or blameworthy. This is so despite our proclivity to say "she got what she deserved" when someone loses on a foolhardy risk. We wouldn't say, however, that a mountain climber deserves to fall because of the high risk of doing so that she assumes.

What this shows, I think, is that risk taking is not itself sufficient ground for deserving anything. It depends completely on the point of a person's taking a risk. Risking one's life in battle is often thought of as grounds for praise or decoration but only when the intended outcome of the behavior is itself noble or worthwhile. Taking the same risks for some evil or selfish end, or just for the hell of it, would not support a claim for deserving anything (except perhaps disdain or ridicule). Moreover, it is often the case that the relation between risk taking and deservingness diverges (and indeed runs counter to what desert demands): when the level of risk a person assumes becomes too high, the strength of the claim to deserve something (like praise) diminishes. We call an overly risky person foolhardy, for example, and hence *less* deserving of the praise that a more cautious individual would merit.

Similarly, the relation between the riskiness of some production venture and the return of a positive rate of profit is a complicated one, and not always in line with the presuppositions of the argument under discussion. For often highly risky ventures return relatively low rates of profit, and so-called sure-things—where the initial venture capital required is low and the probability of market success is high—can return a high rate of profit. And as we said, rewards received and desert bases that ground them must be proportional, so it cannot be the mere assumption of the risk that grounds the claim for deserving profits. It must be established that the risk is taken to achieve some beneficial or praiseworthy end.

This then brings us to the second proposal. This claim is that the basis on which entrepreneurs deserve their profits is that a benefit is provided by the production and sale of a good for which there is sufficient consumer demand. After all, those who buy the product in question, at a price that results in a profit for the entrepreneur, must have wanted or even needed that product, since we assume that consumer actions are voluntary. This provision of a benefit, at the cost of the entrepreneur's time, effort, and creative and organizational skills, is the kind of activity which would ground the claim that the entrepreneur deserves any resulting profits returned to the firm. So the claim amounts to this:

> An entrepreneur E deserves some profit P by virtue of the fact F that E has provided a benefit to a set of individuals, and the relation between the values of F and P meets the propriety and proportionality conditions of desert claims.

As I presently argue, my denial of this claim rests on the contention that the factors determining the magnitude of the profit returned after a cycle of production and exchange necessarily run afoul of the proportionality requirement for all desert claims set out above. That is, while we are assuming for argument's sake that the entrepreneur performs a service to the community of people that purchase her product, and thus might deserve some positive response, the *profit* she earns cannot be that deserved response. This is because an essential part of what determines the magnitude of profit for the production cycle is the proximity and capacity of potential competitors, and these factors are independent of the bases upon which the desert claim is purportedly made.

Recall that one of the essential factors in the determination of market prices for goods is the unmet demand for those goods in that sector of the market. And what affects that unmet demand are the various barriers to entering the market that face other potential producers, whose competitive presence would drive prices below what could be offered by the original producer-entrepreneur. The profit returned, then, which is a function of the market price, is directly determined by these barriers: such things as monopolies held by the entrepreneur—on resources, information, or technology (including patents and copyrights); lack of attractive credit opportunities for new producers; other high transaction costs (like the cost of physical relocation); and the like. And, again, these are conditions that the entrepreneur did not herself create; and more important, they are not part of what we have described as the beneficial effects of entrepreneurial activities (the desert bases F).

Frank Knight has put essentially the same point this way: "Nearly all supplies of goods and services . . . enjoy some degree of monopoly. Each has a monopoly with a certain *market area*, and competition is effective only at the boundary between market areas."[21] In other words, the size and scope of that limited sectoral monopoly determines the size of the profit margin returned on the sale of the commodity produced. And the various factors listed above determining the profit margin are not part of the value of entrepreneurial activity (which is limited to meeting demand).

That value, after all, amounts to the provision of a beneficial good or service to a group of consumers willing to pay the market price for the commodity. This benefit is not affected by the *source* of the product (except insofar as the source affects prices). So whether or not the good is provided by our original entrepreneur or by some competitor, the benefit (the product's being consumed) remains the same. In fact, since the existence of competing producers effectively drives the price down, the benefit of the entire enterprise to individual consumers is increased when profits to producers decrease.

My main point, however, is that the size of the profit is not *determined* by the magnitude of consumer benefit upon which the purported desert claim is made. Imagine an analogous case of a criminal who deserves some punishment. For it to be the case that the criminal deserves the particular sentence given to her, its severity must be proportional to the harmfulness of her criminal acts. If, for example, prison sentences were randomly pulled out of a hat, we would not say that the prisoner deserved that punishment, for the severity of the sentence was not determined by the harmfulness of the crime. To make the analogy closer to the present case, imagine that the sentence was determined, not by chance, but by the availability of prison space in the area, or the numbers of guards employed by the facility. These factors are not related to the severity of the crime; so, if they determine the punishment, we would not say that the criminal deserves that particular sentence. As we saw, desert is a fundamentally non-consequentialist moral notion: what is deserved can only be determined by the value or disvalue of the factors that are the basis for the desert claim.

Rawls makes a similar claim when he writes that "the extent of one's contribution (estimated by one's marginal productivity) depends upon supply and demand. Surely a person's moral worth does not vary according to how many offer similar skills, or happen to want what he can produce. No one supposes that when someone's abilities are less in demand or have deteriorated . . . his moral deservingness undergoes a similar shift."[22] Although my claim is similar, it does not concern the varying moral worth of the character of the entrepreneur, but rather it is based on the arbitrary relation between the entrepreneur's supposed contribution to the benefit of others and his profit margin.

Now it may be objected here that the presence or absence of other producers of the same product actually does affect the value of the contribution of the initial entrepreneur's product. This is because the marginal value of the product (which, it is assumed, is equal to the benefit received by a purchaser of a single extra increment of it) increases or decreases with the competitive threat posed by other producers. So the benefit provided actually is proportional to the profit. This line, however, goes astray in two ways. First, it can plausibly be argued that the marginal value of a particular product is not a proper measure of the welfare increase in its consumption.[23] It is an economist's fiction that the "equation" between price, marginal value, and welfare is in fact an equation. The various fluctuations in the relative values of consumable products, from Edsels to hula hoops to heroin, most often have little to do with the relative utility gained by consumption of those products, or more generally with the good consumers receive from them. This is not exactly to deny our earlier assumption about the benefits of consumption but to say that even if the purchase of the product reflects a welfare increase for the person, that increase is not *measured* in any precise way by its price (at least in the real—imperfectly competitive—world).

Second, this objection ignores all of the arbitrary ways in which products' marginal values, as well as corresponding profits, can fluctuate due to competitive pressures. Imagine that a particular firm can take advantage of a sudden drop in the price of a single input factor, a price change that competing firms lack access to (a favorable wage arrangement with a non-unionized labor pool, for example); and imagine that this drop does not induce a price change for the firm's output. (Since competing firms lack access to this cheaper factor, its price will not be bid upward, at least for a while.) Under these conditions, where production prices decrease but market price for the good remains constant, the profit margin thereby rises. And this takes place without a corresponding change in the benefit enjoyed by consumers of the product. Examples such as these illustrate the indirect relation between profit margin and benefit, a relation which must be direct if the profits are to be deserved.[24]

If there could be a measure of pure demand shift, a shift in the demand for some product on the part of consumers alone (and if profits were directly determined by this change), the above objection might have some force. But demand can fluctuate because of natural disaster, monopoly formation in a market sector, advertising strategies, and the like. To say that the corresponding shift in marginal product value is proportional to a shift in the benefit received in the product's being consumed is flatly implausible. Recall, and this is the crucial point, that the proportionality condition requires a *direct* link between the benefit delivered, upon which the desert claim is made, and the size of the reward deserved. I am arguing here that there is no such direct link in the case of profits and consumer benefit. To say that there is ignores the various factors external to the benefit provided to consumers by the purchase of products that determine the profit margins of entrepreneurs.

David Miller has addressed an argument similar to the one I make here and has criticized it.[25] He admits that markets operate in a way that rewards individuals on the basis of a number of contingencies not directly under that individual's control (contingencies that enter into the determination of price and hence reward). He responds, however, that since these contingencies are reflected in the market price of goods or services, they in fact affect the resulting benefit provided by the participant in the market. They are therefore not irrelevant to the desert basis but indeed help determine its magnitude. He writes, "Desert isn't merely a matter of good intentions; it also has to do with how much benefit you create for the recipients of your services, and in nearly every case that depends on the configuration of the world outside. A fall in the price of a commodity or a service [is] a signal that the good or service in question has become less valuable, in the short term at least, as a result of what other people have decided to do."[26]

I would argue, however, that this reply essentially gives away the game: it amounts to admitting that rewards in a market become detached from the intentional, benefit-conferring activities of the agent. If I give you a lottery ticket that I think is worthless (just to indulge your addiction to the lottery), does my desert of some reward (morally speaking) go up or down depending on whether the ticket turns out to have the winning number? I don't think so.

Similarly (though not precisely so), participants in a market play a kind of constrained lottery whose variables include the presence of other competitors, the transaction costs those others face, the transaction costs they themselves face, and the fluctuating demand from consumers. My rewards, despite my best (or worst) efforts, turn on such contingencies and not directly on my intentional activities.[27]

Miller attempts to counter such a reply by pointing out how market participants often engage in resource-developing strategies or in life plans that include the development of particular talents. These are often undertaken in response to perceived demand and contingent market conditions and are rewarded or not by those very contingencies. But such an acute critic of capitalism as Miller well knows that such talent-developing strategies *need* not be part of the life history of successful market participants. The best laid plans of many an entrepreneur have been flushed down the toilet of market contingencies as often as they have been rewarded, and this happens for reasons having nothing to do with the agent's diligence in pursuing his or her goals. Concerted effort is not at all necessary for market success, and it is certainly not sufficient. So again, the market doles out rewards and failures in ways that systematically diverge from the kinds of intentional, planned, beneficial behavior in which individual participants engage.

So my argument amounts to this: entrepreneurs do not deserve their profits because (in a manner analogous to the prison sentences in the example above) these are not determined by virtue of the magnitude of the benefit upon which the claim is based. This is so because profits are determined by such external factors as the proximity of competing firms, general availability of production technology, and other circumstances. And since such variability amounts to a violation of the proportionality condition set out above, it cannot be held that these profits, determined in this way, are deserved.

V. Deserving Market Income in General

So much for entrepreneurs. The extrapolation of the above considerations to apply to allocations of markets generally, and by implication to liberal ownership, is actually quite straightforward. Whenever allocations of resources in market settings are the result of competitive forces external to the direct relation between desert basis and reward, then the rewards received (or the costs incurred) are not deserved. Whenever the barriers to perfect competition are part of the explanation of the magnitude of market shares received, then the proportionality condition for desert claims I explained above will not be met. Therefore, in such cases, whatever moral reasons can be brought to bear on the question of who gets what, these should not include reasons of desert.

Indeed, what I have said would also help support a general skepticism about the possibility of evaluating, in morally relevant terms, the benefit that is provided by the producers of resources in a market apart from the price of that resource. Desert requires that such an evaluation be made, since there must be a relation between that value and the value of the reward returned to those who produce that resource. What I say here might indicate that the evaluation on either side of this relation would be forbiddingly vague, and thus the question of who actually deserves what in a market is useless. To see the force of this skepticism, one need only ask which is of greater magnitude, in morally relevant terms: forty hours of dull and difficult work on an assembly line or the same time spent as a corporate executive in an office, *apart from the market values of these tasks* (their prices). In order to even begin to claim that the market is allocating to such persons the resource bundles they in fact deserve, one needs to be able to make these evaluations. One must then make the *further* claim that the sizes of these resource bundles are indeed determined by (are proportional to) the effort expended (or benefit produced). The foregoing shows just what an impossibly tall order this is.

The foregoing is also relevant to the arguments considered in section I concerning desert and first acquisition. In the argument put forth by Becker, the driving idea was that insofar as a person produced something of value to others, and insofar as the enjoyment of this new thing via the ownership of it was a proper and proportional reward (and subject to other conditions), then that person deserves to own the thing. But a crucial premise in this argument is that the value produced in the original laboring activity is some constant and determinable quantity and that the benefits of ownership somehow mirror this value. But the points pursued in this section should make it clear that values are inseparable from the happenstance of the tastes of valuers and (more important) the accidental presence of other producers. So while one may have at one time deserved some X for the services rendered by one's producing activity, that X is neither fixed over time nor commensurable with the varying levels of benefit that others might enjoy pursuant to one's activity.

The way that these arguments apply specifically to the structure of ownership brings us back to another important lesson: the profits generated by market competition, which I have argued are not deserved, are covered particularly by the right to income contained in the liberal ownership bundle. That is, since income is not deserved, income *rights* are not deserved. The supposed right to retain whatever is given to one in a market transaction cannot be justified by reference to what one deserves based on a benefit one has provided, or so I have argued. So once again, liberal ownership founders on the weakness of the income rights component.

That is not to say that, in principle, use and possessory rights could not somehow be justified on the basis of moral desert (though my criticisms of Becker's Lockean argument would raise questions about those cases also). But in response to any such argument, I would register a more general skepticism concerning claims of desert of material goods. Desert claims are valid only when made from within a well-established and widely accepted system of performance and reward, where equivalence rules fixing the levels of desert are unquestioned. In this way desert claims are fundamentally conventional.[28] But when the rules governing the connection between activity that purportedly grounds desert and rewards stemming from that activity are contentious or ill-defined, then no solid claims can be made for such rewards.

These conclusions fly in the face of popular ideology as well as philosophical or political principle. That popular ideology—that what one earns is commensurate with one's value or effort and hence just—is pervasive and dangerous. This is especially so when such claims are confused with consequentialist arguments concerning what it is necessary to pay someone to produce the results one wants. We might well be put into a situation where the best thing overall for everyone is to allow someone some benefit or punishment, but this does not imply that the person deserves that treatment.

This chapter brings us to the close of the generally non-consequentialist and direct attempts to justify liberal ownership. I say this realizing that one important strain in the argument from liberty was an indirect one; but the abandonment of direct arguments for liberal ownership is itself a significant conclusion, for it implies that ownership must be structured in whatever way is necessary to produce the results one favors or which are considered constitutive of the public good. Such indirect strategies are fundamentally different from those that claim that the production of just outcomes must be *built upon* or *constrained by* respect for liberal ownership. This latter idea is a major weapon in the fight against egalitarian distributions.

And furthermore, giving up the idea that there are direct and non-consequentialist reasons supporting liberal ownership means that one's ownership of one's goods is fundamentally conventional and irreducibly contingent on the justice of the overall state of affairs. The ever-changing nature of such states, as well as the contending views about which are the worthiest to pursue, makes the status of one's ownership much less independent of the condition and prospects of others in one's community. I would contend that this conclusion thereby dislodges a crucial brick in the foundations of liberal ownership, and the walls that block the development of egalitarian economic policy seem consequently to be starting to crumble.

6

Ownership and the Maximization of Utility

The previous three chapters have established the extreme weakness of direct arguments for liberal ownership. The present chapter, however, will take up the most familiar of the *indirect* arguments for economic arrangements, namely, arguments that include as a major premise the claim that institutions should maximize utility, and further, that only liberal ownership structures succeed in maximizing utility. Such arguments will perforce include a variety of empirical assumptions, and hence my conclusions, like the arguments themselves, will be characteristically incomplete. As in the previous chapters, it is difficult to show that there is *no* justification for liberal ownership along these lines. All I can do here is, again, to appraise a sampling of some of the most powerful attempts at such a justification and to localize the crucial claims along the way.

My procedure here is to divide these kinds of arguments into three separate strategies. The first is the Bentham-inspired argument that because of considerations of reasonable expectations, only when owners have liberal ownership over their goods is utility maximized (section II). The second surrounds the variety of claims that have been made connecting property arrangements with economic efficiency, in particular microefficiency. I discuss these in section III. And the third, treated in section IV, is the argument that only liberal ownership and attendant free markets can guarantee maximum productive efficiency, which in turn maximizes utility. At various points, I subject the presuppositions of these arguments to critical scrutiny (for example, what utility is, whether it is worth pursuing as a unilateral goal, and whether microefficiency is a plausible normative measure of aggregate utility).

The question of what will be the best outcome of some property arrangement is, of course, extremely complicated, as the number of combinations of property rights and the kinds of items they will cover and the background conditions they are found in can be endless. As I have since chapter 2, I understand private liberal ownership to be comprised of use, transfer, and income rights. So the question we are asking here is whether utility is maximized only when owners have complete use, transfer, and income rights over their goods. The conclusions I reach are these: whether or not maximizing utility can be thought of as a worthwhile social goal, efficiency (either microefficiency or productive efficiency) is tenuous as an indicator of the desirable aspects of that goal; even if efficiency is a valuable goal, markets aren't always efficient; even if it might be admitted that markets are necessary to achieve efficient outcomes (if and when these are valuable), it is not generally the case that liberal ownership is necessary for those markets to function; and finally, even if the combination of liberal ownership and competitive markets is locally needed for the production of socially desired outcomes, the shortcomings of this combination as a general allocative arrangement are so great that liberal ownership will not be the optimal *general* property institution in the society. So the argument supporting that structure along these lines is not sound even if many of its very questionable premises are accepted along the way.

An additional introductory word: it will not do to argue that only *in some instances* will liberal ownership be necessary to maximize utility. Liberal ownership is an ownership *system*, and I am interested to investigate here whether this system is needed to maximize utility (if indeed that is a good thing). We could all imagine rare circumstances where some act or decision will be necessary for some needed goal—paying a ransom to a kidnapper, for instance—but which would be disastrous as an overall or broad policy. The claim being tested here is that in general, or as a matter of widespread policy, liberal ownership is recommended on these grounds. If our conclusion is that that structure is recommended for only some narrow cases (and not generally), then this is *ipso facto* an argument against liberal ownership.

I. Preliminaries: Utilitarianism, Utility, and Efficiency

Utilitarianism is a global moral theory. It is best understood as being comprised basically of three components: consequentialism, welfarism, and sum ranking.[1] Consequentialism is the view that only future states of affairs can be taken into account in moral calculations (not, for example, the intrinsic character of acts or intentions). Welfarism is the principle that the only aspect of states of affairs that can be taken into account in moral evaluations is the well-being (welfare) of individuals in those states. What "welfare" turns out to mean is a matter of great controversy, and I will return to this question presently. Sum ranking, or the aggregative principle, is the directive that states of affairs must be ranked according to the *maximum* level of welfare contained in them. The combination of these three principles amounts to the famous utilitarian dictum that one must always act so as the produce the greatest happiness (welfare) for the greatest number.

I will not concern myself here with the consequentialism and sum ranking principles, but only with welfarism, the view that people's happiness or pleasure or desire satisfaction is all that matters, morally, about them or the situation they are in. Classical utilitarianism, of which Jeremy Bentham is a paradigm exponent, views "welfare" as pleasure, the actual psychological state characterized by good feeling, which varies only by its intensity and duration.[2] On this view, utility or welfare can be measured according to a cardinal scale, and hence the degree of any one person's utility can be compared to anyone else's. Later theorists in the utilitarian tradition, and those economic theorists who took over these notions, were bothered by the difficulty of measuring such an elusive and mysterious property as the mental states of individuals. Consideration of this difficulty gave rise, among theorists, to a more behaviorist approach to utility, defined in relation to people's choices rather than their feelings. This view is that welfare means desire satisfaction, and desires are those things that move a person to choose one thing rather than another. What results is a picture of utility as a function of an ordering of preferences. Those choices, moreover, need not be observed in the agent's brain, but can be taken as the behavior exhibited by the person when faced with the object of choice.[3] Being better off by this measure means having more of the things one prefers, and/or having things that are ranked higher on the list of desired items.

This measure of utility, which does not admit of any interpersonal comparisons and which can only be expressed ordinally, is one associated with neoclassical economics. As I discussed in chapter 2, the definition of efficiency is associated with Pareto rankings of states of affairs. In this picture utility is maximized in a social state when some person in that state is better off, by her own lights, and no person is worse off. If someone were to lose in the change, then there would be no way to say that utility was maximized, since it is not permitted to compare the levels of satisfaction (expressed in the rankings) between the winners and the losers. My getting my first choice cannot be compared, in utility terms, to your getting your third.

So in economic theory welfare is measured in this austere manner. This implies, of course, that a great number of states of affairs will not be comparable by these measures. There are countless pairs of states wherein at least one person is made worse off by moving from one to another—making the two states non-comparable by the Pareto standard—but by an extent far less than the level of improvement experienced by others from the move. Labelling such pairs non-comparable severely limits the applicability of efficiency tests. To alleviate this, another method of comparing utility levels in different states has been developed. It is called the Kaldor-Hicks test, after two economists who developed it.[4] According to this criterion, a state of affairs, A, is Kaldor-Hicks (KH) superior to another, B, if those who gain in A could compensate those who lose to an extent that would make no one worse off by the change. These compensatory payments need only be hypothetical, in that *should* they be made, the resulting state A would be a Pareto improvement over B.

Defenders of KH efficiency argue that actual payments need not be made since often what prevents them is transaction costs. That is, imagine a situation that would benefit me to an extent that I could compensate you amply for whatever losses you might incur, but *finding* you will cost more than I gain. In such a case, demanding that compensatory payments must actually be made would result in a worse state, or more precisely, would mean that the change would not occur.

The implicit motivation behind the KH efficiency test, however, is that it surreptitiously allows interpersonal comparisons of utility back onto the scene.[5] If P could pay Q out of the gains that P receives from some change, then it must be that P values the change more than Q does. This introduces a standard of welfare measure called "willingness to pay" and presupposes that there exists a currency in which these payments could take place. If we assume, for example, that how much I am willing to pay for something reflects how badly I want it, then we can compare the "intensity" of desires across persons by this method.

The KH measure has been criticized from many quarters. One acute problem with the measure is that it can be shown that under some conditions, the KH test does not determine a unique result. In fact, some states of affairs are KH superior *to each other*. This is called the Scitovsky paradox.[6] More relevant to our discussion, I think, is the problematic use of "willingness to pay" measures of well-being that KH must invoke. This measure is problematic since it can easily be shown that how much a person is willing to pay for something, or how much she is willing to accept for it, is not strictly a function of her evaluation of the thing itself. Often, how much money a person *has* will determine or affect how much she might be willing to pay. Moreover, when the state in question is not a certainty, one's willingness to pay to bring it about or avoid it will poorly reflect one's true valuation of that state. You might well pay a dollar to avoid a one in ten million chance of being killed, but your payment to avoid certain death might be greater than ten million dollars; it may well be infinite!

We will mention details of these measures of utility as well as problems they have when it becomes relevant. I now want to back up a few steps and return to the Benthamite conception of utility as merely pleasure and absence of pain. For it is this notion that Bentham utilizes in the arguments to which we now turn.

II. Bentham's Argument

Jeremy Bentham is the father of modern utilitarianism, and as such he was also an explicit champion of free trade and full ownership. But, paradoxically, he can also be thought of as a derailed (utilitarian) egalitarian. For although maximizing utility was, for him, the only guide to action, he developed quite subtle and powerful arguments for the diminishing marginal utility of one's goods. The claim of the diminishing marginal utility of goods amounts to the view that the utility (pleasure) that one gets from the first unit of any good is always some degree greater than that received from the next unit. The pleasure that a rich person gets from a single dollar is less than the pleasure a poorer person gets from a dollar.

Bentham used this assumption to argue that "[t]he more nearly the actual proportion [of people's wealth] approaches to equality, the greater will be the total mass of happiness."[7] On the other hand, he was staunchly *opposed* to instituting any government policy designed to bring such equality about, primarily because he thought that equal distributions of goods would be unproductive.[8] But he used another line of argument that rested on his views about the connection among full property rights, security, and happiness.[9] It is these arguments that interest us.

For Bentham, attachments made between an individual and her possessions, as well as expectations concerning future projects (which depend on continued possession of her holdings), are seriously threatened when the state invades her share of goods in order to redistribute wealth to achieve equality. "Every thing which I actually possess, or which I ought to possess, I consider in my imagination as about to belong to me forever: I make it the foundation of my expectation—of the expectation of those who depend upon me, and the support of my plan of life."[10] Moreover, he claims that a person will develop certain expectations concerning the gaining of advantages from this possession, which may come from trade, rent, or productive development. Establishing and maintaining security in possession is one of the principal aims of the civil code, for Bentham, and attempts to institute equality are in direct violation of this aim. He sums up this opposition rhetorically this way: "For how shall a different [more equal] distribution be made, without taking from someone what he possesses? how shall one party be stripped without attacking the security of all? When your new distribution shall be disarranged, which it will be the day after its establishment, how will you be able to avoid making a second? Why should you not correct this also? and, in the meantime what becomes of security? of happiness? of industry?"[11]

The claims implicit in these questions involve an array of arguments, some of them slippery slopes about the need for greater and greater government control of property and some of them incentive arguments to which I attend later. But the central claim is that no one could enjoy security in one's possessions if property rights were curtailed (through taxation, for example) for redistributive purposes.

But the rebuttal to this argument is obvious, and indeed a version of it was supplied by Bentham himself.[12] All one has to claim is that the system of taxation—ownership structures shaped with distributive goals in mind—be public, stable, and consistent. For security in possession is gained merely by the stable prediction one can make about one's present and future holdings ("established expectations"). If I know that I have to subtract my tax liability from my paycheck every month, and I can easily figure out what that liability is, I have no uncertainty about my income.

Much of Bentham's argument turns on the slippery slope of greater and greater interference once the government gets its foot in the door. It is also assumed that the tax structure will be shifting about unpredictably, perhaps in reaction to the ever-changing needs of the poor. But these assumptions, of course, need not be accepted, and the experience of the U.S. tax code might provide ample evidence for the slowness of change. There is no necessary, or even close, connection between redistributive programs and instability and change. Additionally, there is no reason to suppose that the needs of the less well-off will be so uncharted and shifting that the general government strategy to alleviate them will need constant revision.

Moreover, the interest in security in possession hardly supports a right to *increase* one's share of holdings, since having expectations for greater wealth must be weighed against those unsatisfied desires of others that result from the first person's getting such wealth (and not the others). Bentham's claim that *actual* possession creates the psychological bond that grounds the expectation in question does not apply (directly) to increased income from property. One cannot plausibly form an important psychological attachment to wealth that one can only hope for, at least not one that grounds a *unique* claim to such wealth.

All that has been justified in Bentham's argument is the need for a consistent and sufficiently public institution of property rights over some objects.[13] These property structures could vary greatly from liberal ownership as long as the structure is public and consistent.[14]

In fact, the danger of an ever-shifting tax structure of the state, in many instances, pales in comparison to the *in*securities that are introduced and go unprotected by the happenstance of market demand. Such insecurities are the grounding for market-supplementing devices like the FDIC, which insures bank deposits in the United States. If security is what we are really after, unimpeded market activity is hardly the most reliable place to find it.

Considerations of security and consistent expectations may be relevant to some components of property rights, but they do not support liberal ownership. In fact, there is reason to believe that insofar as liberal ownership allows free markets to emerge, many people will be *less* secure in their possessions thereby. For the happenstance of market gain is at least as unpredictable as is the bureaucratic mechanisms of (say) a redistributive economic policy. And there is some reason to believe it is significantly more so.

III. Efficiency: The Microeconomic Case

I now move to the question of the overall efficiency of economic systems involving liberal ownership, efficiency that allegedly is a stand-in for maximum utility. As I explained in section I, the conception of utility that can be appealed to in utilitarian arguments, the maximand, is widely variable. Neoclassical economics is built on notions borrowed from utilitarianism, but the notion of welfare that is invoked there is a departure from the psychological state view of Bentham and his followers. For economists after Pareto, and those who ushered in the "marginalist" revolution, social states were no longer measured according to interpersonally comparable standards of welfare. Pareto measures of efficiency, and the underlying conception of utility as a function of preference orderings, are all that can be appealed to on these views in ranking social states.

Where distributive questions are concerned, the only recommendations from these quarters will be based on notions of equilibrium and Pareto Optimality. In particular, the argument will be that some political arrangements facilitate achievement of these optimal states better than others. This claim rests on a notion of efficiency from the "micro" perspective, or from the perspective of individual agents and their utility levels. The *moral* status of such arguments depends, of course, on how one interprets and evaluates efficiency as a measure of social desirability.

In the case of liberal ownership, the argument is that only when the full package of use, transfer, and income rights (over determinate goods) is vested in single individuals are efficient outcomes achieved. More generally, it is always better, from the point of efficiency, to "internalize" some effect or factor—to give people property rights over it—than to adopt some alternative, an attenuated rights structure or a more centrally coordinated use arrangement.

This approach to various economic problems, in particular the problems of externalities, has gotten much attention from those economists, discussed in chapter 1, who label it the "property rights approach." As I touch on below, such writers have put forth models designed to show how externalities can be reduced and greater efficiency achieved when internalization takes place (when property rights are extended over the goods in question).

Before revisiting those arguments, I need to define terms. First, an "externality" is any effect that a transaction has on people other than the transactors, and hence is not considered in the bargaining of those transactors. Externalities can be either positive, as when a neighbor paints her house so attractively that it makes yours look good, or negative, such as air pollution. The focus is usually on negative externalities, since they are the effects that taint the benefit that mutually voluntary binary exchanges are meant to produce. Another characteristic of externalities, though not one that everyone agrees is essential, is that they are unintended by the contracting parties, that they are side effects of market behavior.[15] It is also true, and important, that externalities are not paid for by the contracting parties. The side effect, which may be costly or beneficial, is not taken into account when the price of the good or service is calculated. Your neighbor's painter didn't say to her, "Look, I'll have to charge you extra since the people next door will also benefit from this new color. It's up to you to collect." And we all know who pays for the unchecked air pollution that is caused by nearby factories.

Externalities can be pecuniary or not, depending on whether they are inside or outside the range of market interactions. The benefit of your neighbor's beautiful house may merely give you pleasure (a non-pecuniary gain), or it may increase the market value of your house (a pecuniary one). Most economists either disregard or define out of existence pecuniary effects, since they do not in principle violate anyone's (property) rights and do not automatically involve inefficiencies. The important point is that the costs of externalities, either positive or negative, are absorbed by people other than the contracting parties who produce them and who can therefore ignore them in their negotiations and price agreements. This implies that the cost-benefit formula used to assess the transaction, if it refers only to those contracting parties, is seriously incomplete.

In chapter 2 I briefly discussed transaction costs, defining them as the costs of making exchanges. But it is important to keep in mind how wide is the range of phenomena that this definition covers. For whatever the difference—in time, effort, resources expended, or the like—between an instantaneous, effortless transaction and one that takes place in the real world, it counts as a transaction cost. If I have to find customers for my product, or pay others to do this, or if I lack information about technology or availability of resources and have to pay to get it, then I face transaction costs. Some economists are trying to take better into account the pervasive nature of these costs and have built models that include them.[16] But for the most part, any talk of efficiency of market interactions is functioning under the assumption of zero, or at least low, transaction costs.

Now back to property and efficiency. There is a straightforward line of argument for the conclusion that granting individuals property rights over resources increases efficiency in comparison either to collective control of the resource or to the condition of no individual rights at all. If aspects of the environment have an effect on individuals living in that environment, but there exists no rights in regard to those environmental factors, then the factors can be regarded as a type of externality. When rights of use, possession, and exchange (ownership) are granted to individuals in relation to the factor, that factor can be said to be internalized. Economists such as Harold Demsetz and others have developed the argument that property systems emerge because externalities are always best (more efficiently) alleviated by the ascription of private rights to individuals over the inefficiently used factors.[17] On this view, the air that is soiled by the pollution of the factory next door should, if possible, be owned so that the true costs of the pollution can be calculated and paid for.[18]

The upshot of this argument rests on the view that efficient outcomes should be promoted; that is, it rests on the assumed equation between efficiency and utility maximization and the assumption of utilitarianism as a moral theory. As an argument for liberal ownership, this approach must make the claim that only when individuals are given private rights over previously unowned resources and, more particularly, they enjoy the complete package of possession, use, exchange, and income rights, will these outcomes be efficient.

The operative assumption in such arguments is that the activities of fully informed, rational, and self-interested individuals will be the best mechanism by which to distribute resources (and environmental factors) to those who value them most. Granting private ownership rights and freeing up the wheels of trade (of these rights) ensure an outcome that is a Pareto efficient equilibrium.

Defenses of privatizing factors in this way are often made on the grounds that the costs of negotiation, of coordinating the bargaining among all affected parties, will be lower if private rights are granted to individuals and trade is then allowed. The view is that, no matter how the resources are initially distributed (who initially gets the rights to the factors in question), free trade among rational agents guarantees an efficient outcome. This result is what the famous Coase theorem is purported to show.[19] The alternative is thought to be collective regulation or control of the factor, in which case negotiation must take place among all the actual and potential users of the resource. Alternatives such as these are, it is claimed, much more costly than the privatization arrangement.[20]

But will granting individuals rights over such factors predictably result in liberal ownership structures? There is good reason to think it will not. Imagine, for example, that the unowned resource is land, and that some people want to use the land for housing, others for timber, and others for food production. It seems highly likely that the most efficient solution to this conflict is the *disaggregation* of the liberal ownership bundles over parcels of land. The hunters will take the pelts of killed prey while the food harvesters will take the meat; and the timber gatherers can arrange to ply their trade as well. What results is a system of use and transfer rights much more complex and fragmented than liberal ownership.

So if we step back from this argument, we see that it does not support liberal ownership as a unique property structure at all, for it cannot be assumed *a priori* that the bundle of use, transfer, and income rights will hold together if individuals are given the widest possible range in bargaining over rights. In fact, it is very likely that disaggregation of property bundles will be favored in many situations. It will more often be optimal to separate (and trade separately) the rights to use a resource from the rights to exchange and gain income from it (or indeed the various rights to use the factor in different ways). In such cases, no person will have liberal ownership rights over the resource when bargaining reaches a Pareto Optimal equilibrium.[21]

The possibility of property structures other than liberal ownership as a solution to these efficiency problems is only passingly mentioned by defenders of this line of argument, though the alternate possibility often considered is state ownership (state control of use).[22] But there are a plethora of varying property structures that can be instituted to utilize the available resources most efficiently. And state ownership is certainly not the only alternative to liberal ownership that could be sensitive to distributive concerns as well as maximization of utility.[23]

Underlying many of these arguments are assumptions about human motivation, namely, that behavior is motivated only by the desire to maximize one's own utility (defined independently of the desires of others), an assumption that I will discuss shortly. Moreover, efficiency arguments of this kind attempt to show that property rights over resources (even air) allow the smooth workings of a market to take over and direct the action, and as we all know (they argue), markets guarantee efficiency. Well, perfect markets might do this (this is a theorem of welfare economics), but perfect markets are impossible to find in the real world. In the next three subsections I explain the ways that real-world markets differ from the abstract models that provide the promise of efficiency and show how these differences tend to cast doubt on the promise of efficiency from markets.

I have been concentrating on the thesis that liberal ownership is necessary to allow efficient markets to emerge, which in turn are necessary to best solve problems of externalities and waste. I have been arguing that liberal ownership is in fact not uniquely necessary, and may not be sufficient, for these ends. This line of argument may indirectly suggest a favorable attitude about such markets and their results. But as many have pointed out, there are problems that markets themselves introduce as a process of allocating and transferring goods. Although I certainly think that markets are *sometimes* the best such mechanism (few outside Havana and Beijing now deny that), markets do have their own shortcomings and limitations. So my view here is not that markets should be avoided, but rather that their usefulness is *limited* and *local.*

Transaction Costs and Hidden Externalities

Recall that for all these arguments to succeed, it must be assumed that the negotiators in question can costlessly (or at least very cheaply) get together for the bargaining process. But of course transaction costs are *never* zero and are often maldistributed. The differential costs faced by participants directly determine the eventual distribution after bargaining and trade. I may well value pleasant-smelling air more than the incinerator owner values producing foul-smelling stuff (that is, I am willing to pay more to avoid it than the owner's marginal profit from not correcting it), but since I can't afford the costs of negotiation (and she can but prefers not to engage in negotiations), then *I* suffer the extra costs (smell) and she keeps the extra profits. And next year when the same factory fouls a stream I use, the income differential will be that much greater and the cycle will likely repeat itself. Since transaction costs can always be paid for, their "placement" is always a function of differential wealth, so their presence always benefits the comparatively wealthy.

It is similarly important to keep in mind that the inequalities produced by market forces tend to snowball with every round of bargaining and trade. Such snowballing is inevitable because those with greater wealth can always outbid their competitors for some scarce good. Indeed, if we assume diminishing marginal utility of wealth, then the relatively rich stand to loose less (utility) in paying some amount that they offer than does a poorer person in paying the same amount. In both cases the poorer person can make fewer favorable deals (or has less access to the most favorable deals) and hence reaps fewer benefits in each cycle.

Add to this the phenomenon of *differential* transaction costs. If these are initially randomly distributed, it will nevertheless always be to the advantage of the relatively wealthy since they can better afford the cost of overcoming them than can the poor. I can't afford a marketing consultant, for example, to find out just what the next consumer rage is going to be, so those that can will get in before me in setting up production. And since this disadvantage increases with every cycle, the array of costs faced next time is *not* random but favors the first round's winners. Hence, inequalities tend inexorably to increase.[24]

Also, it would not be too far afield to think of this phenomenon, the resulting inequality of market trades, as a kind of externality. When A and B trade to their mutual advantage, it affects C, who may then be in a worse position than, say, B in the next round of competition. So C is negatively affected by the private transaction between A and B in a way that they need not take into account. Of course, C could have bid the price up if she wanted the good bad enough, but if her funds are lower than A's and B's, then she loses and the process of comparative disadvantage begins.

Such an externality is of course a pecuniary one and, as such, is not considered a diseconomy by most commentators. The reason for this, which is not always explicit, is that even if there are losers in a set of transactions (those made worse off in bargaining power), as long as those losers could in principle be compensated by the winners, then there is still a Kaldor-Hicks efficiency gain. This response of course brings into sharp question the usefulness of that measure of efficiency, especially when one realizes just how severe and pervasive pecuniary externalities can be.[25] But it similarly underscores the difficulties in applying the test, as I mentioned in section I. For if segments of the population find themselves consistently to be members of the disadvantaged, uncompensated, "loser" class, it hardly seems accurate as a measure of overall good to remind these people that were they to be compensated they would not complain.

The consideration of comparative disadvantage is especially relevant to the strategy considered earlier of justifying property rights by virtue of efficiency. For if there are always losers in the game of internalization, either one must rely on the questionable Kaldor-Hicks test of efficiency or one must face these distributive questions head on. And when transaction costs are both non-zero and unevenly distributed, as they always are, then granting private rights over a resource creates a contentious distributive pattern that cannot be set right without tampering with the market later. There may be efficiency arguments for property rights along some lines, but it is implausible to claim that internalization makes no one worse off.

The final line of criticism of this strategy is one I borrow from Frank Michelman, who argues that the alleged efficiency of privatization depends heavily on contentious assumptions about individual preferences and motivation.[26] For example, these efficiency arguments always must assume that people prefer achieving desired results through private exchange in a market rather than by public decision through politics. For if there is widespread preference for the latter form of resolution, markets will not be efficient at the microlevel. In the case of property rights assignments, these assumptions are particularly contentious since adopting a private exchange regime for the production of socially favored outcomes effectively *prevents* reversion to these alternative methods. This last point brings up, yet again, the deep and pervasive problem of equating microefficiency with a morally relevant conception of well-being.

Failure to Provide Public Goods

Another well-known feature of market mechanisms is that they are very bad at organizing people to provide those goods for which cooperative behavior is essential. "Public goods" are goods for which cooperative (though not unanimous) participation is necessary for their production (at some cost to participants); they are a good for everyone; those who do not participate in their production cannot be excluded from enjoying them; and, in the case of a pure public good, one person's enjoyment does not reduce the total supply of the good.[27] The famous example of such a good is a national defense, where a general fund is pooled to provide an army that protects contributors and non-contributors alike, and my being defended doesn't reduce your level of protection. Public parks, clean air, beautiful landscapes, and general social stability are other examples.

It is widely understood that social interaction built on market relations alone would result in there being few if any goods of this kind. This conclusion rests on the claim that everyone in a market, by assumption, is aiming to maximize his or her own well-being independently of others. So either one's participation in the collective effort to produce the good is not needed, in which case it is in one's interest not to participate whether or not others do; or one's participation is useful only if enough others participate, in which case one would not participate short of assurance from others that they will do so also (and in a market full of selfish actors this assurance cannot be provided). In either case, the best thing for everyone (individually) to do is to be a "free rider," to stay home while others (if they choose) get together to provide the good. But since everyone reasons this way, no one does anything and no goods arise. So if markets reign supreme, there are no parks, no national defense, no beautiful scenery, and so on (the list is very long).

In the extensive discussion of this problem, the pervasive conclusion is that, for such goods to be provided, the market must be supplemented as the sole allocative mechanism of society. The government, for the most part, must be utilized to enforce cooperative behavior necessary to provide public goods, usually in the form of a tax subsidizing the production of the good.[28] This way of solving the problem, however, reveals the pervasive *in*efficiency of markets as the sole allocative mechanism of society.

Markets, Preferences, and Well-Being

The translation of arguments for efficiency into plausible moral arguments must proceed by way of a claim that the property of persons that is maximized by such efficiency bears a close relation to well-being, in a morally relevant sense of that term. Usually, this claim is understood as the view that what is maximized is preference satisfaction (utility). But there are numerous criticisms of preference satisfaction, and in particular the *maximization* of preference satisfaction, as a plausible measure of either individual well-being or social desirability. I agree with much of those criticisms, and in chapter 9 I will add to them. But my point here is a bit more narrow. I draw out just how the *market* affects the range and nature of individual preferences and as a result affects well-being.

The first problem to be raised concerns the authenticity of preferences displayed in a productive market. I assume that for the equation between choice behavior and well-being to be a valid one, it must be the case that those choices truly (or very nearly) reflect the agent's real or authentic judgment about her own good. If, for example, the market could operate only if hypnotists went around inducing people to subconsciously desire the goods for sale, we could hardly conclude that their well-being was being advanced by such purchases. So it must be the case that the preferences revealed in the market are, at least in some loose sense, authentic.

But markets operate, in part, in ways that discourage the authenticity of preferences. It is a familiar point that markets are structured so that they function most efficiently when they expand. This need to expand creates a structural inducement to search for greater and greater demand for products. Individuals producing and selling products, then, have a strong incentive to "create" this demand in a population by convincing people that they truly desire the product in question. Hence, products are advertised.

Now since there is no difference in profit from sales based on authentically produced new desires and from those based on artificially produced ones, owners of productive operations have an incentive to create demand in whatever way possible. That is, there is no incentive to discriminate among the kinds of preference formation processes that manifest themselves in the market. Advertising, then, is a way to induce buyers to change their preferences, even if this means doing so in ways that undercut the connection between their purchasing choices and well-being. When Brooke Shields said on television that she wasn't wearing any underwear under her Calvin Klein jeans, suddenly millions of people "decided" that those jeans were a much better product than they had previously thought, and sales skyrocketed.

Now I can make this argument without entering into a complicated empirical debate about the effectiveness of advertising in changing preferences or about the methods of this change. I claim here only that there is a *structural incentive* for producers to change preferences in ways that subvert authenticity in order to increase demand. The market not only includes no intrinsic check on this type of preference production, but is organized so as to encourage it. We have only to assume that it sometimes succeeds to begin to doubt the claim that market behavior reflects rational, autonomous behavior on individuals' parts. This conclusion further disturbs any remaining faith that market efficiency maximizes well-being.[29]

Also, private-ownership market economies presuppose and promote the *individual* pursuit of ends. That is, since income flows return to owners of inputs in trades and production, rewards are structured according to separate and individual activities. Moreover, the efficiency promised by such systems depends on these motivations (as I discussed in chapter 2, only when preferences are non-tuistic do markets become competitive under private ownership). Indeed the competition among suppliers of goods increases the motivation to disconnect oneself from others in the pursuit of one's goals. The market system works best when individuals choose optimal strategies independently of the announced preferences of others. This pattern of choice keeps the cogs of the machine turning and by the invisible hand produces the alleged benefits of the market economy (as well as the defects). And as we saw in the examination of the public goods problem, when people act individually (whether or not their preferences are selfish in an everyday sense), relations of interconnectedness and trust are pervasively unstable.

But there are other goods, other preferences, whose structure and object are in sharp contrast with these. They are what could be called "collective preferences." These are desires that are not settled for an agent until interaction or negotiation with certain others has taken place. Examples would be the interactions of family members, lovers, or closely knit groups.[30] What characterizes the preference sets of these people is that they are fluid and ill-formed prior to interaction. Hence interaction cannot be, as it is assumed to be in formal bargaining theory, merely the exchange of information about preference sets. When I am involved in such a connection, I am not sure what I really *want* until I discuss the situation with my partner(s) and hear about her (their) perhaps equally provisional preferences.

The unique aspect of these sorts of preferences is that they cannot arise under conditions of unstable personal relations, where trust and cooperation are always contingent upon individual self-interest (that is, defection is always an option). And it is also clear that having such preferences, and having them satisfied, contributes uniquely to the well-being of people. Just consider how arid your life would be without the kinds of close connections constituted by non-individualistic preferences that surround you. So insofar as these sorts of interrelations are systematically discouraged in private market economies, and insofar as these goods would enhance well-being were they live options for people, then the connection between preference satisfaction and well-being is made more fragile under pervasive market systems.[31]

What follows from these arguments is not the radical conclusion that markets should be abandoned on grounds of well-being. Rather, these considerations suggest (what most agree to be true) that markets as allocative devices must be limited in scope and selectively utilized. Such a conclusion is the crucial blow, however, to the line of argument being considered in this chapter for liberal ownership. For pervasively allowing liberal ownership is exactly contrary to the goal of limiting the scope of the market. To provide the public good of a city park, one must restrict the right of purchase of those who may want to buy part of it. To protect consumers from being moved by inauthentic or misinformed preferences (from advertising and the like), producers must be prevented from selling products in some of the ways that they might wish. To overcome transaction cost problems, the rights of some owners must be restricted (or taxed) in order to loosen up trade for others. In all these ways (and many more) the public policies necessary to correct for inefficiencies of imperfect markets precisely amount to selectively limiting ownership structures.

To recap this section, I have argued that the strategy of claiming that property rights are necessary for microefficiency has failed on many counts. It does not show that liberal ownership is necessary for these efficient outcomes; nor does it show that these outcomes are efficient in a compelling sense of that term; it faces the problem of accounting for the pervasiveness of transaction costs and externalities that render the results of market exchange questionable; and it can plausibly be questioned whether market outcomes systematically reflect individual well-being in a morally relevant sense of that term.

But there is a line of argument here that is still available to a consequentialist-minded friend of liberal ownership. That is that *productive* efficiency, which is socially desirable, cannot be achieved without full liberal ownership of the factors of production. This argument involves several claims, one of which operated in the previous arguments and was there left untouched, namely, the claim that individuals are motivated in such a way that only liberal ownership will provide the right incentives for them to act in socially optimal ways. I now turn to these claims.

IV. Efficiency: The Question of Productivity

It has often been claimed that the maximum productive capacities of market economies can be obtained only by structures recognizing liberal ownership of productive factors. The argument is that only classical capitalist property rights (no taxation of profits, private control of productive decisions, and so on) allow for maximum efficiency at the macrolevel and thus the production of maximum social benefits.

I consider these claims only briefly, because the debates about productivity and organizational optimality are ongoing and unresolved (not to mention their being reevaluated in light of the upheavals of economic systems in Europe). Moreover, such debates involve the sometimes unwieldy question of comparing alternative economic systems for their productive efficiency.[32] My focus is the general and abstract claim that, because of considerations of information and motivation, the owners of productive factors must have liberal ownership rights over their goods for the system to operate efficiently.

Before I discuss this issue it is necessary to put the question of productive efficiency into the proper context. Productive efficiency (PE) is a measure of the ratio of the total output of an economic system to its inputs, as well as the system's tendency to find or generate new inputs (natural resources and the like). A system is productively efficient (relative to some alternative) when total output is at a maximum for a given set of inputs (or is greater than any alternative). To make these comparisons, it is necessary to assume some common type of output that two systems are producing which can be consistently measured, such as tonnage of steel or coal or the like, or some currency in terms of which outputs can be valued. The ability of a system to generate new sources of inputs is also important for productivity since the aim in such measures is to evaluate maximum total productive output over time.

This measure, which is often referred to by the simple term "efficiency," is thoroughly different from the notion of efficiency that I have been discussing so far. Microefficiency (or welfare efficiency) relates directly to individual preferences and (with qualifications) individual well-being. All that productive efficiency measures is total amount of physical *goods*, saying nothing directly about the effect on individual welfare that these goods might have.

Indeed, it has been argued by many that too great an emphasis on the productive efficiency of a system has obscured the merely indirect relation this has to individual good; and this overemphasis has proven counterproductive in this regard—overproduction of many goods has had serious detrimental effects on well-being. The mere fact that goods are produced at greater rates, or that more of any good is produced in total, clearly does not imply greater well-being of individuals in the society.[33]

Growing attention to the ecological damage of industrialization in the United States and elsewhere is testament to the divergence between productivity and social welfare. Especially if part of the measure of productivity is the ability of the system to produce *new* inputs (natural resources), the danger of eclipsing the harm that such production does to other sources of human welfare (such as wilderness areas, non-acidic rain, non-carcinogenic drinking water, and so on) is well noted. So while I consider seriously whether market capitalism is superior to relevant alternatives on productivity grounds, it must be stressed that productivity is not all it's cracked up to be (in terms of overall utility levels) and often may be a dangerous measure of social progress.

What is relevant here is the claim that only liberal ownership of the input factors used in production can guarantee acceptable levels of productive efficiency. This question can be approached by imagining how the production process works and in particular the number of decisions that must be independently made for producers to organize the process. Recall that the price of any item is defined as the ratio of the respective opportunity costs of the items being traded, that is, the cost of the next best alternative use of the items for each agent. When production is organized, it must be determined how much of each input factor is to be purchased and at what price. These determinations are all relative to the supposed selling price for the produced good. To frame the question of the efficiency of capitalism, it will help to consider the contrast between it and a completely planned production process.

Imagine such a planned economy. Say we wanted to produce some tractors for our society, perceiving a general desire for tractors in the population. We must first determine how many tractors to produce and at what price to sell them by measuring the substitution curves of the consumers (the relation between their desire for this item and that for any other item). In a market economy, of course, this would be done by observing purchasing behavior and letting prices find a market-clearing equilibrium. In a centrally planned system this mechanism is not available, so some other method of measuring consumer preference must be used. Moreover, it must be determined how many of the various parts of each good to gather and how much to pay for them: spark plugs, seats, tires, and the like. And finally, one must decide how much to pay for the "fixed capital" goods (machines) as well as the labor to put them all together. What must be solved, then, is an enormous number of calculations and price equations. If a central planning bureau had to make these determinations, not only for tractors but for all other goods in the economy, the calculation problems would be nearly impossible.

Nearly impossible, but not theoretically so, as Enrico Barone showed as early as 1908.[34] This result sparked the well-known "calculation debate" over centrally planned socialism. Ludwig von Mises and others responded with the argument that the solution of all of these equations, while theoretically possible, was not *practically* possible, and hence for any system that did not rely on markets, both for retail sales and for input factors (including labor), productivity at optimal levels could not be achieved. Unless there existed a competitive market for production goods, no rational calculations could be made concerning the proper levels of efficient production of any good (let alone for several goods). This argument seems, then, to imply that private liberal ownership of productive factors is essential for productive efficiency of an economy.[35]

But this line of argument presupposed that since under socialism there is no private ownership of the means of production, there can be no markets. However, if one allows some markets to operate, in particular markets for labor and consumer goods, then socialist productive organization could be made rational and efficient. This is essentially the step taken by Oskar Lange in a famous work, *On the Economic Theory of Socialism*.[36] In Lange's scheme, there would be a market for consumer goods, where individuals' substitution rates for different goods could be expressed, thereby revealing their preference orderings for those goods. Three levels of productive organization would then be necessary: enterprise managers operating plants (who are directed to produce at optimal levels, bringing marginal costs into line with price at the lowest possible short-run marginal cost curve for the enterprise); industry managers who decide entry and exit of plants; and a central planning board in charge of setting investment and savings rates. Lange showed that such a system is technically efficient despite eschewing the private ownership of the means of production (all profits generated, as well as economic rents, go to society at large in this system). For our purposes, this argument would show that liberal ownership is not uniquely required for productive efficiency. This is another instance, in fact, where the operation of markets is postulated while the agents of market competition are not the owners of the factors traded. As discussed in chapter 2, markets can exist without liberal ownership.

There has been much critical discussion of this question over the last several decades. People have pointed out that while Lange may have solved the "cognitive" problem of productive efficiency (that is, he may have explained how the information necessary to run the system could be gathered), he did not provide a solution to the motivational difficulty that must accompany it. In other words, Lange did not provide a theory of how the managers in the system (who are instructed to run their organizations at efficient levels) could be motivated to economize unless they had rights to the output (profits) of the enterprise.[37]

Another major problem charged against such market socialist systems[38] is that although the plan might establish the possibility of static efficiency, there remained a serious problem of dynamic efficiency. Static efficiency is the optimal use and allocation of existing resources. Dynamic efficiency is the optimal creation of new resources. In particular, the argument goes, there will not exist proper incentives for entrepreneurial activity in which innovation of technical methods of production would be sought.

The argument comes from Joseph Schumpeter and is fairly straightforward.[39] Consider the entrepreneur as described in the last chapter (although Schumpeter's definition is narrower than mine since on his view entrepreneurs borrow all venture capital and thus do not risk their own fortune). Recall also that while in equilibrium, all factors of production (labor, capital, resources) are paid at their marginal rate of contribution. But profit emerges when the development of a new technology, or the exploitation of a new, cheaper resource, can make production costs lower without (significantly) lowering market price. When this cost reduction occurs, the profit is returned to the firm until competition drives the price down again and another equilibrium is achieved. This is how new technologies, new combinations of existing technology, and other innovations are introduced to society.

Schumpeter lists several possible motivations that may drive a person to search for and pursue such entrepreneurial activities (the development of new productive combinations).[40] One of the principal motivations is, of course, self-interested pursuit of economic gain. This being the case, a potential entrepreneur will seek out new technologies at a maximum effort only when the promise of profits from the (successful) new venture revert completely to her. Otherwise, her costs (chiefly the probability of failure, given that she bears all liability for losses) will not be covered by the promise of gain, and it would not be rational for her to proceed.

In a simple socialist economy, by contrast, where all surpluses are distributed to all workers, this incentive would not exist. What is usually envisioned is that some "leader" might be simply assigned the task of finding innovations. But, the argument goes, this person would not be as motivated as the capitalist entrepreneurs to come up with new technological ideas. Indeed, if the leader succeeds in producing a surplus-generating discovery, she is exploited during the period of the generated surplus. This is because her activity (her input) creates the surplus, yet she receives only a per capita share of the proceeds. But more important, she would not be as motivated as her capitalist counterparts who, *ex hypothesi*, stand to gain a disproportionate amount from their successful endeavors. The result, then, of denying liberal ownership rights to these entrepreneurs is an economic system that is dynamically inefficient since it produces less economical output over time (as compared to a fully capitalist system).

The cogency of this argument, stated here in its barest essentials, depends crucially on several contingent factors, which have received much attention by economists in the last several years. First, does research and development (the principal activity of the entrepreneur as we have described her) achieve its best results from this kind of individualistic, profit-driven activity? Or will R&D become routinized as ongoing aspects of larger corporate entities? Are innovations best explained by a "demand-pull" or a "technology-push" model?[41] What exactly is the best market structure and firm size for the production of new technologies?[42]

There is much empirical work, of course, on the rate of technological innovation in various kinds of industrial organizations. At the theoretical level, questions have been raised about whether any monolithic theory of motivations, whether the neoclassical model of rational choice or the Schumpeterian vision of the wealth-seeking entrepreneur, will account for both the rate and the direction of technical change.[43] It has become clear, however, that in a modern, complex corporation under capitalism, there is little room for the single independent entrepreneur of Schumpeter's model. The R&D division of any firm is peopled by salaried personnel whose remuneration only indirectly flows from profit increases due to innovation. Moreover, the incentive structure of the independent entrepreneur, if she exists, is not easy to determine, since often she may already be in a high income bracket where risk taking is less costly, returns from profitable ventures have comparatively less marginal utility, and residual returns are not clearly differentiated from interest on loaned capital.[44] Finally, there is much evidence that cooperative enterprises, organized without private ownership of input factors, could spur development at least as efficiently as capitalist firms, if not more so. For the cooperative nature of such firms more effectively *disseminates* new technological information, and this new information is produced by hands-on engineers and experts (rather than the financial wizards of capitalism). Together these factors suggest a more optimistic long-run picture of innovation and technological change.

But common to many of the arguments I am considering here are disagreements about the motivational structure of participants in economies. Hence, it is necessary to give the general issue of incentives and rational choice sustained attention.

Incentives

A recurring claim in contexts such as these is that unless people receive the maximum return that the market allows for their efforts, they will not produce at optimum levels. This claim applies to factor owners, in that the prices of those factors will reflect their true demand only if individuals supplying them compete with one another, and they will do so optimally only if they can be assured of maximum profit from sales. Similarly, it is claimed that workers, at any level of production, will exert suboptimal degrees of effort if the income they gain from working is in any way interfered with by non-market factors such as taxation. This phenomenon ranges from so-called shirking at the production site to diminished managerial or entrepreneurial activity. These factors all have a variety of negative effects on efficiency, or so the arguments I am discussing purport to show.

For this reason, the aspect of liberal ownership that we are focusing on in this discussion is the right to income from trades. This right is what allows individuals to reap the maximum amount of return for their participation in market competition, given the conditions they face in their market sector. Therefore, we again train our eye on this component of liberal ownership as an element meriting separate and particular attention.

Underlying many of the claims about optimal activity lies a claim that people, as a matter of human nature, are maximizers of utility. But as I discussed in chapter 2, the strength of that proposition depends on what it is that is allegedly being maximized. If it is the abstract notion "utility," then there may be little argument,[45] for then all that is meant is that people strive to satisfy their most favored preferences, leaving open what those preferences are for. But this claim is too weak to support the various incentive arguments. For "utility," on this view, could mean the satisfaction a person receives from commingling with her co-workers, or supporting the state production quota, or spending time at home with children. Nothing predictable concerning production levels follows from the claim that people maximize their utility in this abstract sense.

But if the claim is made stronger, if what is being said is that people always act to maximize their economic well-being, or only act for selfish motives, then while the conclusions about incentives would indeed follow, the arguments would be unsound, for such claims are demonstrably false. The inaccuracy of the proposition, as a claim about human nature (an empirical claim about people generally), is shown by the fact that very few people actually act this way. Most workers, for example, have fairly fixed salaries or wages, and their performance levels are controlled by on-site managers or supervisors, not the promise of increased pay. Fairly few people have their income directly tied to their performance. This claim takes into account such things as merit raises and the like. When I consider the academic colleagues that I know, for example, they are highly motivated based on the intrinsic character of their projects (in the choice of which they have much discretion). Why should we assume "homo economicus" (the self-interested maximizer of neoclassical theory) instead of "homo universiticus"[46] as the model of motivation? Indeed, most people can predict their income with high probability independent of their performance (as long as this is within a specified range). So unless all of these people are working at suboptimal levels, it can hardly be claimed that human nature is such that people need the promise of economic reward in order to work hard.

Motivational structures, whether characterized by narrow self-interest or by the desire for cooperation, tend to develop along with the organization that presupposes and fosters them.[47] So in liberal ownership (capitalist) society, what some call the duty of self-interest may indeed become inculcated in the motivational framework of the general population, and this inculcation may facilitate the efficiency of the organizations in the manner of a self-fulfilling prophecy. But it can hardly be claimed that such organizations are more efficient if we assume those motives, since an alternative organizational structure might achieve efficiency also if it assumes an alternative set of motivations (which it also promotes and fosters). Indeed, since there is no simple general pattern of motives for people—they may be hard-bitten individualists at the office, where this is expected, but altruistic and cooperative in family and social settings—there can hardly be a general efficiency argument based on a single set of motivational assumptions.

But consider further what is being claimed in the view that individuals gauge their effort levels strictly according to *income* expectations. This claim implies that those at the top income levels in the United States, who earn, say, several million dollars a year, must put *hundreds of times* more effort into their jobs than the average worker, since that is the ratio of their incomes. I have observed many of those who work for incomes at or below the average, and I can testify that it is inconceivable that anyone could possibly work hundreds of times harder than they do. Moreover, this claim becomes more ludicrous when we observe that the ratios between highest paid and lowest paid vary widely from country to country. Is the difference in effort levels between highest paid executives and the average worker in the United States really eight times greater than that difference in, say, Japan? Moreover, since the ratio of the salaries of top CEOs in the United States to that of the average worker is estimated to be around 160 to 1, the claim would have to be that some people put in *160 times* the effort of a typical worker in carrying out their employment duties. This is, of course, preposterous.[48]

Furthermore, these arguments ignore the huge preponderance of labor that is done for no economic reward *at all* (at least no direct income and certainly none directly tied to performance), labor which is not only pervasive but upon which the very structure of society is built. What I refer to here is the kinds of domestic work, including the rearing of children, that traditionally have been the job of women. This kind of activity, which again is undertaken completely independently of income (lamentably so, according to some), is certainly more widespread than any modern public workplace activity. So if the claim about the need for pecuniary incentives is meant as a proposition about human nature, one must conclude either that mothers do not work very hard (an absurd claim) or that "human" in "human nature" has been surreptitiously restricted in scope. Or one must conclude that the proposition is simply false.

One could concede all this but then argue that the *workplace*, where efficiency arguments are focused, is at least one place where there is a direct relation between pecuniary gain and work output. The more precise argument is along the following lines: when workers decide on the amount they wish to work—a purely subjective decision—their decision is based on the promise of income and the utility of the work itself as well as the preferred trade-off between work/income and leisure time. When income rights (from the transfer of labor time) are restricted, then that trade-off is altered, and the total labor output will be lower. (People will prefer more leisure at lower income levels.) So maximum productive capacity (a function of labor inputs) is reduced with such restrictions on income rights. What results, it is claimed, is shirking.

It must be stressed that the efficiency argument concerning labor and limitations on income rights is, at best, a productive efficiency argument. Restructuring income rights induces changes in behavior that reflect changing preferences. To say that these changes represent a loss of total welfare assumes strong interpersonal utility comparisons of the sort that are disallowed by measures of microefficiency. Moreover, if the income generated by redistributive or egalitarian measures makes some people better off, then changing that system produces some losers, hence barring a well-defined Pareto comparison.

The shirking argument is flawed in other ways. First, it assumes that the source of satisfaction from work is purely the income earned from that work. I have already cast doubt on the generality of this assumption. Furthermore, it assumes that the decisions about welfare returns from work are *independent* for all workers, that is, that these decisions are not made cooperatively according to the collective desires of co-workers. But there is good reason to think that cooperative behavior among workers not only is common, but is encouraged by management, which know that greater levels of productivity result. Indeed, the very stability of economic systems depends on an initial cooperative impulse necessary to overcome the Prisoner's Dilemma–type relations of the state of nature. Unless I can trust you at least minimally, we could not have stable enough sets of possessions for a market system to get off the ground.[49]

Moreover, there is much empirical evidence that the *cooperative* spirit among workers is much more effective in increasing productivity than mere income incentives. In a study of the worker cooperatives in the plywood industry of the Pacific United States, it was shown that these co-ops have a better record on absenteeism, productivity, and strikes than comparable privately owned firms. The study concluded "that productivity in the plywood firms is higher (a) the higher the effective participation, (b) the higher the ratio of worker-owners to all owners, and (c) the higher the ratio of worker-owners to the total work force."[50] So insofar as these incentive arguments presuppose only independent, selfishly (and economically) motivated individuals, they have little application to the real world where motivations are much more varied.

The conclusion that these observations support, I think, is one of indeterminacy. This conclusion of course is rather weak, in that it provides no alternative robust theory of human motivations. All I argue here is that the range of observable human motive structures is too variable to support any normative conclusions of minimally general scope. Those that rest such arguments on the postulates of general selfishness or pecuniary acquisitiveness must face a plethora of observable counterexamples to that postulate. So the incentive arguments that lie behind justifications of liberal ownership capitalism suffer from this defect.

V. Summary: The Utility Argument for Liberal Ownership Defeated

This chapter is intended as a critical discussion of a variety of arguments purporting to show that only private liberal ownership structures could, under realistic general conditions, produce maximum social utility of a sort which is a significant reflection of individual well-being. In surveying these arguments, however, I have not pursued several relevant issues. Many such issues are connected with the fact that liberal-ownership market economies produce *inequalities* of wealth. Distributive considerations such as this have several implications for utility arguments. First, it is difficult to separate individual welfare from the individual's place in a distribution of goods. Many people have external preferences such that the overall distribution itself makes them better or worse off. (Some denigrate this consideration by dismissing it as mere envy.) This claim of course approaches what many see as the major defect of utilitarian arguments generally, namely, that maximizing good consequences by any means gives insufficient weight to distributions of satisfaction. But even on utilitarian grounds, there are numerous negative effects of massive inequalities for the population at large. (I have already touched on this issue to some degree; see pp. 106–7.)

Moreover, I have been ignoring a consideration that has often been adduced against (unequal) market distributions on grounds of utility. These claims are based on the observation, mentioned in the discussion of Bentham, that goods produce decreasing amounts of utility for people the more wealth they have. Such arguments based on the decreasing marginal utility of all goods will militate against conclusions concerning the ability of markets to actually maximize utility.[51] However, the rejoinder to such claims—that the unchecked inequality of the market produces less total utility than a more egalitarian alternative—is that these inequalities are necessary for the greater efficiency of the system. And this rejoinder leads us back to arguments that were discussed.[52]

Finally, these cursory remarks about macroefficiency have been based on the presupposition that such comparisons of productivity can meaningfully be made. But this is a very complicated assumption.[53] One must compare the resource base of each economy (since productivity is a function of input-output ratios as well as total output), which requires finding a common currency to make the translations between kinds of resources. One must also find a way to factor out all of the extraneous forces, such as military spending, that are exogenous to the workings of the economic structure but relevant to actual economic performance. And finally, one must assess the welfare effects of the productivity itself, since often seemingly less productive methods involve important traditional organizational arrangements that are of fundamental importance to the participants.

In the end, there is little room for anything near a conclusive argument that private liberal ownership of even the productive factors of the economy (nothing has been said beyond that) is necessary for acceptable levels of productive efficiency. And remember that even if isolated examples could be constructed or imagined where this conclusion held, these are not of sufficient generality to support a *system* of liberal ownership, which is, after all, what is at issue.

To sum up this rather wide-ranging discussion, it may be helpful to lay out the arguments that have been treated here schematically, keeping in mind the simplifications in doing so. Following this are the lines of criticism I pursued showing the argument strategy to be unsound.

The general argument for liberal ownership: (a) Utility maximization is a morally valuable social goal; (b) Economic efficiency is a plausible measure of maximum utility; (c) Competitive markets are uniquely necessary to produce economic efficiency; (d) Liberal ownership, as a general property institution, is uniquely necessary for competitive markets (either directly and generally as argued by Demsetz, or indirectly in that liberal ownership over production factors is necessary for productive efficiency, which is, in turn, an indicator of economic efficiency more generally); (e) So liberal ownership is necessary for the maximization of utility; (f) Therefore, liberal ownership is morally justified on utilitarian grounds.

My response to this argument deals with each of its four chief premises. Concerning (a): this can be accepted only if utility and well being are plausibly equated, but they are equated only if authenticity and rationality of preferences is maintained; but (this concerns [b]) efficiency reflects an austere notion of utility, and given its insensitivity to authenticity and rationality, it severs the connection between utility and well being (and Kaldor-Hicks measures of efficiency loosen the connection even more since willingness to pay is not reliable as a measure of strength of desire). Concerning (c): Markets are efficient only under highly artificial assumptions; transaction costs, information shortages, endogeneity of preferences, and market failures (failure to provide public goods, the presence of externalities) make efficiency in real-world markets an elusive goal. Also, there are negative aspects of the use of markets as a general allocative social mechanism, since many preferences do not get expressed in the market. Concerning (d): liberal ownership is necessary for markets to function efficiently only under special and localized conditions (concerning motivations of participants, absence of transaction costs, preferences of a certain special sort, and the like). So although liberal ownership may be *sometimes* necessary for markets to be competitive, they are not generally. So liberal ownership is not uniquely necessary for the solution of externality problems (and it generates some of its own). Also, liberal ownership of factors of production is not generally necessary for maximum productive efficiency; productive efficiency is not correlated with utility maximization—microefficiency—so is itself of only local and particular value; so (e) is false.

I do not jettison considerations of utility from the horizon, nor have I shown that markets are not useful for a variety of social goals. I argue only that neither of these qualified and piecemeal conclusions (that utility has some weight, and that markets serve some circumscribed function) provides sufficient justification for private liberal ownership as an institution.

VI. Epilogue: Summary of Negative Arguments

This completes the survey of the argument strategies attempting to support liberal ownership. I have not said that the principles that guide those strategies must be abandoned. I have not argued, for example, that liberty or natural rights should have no weight in the determination of the correct ownership structure for a society. I merely claimed that these considerations did not support liberal ownership. I will say a brief word, then, about what has survived of those principles from our critical discussion of them.

In chapter 3 I claimed that the natural right to one's body and labor was not sufficient to justify full ownership of external goods. But does the natural, preconventional right to one's body and labor exist? If so, does it carry enough weight to justify *some* property rights? Which ones? These questions are sufficiently complex and important that I give them a full chapter's worth of attention (chapter 8). I recast them, however, into the language of self-ownership, and what I want to say about self-ownership cannot be made fully clear until the distinctions introduced in the next chapter are laid out.

Liberty is certainly a consideration that cannot be dropped from view in the discussion of property structures for a society, and little that I said in chapter 4 indicates that it should be. The distinction I stressed there, however, between normative and non-normative conceptions of freedom will circumscribe the role liberty plays. For liberty in the normative sense, where that is understood as the liberty that individuals have a right to by virtue of other, more basic moral principles, will not play a separate role in determining property rights. The parameters of liberty in this sense just *are* the array of rights (property rights and otherwise) that justice determines that people should have. Non-normative liberty, on the other hand, if that is determined by separate argument to be a value in the society, might play a role. I assume that a principle protecting and promoting maximum equal liberty for individuals is an aspect of just political principles as I understand them. Similarly, basic political freedoms (freedom of speech and religion, for example) are part of the democratic structure of society that such principles demand. These considerations arise, in our discussion, under the guise of the trait of autonomy, which is covered in chapters 8 and 9.

As for moral desert, I am far less sanguine about the usefulness of such a principle in political principles. This is because, as I argued in chapter 5, the equation between the valuation of the desert bases (the actions or traits that ground the claim of desert) and the deserved response must be fairly exact and fixed for desert claims to have independent, non-conventional, weight. (And I argued there that market interactions do not establish such a fixed equation.) While I cannot argue for this point here, my view is that claims based on moral desert have weight only in contexts that include quite well-established and uncontested practices and rules which define the value of desert bases and fix the algorithms of deserved responses (such as some aspects of criminal punishment). Outside of such contexts, there is little to appeal to in spelling out what exactly might be deserved apart from impressionistic and malleable intuitions about moral merit (established in other, perhaps quite different parts of social life). And I would submit that in such contexts, these claims would always take a backseat to better established and more basic considerations of overall distribution.

Utility and efficiency make a reappearance, however. And although I suggest that utility maximization should get weight only when understood in a more narrow and circumscribed way, the goal of economic efficiency (either microefficiency or productive efficiency) is considered relevant in the final structuring of ownership for a just society, insofar as the things I say in the final chapters aid in spelling out such a structure. But as I argue there, efficiency is a value for a society not because utility maximization itself (in terms of which efficiency is defined) has independent value, but rather because productive and efficient economic institutions are what independent and equal citizens will presumably desire for their society. Understood this way, it will be fair to say that utilitarianism, as a pervasive moral and political theory, will have been abandoned.

So the negative arguments adduced have not failed to leave traces to be attended to in the final analysis of political principles. But the final analysis is still somewhat ahead of us. Our business now is to conduct a reexamination of the concept of ownership in light of the rejection of the traditional liberal paradigm.

III

A NEW MODEL OF OWNERSHIP

7

The Abandonment of Liberal Ownership

> That art [of property acquisition] has two forms: one which is connected with retail trade, and another which is connected with the management of the household. Of these two forms, the latter is necessary and laudable; the former is a method of exchange which is justly censured, because the gain in which it results is not naturally made, but is made at the expense of other men.
>
> Aristotle

The arguments of the last four chapters, incomplete and provisional as they are, support the conclusion that private liberal ownership should be rejected as the general pattern of property rights in a society. However, does the failure of those arguments imply that no aspect of liberal ownership can be maintained? As I claimed in the introduction, my purpose here is not merely to reiterate criticisms of private property per se but rather to analyze the complex *structure* of property rights. And as I mentioned at the end of chapter 6, there are elements of liberal ownership that were untouched by the arguments aimed at the entire package. Indeed, and this is the important point, the moral considerations motivated by the various arguments connect with the different elements of ownership *in different ways*. I want to use this lesson to motivate the new understanding of ownership I will now present.

However, while I underscore the rejection of liberal ownership—to emphasize that the rights that owners have over goods should not be the entire package of (distribution-insensitive) rights—I also keep the focus on ownership as a distinct component of the juridical and political picture of a society. Recall that in chapter 1 I argued against the full disaggregation view of ownership and claimed that an invariant conceptual core of the concept can indeed be found. What I think must be done, though, is to reorganize our thinking about ownership, to understand the concept in a new way, no matter what the most plausible principles of distribution turn out to be.

In that first chapter, I argued that the core notion of ownership, which stood up under the reductionist pressures of the full disaggregation view, clustered around two sets of concepts, one having to do with "primary functional control" and the other with "primary claim to income." Here I go a step further and argue that ownership should not be thought of as a single set of varying rights at all, but rather as *two* sets of such rights. On the one hand, the question of what individuals should own involves the question of what things they should be allowed to possess and use for their own purposes. On the other hand, what people should own involves what they should be allowed to transfer, rent, or share for the sake of gaining income. Principles of distributive justice must weigh these two sets of rights *differently* in determining the manner in which individuals should be able to control and trade goods. The argument for this claim begins here and continues over the next two chapters.

In rejecting liberal ownership, in particular in rejecting the direct arguments in its favor, one could conclude that all property rights in any society will simply be a matter of convention in the sense that they are purely derivative from the contingencies of the social setting and the rules of justice and distribution adopted by that society.[1] For reasons to be spelled out fully in what follows, I do not accept such a fully conventionalist view. There is, in fact, some structure to the kinds of property rights that a society must adopt independent of the particular conditions of the society and, to some extent, independent of the principles of distributive justice operative there. In other words, the rejection of liberal ownership makes ownership conventional in that the complete contours of ownership cannot be articulated apart from normative and descriptive claims about justice and the society in question, but this conventionalism is bounded by structural aspects of ownership itself and by the particular individual and social interests that property rights protect. Every just society will have to adopt a system of rules regulating the control and exchange of physical things; this may well vary with the conventions of a particular society, but the fact that these rules have a particular and unvarying framework and focus will not.

The main focus of this chapter, then, is this reorganization of the concept of ownership, which is attended to in sections I and II. I defend this view further in section III, where I give examples of arguments that are misunderstood or misplaced without such a renewed understanding of ownership. I add to this a discussion of the structure of the modern corporation where, it has been argued, the view of ownership I develop has already become a fact of life.

Before beginning, however, there is one more implication of the rejection of liberal ownership that I now want to underscore. Recall that one of the central aspects of that system is its distribution-insensitive structure. It says that what property rights people have is not a function of the overall distribution of goods in the society. But in rejecting this view, we, in effect, commit ourselves to the position that ownership structures *should* be shaped (in large part at least) by the distributive principles governing the economy. This conclusion implies that we should reject the usual view of the relation between the state and the economic institutions of a society.

In chapters 1 and 2, I indicated that I wished to dislodge the assumption that the governmental institutions whose policies guide the economy are *separable* from the economic activity that is affected by them. The accepted view is that the state often interferes with the economy for the purposes of equity or the common good. But this picture presupposes that there exists one entity, the state, which is disrupting the workings of another, the economy. And I suggest here that this picture is importantly misconceived.

Part of the definition of ownership in any society includes the rights, if any, to gain income from goods afforded to individuals. These rights concern personal items such as houses and clothes as well as capital goods such as shares in a firm. The extent to which agents are granted the right to retain the increased returns on transactions of such goods marks the particular economic policy the state has adopted for its citizens.

It follows from this, however, that it is implausible to claim that the governmental institutions whose policies guide the economy are *conceptually separable* from the economic activity that is affected by them. An economy is that area of social life that includes, principally, the trade of entitlements. The regulation of the economy is thought to occur when the enforcement mechanisms of the state declare that some potential exchange cannot occur, or that it will occur only at significant cost or under restricted conditions. At least this is the usual story. But notice, any definition of "the economy" must make central reference to the *entitlements* of the holders of resources, in particular the rights, liberties, and powers they have to alter and trade those goods. The structure of the entitlements that comprise ownership will make up the structure of the economy. It follows, then, that the specification of what the economy *is* necessarily includes specification of the structure of individual (or collective) ownership in that society. And the governmental policies that play this role specifically reflect the principles of distributive justice by which they are guided. Therefore, the operative distributive principles actually *define* the economy.

Liberal ownership, of course, is a structure where the greatest attempt is made to grant distribution-*in*sensitive ownership rights. Even there, it could be argued, the state allows owners to benefit differentially from the relative placement of natural barriers (to trade), relative transaction costs, and initial holdings, by virtue of granting owners full income rights. This policy, it can be said, is not distributively neutral. On the other side, however, the claim could be made that liberal ownership retains its distributive insensitivity by virtue of the diffusion of information (about preferences, transaction costs, available technology, and the like) away from a central entity like the state. So the state cannot be said to be *directing* the distribution in such cases. Nevertheless, we have rejected liberal ownership and hence have rejected property structures that are totally insensitive to the distribution of goods. So ownership, in particular the assignment of income rights, cannot be separated from the state's distributive policy.

The point is that the specification of the actual holdings of individuals, and hence of the economy of a society, is incomplete without specification of the bundles of property rights they enjoy over their goods.[2] Hence, for someone to claim that some distributive plan (which would be otherwise justified) must be rejected *merely* because it interferes with the ownership rights of individuals (especially income rights) is simply confused.

I. Two Concepts of Ownership

The rejection of both liberal ownership and the full disaggregation view of property rights necessitates the development of a new model. Defenders of full disaggregation erred, I think, in looking for a single idea that would unify the sundry elements of ownership. I argue that in fact there are *two* such ideas, two importantly different aspects of ownership that must be considered separately and justified, if they are to be justified at all, according to crucially contrasting considerations. As I argued in chapter 1, ownership involves a special relation holding between persons and the rest of society vis-à-vis some good. The thesis I defend here is that this relation can take one of two forms: what I call "primary functional control" (control ownership) and "primary claim to income" (income ownership). Where either of these forms of ownership is recognized (in some way), there will be a publicly recognized relation between the owner and others concerning his or her goods. But this relation is so fundamentally different in the two cases that these two kinds of rights clusters should be kept apart in discussions of distributive justice and ownership.[3]

Ownership is usually taken to mean *both* the power to use and consume something as well as the right to exchange it with other willing parties and keep the proceeds from such trades. I claim that use and exchange are different, both in the kinds of individual moral interests they protect and in the effects they have on surrounding others. In short, I urge that ownership be bifurcated into the separate notions of "control ownership" and "income ownership" and that it be understood that these two ideas occupy different places in the landscape of moral and political principle.[4]

I explicate and defend this thesis as a *general* claim about the ownership rights associated with individual property (of any kind). That is, I think that any principle of distributive justice, when it assigns property rights to people, ought to use different arguments in the case of each kind of ownership. And it should not be surprising if control ownership and income ownership over the same goods end up being vested in different individuals under those principles.

As I suggested in chapter 1, the central elements of the ownership relation include the rights to possess, use, manage, alienate, transfer, and gain income from property.[5] Control ownership is comprised of the rights to use, possess, manage, modify, alienate, and destroy one's property. These rights, liberties, and powers all concern interests of owners to *control* the good in question. "Control" here refers to the ability on the part of a person to be the final arbiter over what is to be done with a thing, unless this ability is contracted away by a fixed agreement. Control rights, in particular, are aspects of the person's *independent* powers over the thing owned, for they need not be conditional on the consent of others.[6] The rules that protect these rights create barriers of non-interference within which titleholders can convert the thing owned into utility, by either simple possession, use, or consumption. The central idea of these rights is that the owner maintains primary say over what is to be done with the thing insofar as this capacity affects only the owner herself.

To maintain primary functional control of an item of ownership is to enjoy rights that clear the path between one's own decisions and the state of the object of ownership. The component elements of control ownership are those incidents, such as possession and use rights, which allow the owner the greatest possible say over the placement, nature, physical state, or operation of the object owned. Another way to put this is that the control-owner of the object maintains decision-making authority over the physical state of the item.[7]

This is obviously most clearly the case with tangible objects of ownership. My control rights over the chair I sit on allow me to directly determine (as much as anyone has this power) the physical characteristics of the chair. I can sit on it, chop it into pieces, or paint it green. Even with tangible objects, the physical state of the item may not change when I exercise control over it: I may simply use the chair to sit on, for example. But it remains the case that the events which involve the object are directed by my intentional action.

Where less tangible objects are concerned, the rights included in control ownership must be stated more abstractly: one has control over intangible items when the particular functions of the thing are governed by one's own particular decisions (though it will turn out that most intangible items of ownership, such as stocks and bonds, are such that only income rights will be exercised over them). I can, for example, use my stock in a corporation to vote in decisions by the board of directors. This is the reason for the modifier "functional" in that the control of the item is delineated by the possible functions to which it can be put.

The right to control an item covers not only the right to use it (change its nature, consume, or destroy it) but also the right to exclusive possession of it. This means that the holder of this right has ultimate authority over access to the item. As I noted in chapter 1, this right covers primary control of this sort even if the immediate control is being exercised by another person (I can allow you to use my goods and still maintain primary control in the sense that your permission to use the goods is directly derived from my decision).

Use can be divided into non-relational and relational use: I use an object in a non-relational manner when I engage in an activity involving that object, and the description of that activity makes no essential reference to another person. Relational use involves activities that do include others (by virtue of my permission). This latter power is contingent on the actions of others in a way similar to exchange, but the stipulation I make here is that the relational uses that control rights cover are those which do not involve *mutual* exchanges of goods. I exercise my control rights when I share goods with you as long as this sharing does not take the form of a *quid pro quo*, where my permission to you is directly contingent on similar permission on your part allowing me to use (or come to own) your stuff. That case is covered by the right to income I will turn to shortly. Below I will say more of the distinction between relational use and exchange.

The line that divides control rights and income rights is drawn between alienation and exchange, so a word should be added about the distinction between these two. To alienate an item of ownership is to unilaterally divest oneself of title to it and to declare an intention that another become the owner (such as with a gift). Similar to what was just said about relational use, the difference between acts of gift giving and exchange has to do with the conditional and contingent nature of the latter. I exercise my right to exchange an item—as opposed to that of simple alienation—when I divest my title to it and declare another the owner on the *condition* that that other party does the same for me. Exchange is a contingent and conditional act. Alienation is unilateral, however.

Of course, I can decide to exercise my rights for any number of conditional reasons (as is the case with the exercise of any right). The difference concerns the scope of the two rights: alienation has scope only over the divestiture of title (without mention of a condition involving a similar act by another person); while exchange rights have scope over this bilateral, conditional act of title transfer. The contingencies according to which I might utilize my rights to alienate title are outside of the specific scope of the right itself.[8]

This leads to the other major group of rights I listed with which I want to contrast control rights, the right to the *income* from assets. This group is composed of two separate rights treated here as a combination: the right to transfer and the right to retain goods received in trade (income).

In a perfect market, the trade of goods is an exact reflection of the "substitution schedules" (preference orderings) of the trading agents. The only increase captured by the right to trade is a welfare increase, called the consumer surplus, enjoyed by each rational trader acting voluntarily (that is, but for such an increase, they wouldn't trade). In such cases the rights to income add nothing to the right to bilaterally transfer items.

Even in such perfect markets, however, a distinction can still be drawn between the right to consume (possess, use, etc.) an item and the right to exchange it. Income rights in that case (which are equivalent to exchange rights) still involve different considerations, both personal and social, from those that control rights involve. I will illustrate that point in a moment.

But things are different in imperfect markets, where there are scarcities of goods, transaction costs, and natural barriers to trade. Under such circumstances, the price of some items may be well above what it costs an agent to bring those items to the market and engage in trade. This difference results from artificial scarcities of goods (competitors who could supply more of the good, and hence bid down the price, face transaction costs or barriers in entering the market sector). This is a point I made much of in chapter 5. In such cases, buyers and sellers collect what we are calling economic rent. Hence, (full) income rights afford owners a benefit over and above the rights to exchange goods *simpliciter*, for such full rights give them the right to that economic rent.

The right to income, then, includes rights to what I earlier called economic rent. Although historically the term applied exclusively to land, economic rent is any income from trade of some good (factor) which is over and above the amount necessary to motivate the person controlling the factor to trade, where this surplus is due to the fixed supply of the factor (its scarcity). Since a full right to income gives owners rights to all flows from market transactions, such rights afford owners the right to economic rent. Conversely, if the state *confiscates* all such rent, the state is denying the right to the income (though not all of the income) to owners without touching their exchange rights.

So in an abstract sense, the right to the income derivable from trades amounts to the right to increased *benefit* from (relinquishing) the ownership, where this benefit is derived from others' goods, artificial scarcities, and economic rent. Some forms of ownership—trusts and shares, for instance—confer upon the owner rights *only* to accrued monetary benefits, such as interest. If it makes sense to speak of values of objects apart from their prices, the idea here is that a right to gain *extra* benefits from a holding—benefits different from the use value of the object—is captured by the right to the income.[9] More importantly, however, the right to income allows an owner to trade goods and collect whatever economic rent is available in the market sector as is reflected in the selling price of her goods.

The ways that individuals can be vested with income rights are increasingly various. Shares in a corporation are an obvious example. But also included are investment portfolios of various kinds, from mutual funds to pensions to bonds and stocks, all of which give the owner of these assets the right to the increased economic reward (interest, dividend, or profit) that accrues to them. Another way to describe the holder of income rights is to label her the "residual claimant," where the residual is that amount of revenue that returns to a firm over and above all outlays (all production costs, depreciation, and interest payments on borrowed capital). And as I said, such residuals occur only in imperfect markets and hence result from artificial scarcities.

Although there are innumerable ways to shape and delimit individual income rights, the most obvious mechanism for doing so is taxes. Taxation, at whatever rate, on income, capital gains, property value appreciation, or the like, is, in effect, a set of limitations on individual income rights. So another way of expressing the idea of "income rights structures" is simply "the tax policy (if any) enforced by the state."[10] Granting *full* income rights amounts to allowing bilateral trades with no regulation, taxation, or interference. The attenuation of full income rights takes the form of price regulation, wage controls, restricted interests rates, and income taxation.

Another important aspect of income rights is that they are uniquely *conditional.* While a right to the income from trade or rent of an asset is itself fixed, the *content* of that right—exactly what it is that one has a right to—is not, since that depends on various market factors over which the right holder could make no presumptive claim.[11] Another way to put his point is this: If I hold the income rights to some productive resource, I hold the conditional right that any income from productive uses reverts to me; if I sell a commodity in an area and make some profit from these sales, the right to the income gives me exclusive claim to these profits. But if everyone in my area decides to move away, thus reducing my returns from sales to zero, I do not have a claim against anyone. Hence although I may receive an income from regular transfers of property, this right is contingent on the presence and cooperation of others in an area. This level of contingency does not hold for control rights (over most goods). If my preferences are fixed, then the conversion of goods into utility depends crucially on my own preferences and plans. I can make use of the determinate nature of my holdings by constructing plans and goals (preferences) for which these goods are essential.

This is, of course, a contingent claim, and it does not hold uniformly for all goods. But this much is uncontroversial: control rights *may* be perfectly defined and unconditional when agents consume goods privately and with settled preferences. But income rights are *always* conditional upon the presence and preferences of other agents.

So the rights to possess, use, consume, destroy, and alienate one's property—rights manifesting primary functional control (control rights)—can be meaningfully distinguished from the rights to transfer title conditional upon receipt of goods in trade and the right to increased welfare and income from so doing—primary claim to income (income rights). This distinction may not be unequivocal in all cases. (Sometimes, for example, use and transfer rights will shade into income rights, and the market forces that define the scope of income rights will have the same effect on use, as I discuss below.) In fact, any two rights in the property bundle (indeed, any two rights whatever) may well, under a precise enough specification, not always be fully distinguishable. But the usefulness of the model will not depend on covering every possible circumstance but rather on its success in clarifying and defending economic principles in the general array of cases.

With these conceptual points made, let us turn, then, to the contrasting normative implications of these two modes of ownership.

II. Control and Income: Contrasting Implications

Given the distinction just laid out, I now discuss the contrasting *values* with which each kind of ownership connects most closely. Hopefully, this contrast will further clarify the distinction as well as emphasize its importance, for the difference between control and income rights becomes highlighted when we note the contrasting individual and social interests that the two sets of rights tend to protect. Such a contrast serves also to emphasize the fact that personal control and consumption of a resource need to be justified, if ever, according to importantly different considerations from those that might justify the right to gain income from the resource. If control rights are justified at all, essential reference must be made to individualist interests such as liberty, autonomy, and self-determination; the source of justification for income rights, however, is necessarily principles that govern the pattern of distribution of goods in the economy, considerations that are not reducible to those individualist interests.

As I mentioned, income rights and control rights diverge to a greater degree the more one moves away from perfect market conditions. However, even under such conditions, different considerations arise, but the distinction between income (exchange) rights and control rights can be seen in a fairly straightforward manner (utilizing the austere assumptions of economic models): Imagine two agents, Bob and Mary, who face each other in a state of nature. Bob is in physical possession of a book while Mary holds three oranges. Assume full information, stable preference schedules, no interpersonal comparisons of utility, and that each agent is a strategic rational maximizer of his or her own welfare. Now consider that Bob prefers the oranges to the book and Mary would rather have the book than the fruit. Each would prefer the combination of both packages most and the loss of everything the least. We then can construct a strategic choice situation that, without any enforcement mechanisms in place—without property rules—takes the form of a Prisoner's Dilemma.[12] Schematically, the situation can be illustrated with ordinal preference rankings and two choices:

		Mary's Choices	
		Yield Oranges	Keep Oranges
Bob's Choices	Yield Book	2,2	4,1
	Keep Book	1,4	3,3

Both would prefer to get both things if they could get away with it, though the move from holding their original possessions (the southeast cell) to trading (the northwest cell) is a favorable move for both of them. But without assurance that the other will cooperate (something not afforded them without a property structure), they will not trade and will be collectively worse off.

Now an ownership structure that affords both players both control and income rights would allow the optimal move from southeast to northwest cells. But notice how the different sets of rights impact differently upon the agents' choices: prior to talk of any trades, there is a *primary* interest in the protection of the mere (*de facto*) possession of the goods that we have been assuming. For protecting control rights (excludability) prevents a move from the *status quo ante* (the 3,3 cell) to either the southwest (1,4) or the northeast (4,1) cells, the direction depending on who does the "pinching." Unless use and possession rights are protected by some enforcement mechanism, either agent could take the other's goods and get her or his first preference, leaving the other with her or his last. So trades are only possible (and optimal) if at least minimal control rights are already enforced. That means that even in this minimally described scenario, with no discussion of the objective character of the interests being protected or interpersonal comparisons of utility, control rights are *strategically prior* to transfer and income rights.

Now many claim, of course, that it is the alienability of an asset that strategically is the most basic right in the package, since alienability provides the basis for all bargaining and contract and hence for putting together the optimal package of rights over available goods for the agent. This is the view that gives the full disaggregation view of property we discussed in chapter 1 its force. But this view overlooks the point that exclusive control rights must ultimately vest *somewhere* if goods are to be consumed. And without opportunity for consumption there can be no motive for trades. The right to the exclusive possession and use of a good is still more basic than (that is, it is presupposed by) any interest in the right to alienate or trade those goods.

So this is an aspect of control rights that is not shared by income rights—its strategic primacy. On the other hand, the aspect of ownership that is unique to income rights has to do with the closeness of their connection to the overall distribution of goods in the economy. To make this connection clear, let us now assume that we can compare the well-being of individuals to an extent that makes talk of a distribution intelligible, and also that there are costs (transaction costs) that face other existing traders who would want to enter into the bargain I have described. Assume, then, the existence of a third agent, Carol, who would like to enter the negotiations for the oranges but for the fact that she faces such costs. In such a situation the price for oranges and books is a function not merely of the preference schedules of Bob and Mary but also the barriers facing Carol preventing her from entering the contract.

With no taxation, price regulation, or redistribution of gains from trades, we say that traders enjoy full income rights to their goods. In a world of positive and unevenly distributed transaction costs, there are potential competing trading partners (like Carol) who may underbid the actual traders and who are unable to overcome the obstacles that they face, which may include lack of information about the preferences of agents in the market, technology for information collection, and the like. The structure of the income rights granted to holders of property amounts to a response to these environmental constraints on prices. Full income rights allow such factors to play a maximum role in determining the eventual distribution. It gives traders full rights to the economic rent available.

So the rules protecting individual claims to income from trades serve a distributive function; they serve the social interests in directing (or allowing) the distribution of goods to flow in some direction or other.[13] Patterns of distribution of resources are produced by the granting of those rights (since each new round of trades sets the stage for the constraints and opportunities of the next). My point is one of contrast: control rights do not serve this function, at least at this level of description.

Moreover, it can be shown that the very existence of a market, without which income rights would not exist, creates its own surpluses.[14] These are due to the efficiencies of stability, information transfer, and economies of scale that the market makes possible. When a system of property is set up, that is, when a stable set of rules governing the possession, use, and exchange of property is put into effect, there results a net gain in total social product due to the efficiency increases from such a system. Having such a system solves various collective action problems which, if left untended, would result in less productivity. So the existence of property systems entails a net gain in the social product.[15]

As I showed in the minimal schema involving Mary and Bob, protecting holdings and allowing trades produce such a consumer surplus (which is the difference in utility between the traders' getting their third- and second-ranked choices). The important point here is that the structure of the income rights recognized in the economy serves to *distribute* this surplus. That is, the nature of the recognized income rights (for example, the tax policy) will serve as the distribution mechanism of the surpluses created by the greater efficiency of a property rights system. Income rights determine the distribution of the wealth in an economy that is over and above that which is produced by individuals exercising their control rights (production, say).

More important, because such mechanisms produce a net social benefit, one cannot argue that income accruable from trades of the holding can be simply derived from the value of a holding to the individual possessor (in a way similar to what I claimed in chapter 3). Since the total value of resources in a society increases as a result of the existence of structures that enable trade, no one can claim exclusive control of the resultant surplus on the basis of the value of holdings controlled prior to the creation of these institutional structures.

It is not that protection of control rights will not necessitate political and social structures (such as a police force) that will affect the surrounding distribution. It is rather that the political and social structures demanded by income rights are, by contrast, *constitutively* related to the mechanisms that direct the distribution of resources in the economy. Admittedly, the postulation that there are individual rights of *any* sort will most likely presuppose that there are enforcement mechanisms to protect these rights. In general, the distributive implications of the existence of such institutions are highly contingent. But the set of legal structures necessary in the enforcement of income rights (for example, a tax code) just *is* the distributive policy of the state.

In general, then, the connection between income rights and distributions rests on the nature of prices as set in the real world, where things other than individual preferences (substitution schedules) enter the formula; that is, there is a measure of economic rent. The potential income from any holding varies depending on the presence or absence of other traders with whom one can make favorable bargains. The factors that determine the prices of goods—the terms of trade available to possessors—include the obstacles that face the various other agents who might want to compete in this trading arrangement. Recall that in a perfect market, where there are infinite numbers of traders and no transaction costs (or obstacles to market entry or information shortages), the prices of goods will never go above production costs. For any profit would immediately be undercut by a competing producer of the same good. Or, where there is no production, prices will simply reflect individual indifference curves. In the real world though, favorable trades (and hence income) are a function of the barriers and costs faced by other actors participating in the markets. And since obstacles can always be overcome with enough resources, the terms of trade faced by actors in a market are partially determined by the distribution of resources in the market, in particular the availability of resources to potential competitors.

Income rights also have a *causal* relation to distributions in that the structure of such rights determines, in a diachronic sense, the pattern of holdings in the economy. The consequent distribution of resources is produced by the granting of individual income rights since each new round of trades sets the stage for the constraints and opportunities of the next.

A final word about control rights. We have been assuming that individuals consuming and trading goods in the pictures we have drawn have totally transparent preferences (at least to themselves) which are completely fixed and stable. In chapter 9 I explore in greater depth the question of what further differences emerge between the two types of ownership when this presumption is relaxed, when, more realistically, we assume that people's preferences and values change over time.

Objections and Replies

As a way of further clarifying and defending the control-income split, I now consider some difficulties that such a view might raise and respond to them. First, recall that I claimed that differential sensitivity to distributive factors is one of the normative implications that marks the distinction between control ownership and income ownership. One might want to underscore, then, the distributive implications of control rights in order to dilute the difference in the value implications of the two kinds of ownership. One could argue that control rights do, in fact, affect the distribution of goods and welfare in the economy. For any scarce good that is generally desired or needed, the grant of full control rights to individuals will directly affect the well-being of surrounding individuals. The consumption of many kinds of goods, for example, will detract from the welfare of others in that it often involves the destruction of scarce resources. In these cases, where individual control of a good affects the general welfare of others due to scarcity, the interests that control rights are meant to protect will need to be balanced against distributive considerations. The person's ability to control her life and, as an extension of that, her possessions, may in many cases conflict with others' interests (perhaps of this same sort) for which (scarce) possessions are necessary (for instance, a need for first aid).

It must be admitted that there can be a connection between the granting of control rights and the present and ensuing distribution of goods in the economy. But this connection is far more variable and contingent than will be the case with income rights, whose connection to the distribution of goods is direct. When considering the justification of control rights, for example, one may have to *balance* concern for a particular distributive goal against considerations of autonomy and liberty expressed by control rights. This balancing presupposes two values to be weighed, namely, the interests protected by the individual control of property and the distributive goals of the system. Such a concern still contrasts sharply with the manner in which income rights must be justified, for income rights are *essentially* tied to the distribution of goods. And more crucially, they cannot be said to be a manifestation of the individual's autonomy and liberty, since income is a product of things over which an agent can claim no independent sovereignty. I pick up this point in chapter 9 when I show the connection between control rights and autonomy.

So I am not claiming here that the justification of control rights can do without the postulation of various obligations on the part of the possessors of goods to help promote the interests of others. There may well be Good Samaritan legislation, for example, or a wide variety of restrictions on the manner of consumption designed to protect the public interest, from zoning laws to restrictions on where to burn garbage. But legislation intended to control negative externalities in the use and consumption of goods will not be *simply* a distributive policy. It will be a more complex set of principles that extend respect for individual interests as well as concern for the collective good. In the case of income rights, the principles that undergird the structure of these rights and the distributive policy of the state will be essentially equivalent. In chapter 9 I extend this reply along with a more extensive discussion of the value of autonomy and its importance for the distinction between control and income rights.

It may be argued, however, that the restriction or denial of rights to transfer and gain income from property in effect dilutes or even eradicates control rights. Can I be said to retain the control rights to an object without the right to transfer that thing for a price someone is willing to pay me? Trade might be the very *use* to which I most want to put the object in question.

This objection conflates the regulation of the terms of transfers with their outright prohibition. Recall the contrast between simple alienation and income ownership. The latter is comprised of the combination of the right to transfer title and the right to retain goods received as a condition of that transfer. I have understood rights to the income from property as rights to that extra benefit (defined either in welfare terms or in resource terms) that might accrue to an owner as a result of a trade. In imperfect markets this extra benefit includes a degree of economic rent due to factor scarcities. Even if this extra benefit is heavily taxed (at a level up to 100 percent of the economic rent), it does not follow that the owner has lost the right to trade the object, but merely that she has no right to trade the object except on *those particular terms*.

More important, she didn't have that right unconditionally to begin with. Any given set of terms (prices) is the result of the actions and presence of other people: no one has a right (by virtue of ownership) that other individuals act such that an owner obtains the opportunity to make a certain deal. So if income rights are restricted by, say, state action instead of by the natural placement of human beings and their preferences, it is still the case that the owner retains rights to control the item. To claim that I have a meaningful right to control property only if and when I am afforded the opportunity to make trades that are to my liking means that only the very rich and lucky (who have made nothing but perfect deals with their holdings) have had rights to use and possess their property, and this is absurd.

It is important to keep in mind the distinction between cooperative (relational) use, unilateral alienation, simple transfer, and the right to retain the market-generated income from trade. In the first instance, cooperative uses of an object differ from exchange in that the interests of the parties involved are *coordinated*; they are not competitive. When I share goods with you in an informal (non-contractual) venture, my interests in the use of the object in question are tied up with your own. They are coordinated with yours in that my desires and yours interact; I may adjust my desires in reaction to yours and vice versa.

This is different from exchange, where my interest in your preferences is purely instrumental to the satisfaction of my independently defined desires. Recall the discussion in chapter 2 concerning the non-tuistic nature of market interactions: I do not consider the preferences of the person with whom I am trading in the determination of what I value and whether I want to interact. When we use an item cooperatively, however, this condition does not hold, and we take each other's interests into some account in deciding what value we place on an item or course of action. I discussed these questions under the rubric of "relational use" above.

There are of course many types of goods—so-called positional goods—concerning which the value of one's control rights *presupposes* a certain distribution. With these goods, the value of their possession and use is conditional upon the possession and pattern of use of the resources of others. The objection could be made, however, that insofar as these types of goods are numerous, then the connection between control rights and distributive patterns is more intimate than I have made out. Hence the distinct normative implications of the two sets of rights is thereby diluted.

Notice, however, that the control of items which derive their value from one's place in a distribution of goods does not causally affect the distribution in the manner that income rights do. For any *given* distribution, granting income rights will have a much more direct effect on the surrounding distribution of goods than will granting control rights to those same goods. The value of controlling positional goods (like having water skis) *may* depend on others' having certain goods (a boat), but the value of income rights will *always* bear a direct relation to the overall distribution of goods, for the very specification of my right to that income involves reference to the market price of my goods, and prices, in turn, are a direct function of the relative wealth of others.

A final set of objections come from one of the few writers who actually claim explicitly that ownership is a unified idea. I refer to the work of Richard Epstein, who argues that ownership is necessarily a unified bundle of rights and that anything less than the full bundle should not be seen as ownership at all.[16] Epstein's main concern is the issue of what counts as a "taking" in American law. His overall claim is that any diminution of the full ownership package—of private liberal ownership—is equivalent to a taking and is grounds for full compensation. His arguments apply here since if he is right, if the only coherent sense of ownership is that of full liberal ownership, then the elements of ownership cannot legitimately be separated in the way I am urging.

Epstein's arguments for the necessary unity of ownership proceed by virtue of several analogies that are meant to show how partial takings must be seen as takings per se (and therefore a denial of full liberal ownership is a denial of ownership per se). One line of argument is this: if I take a physical part of your land, I have violated your property rights; by the same token, if I (or the state) declare that some of your property rights to your land (such as the full rights to income) are not properly yours, then I (or the state) have similarly taken some of your property. Another analogy involves cases of divided ownership: Say that A and B share the ownership of Blackacre, where A owns the water rights and B owns the surface rights and the right to rent surface uses to others (income rights). Certainly if the state absconds with A's rights, it is a violation of ownership. And there is no significant difference between this case and one where the state disallows some of a *single* owner's rights of the same sort: if A and B were one person and the state denied that person water rights, say.[17]

Epstein attempts to buttress these claims with what he calls an analytical argument. His view is that analysis of the concept of ownership itself yields a determinate answer to the question of the true nature of property. On his view, possession, use, and disposition comprise the core of the notion of ownership.[18] But even if that questionable claim is accepted (see chapter 1 above for skepticism), it leaves open the question of the meaning and scope of "disposition." If what Epstein means by disposition is the income rights I have been describing, then it is by no means obvious that this is part of the single-core idea of ownership. (There are innumerable things that are clearly one's own but cannot be sold, such as body parts.) If, as is more plausible, Epstein merely means here the right to alienate, then it can be accepted that these three rights are central to a common idea of ownership, but it does not then follow that the *liberal* conception is what is picked out by that common idea (recall the distinction between alienation and exchange). Therefore, the separation of income rights from control rights in the way I am suggesting does not eradicate ownership completely.

Consider an analogy that cuts against Epstein's conclusion: A owns a snowball stand and stands to earn $X from the venture. She has full rights to that income, let us say, and even borrows against her prospective profits. But then B comes along and builds another snowball stand on his adjacent property and sells superior snowballs, causing A's profits to plummet. Now clearly A has no moral or legal grounds for complaint or action against B (as long as B acted in a way that did not violate A's other rights). If B did not take anything from A in this case, then the state takes nothing from a citizen when it, say, taxes profits to the same degree. It will only seem like a taking if the right to the established *market value* of one's goods were the accepted content of the right to income. But that is certainly not intrinsic to the notion of ownership per se.[19]

Epstein addresses this line of criticism in a later chapter.[20] In a response to just the sort of analogy I mention here, Epstein claims that only if a citizen-competitor interferes with the contractual rights of owners and potential sellers "by force or the threat of force" would interference be actionable. Since, he claims, government takings are always "forceful," then this rule applies (and the analogy with peaceful snowball competition does not). But this response merely begs the question. For whether an interference or restriction is forceful cannot be determined without *first* settling the question of the proper scope of the rights in question. My breaking into your house to steal your property is forceful, but a police officer's use of the same method (with a warrant) to gather evidence in a criminal case is not. We cannot say in advance that state declarations about the structure of property rights (which might involve limitations on rights from hypothetical market exchanges) involve force until it is determined what the justified ownership structures are for that community.

Most of Epstein's claims turn on his contentious view that only Lockean liberal ownership—established in the state of nature and holding over into civil society—is the proper understanding of ownership per se. His claim that the partial taking of the object of ownership is analogous to a change in the rights structure of ownership (alteration of the sticks in the bundle) depends on the view that the full bundle is considered already established before the change. But this dependence reveals a circularity in the argument. For we are asking the very question of whether such a construal of ownership is the only sensible one available to us, and I argued in chapter 3 that we need not accept that there were (or even could be) liberal ownership rights established in some state of nature prior to government action defining ownership. In the absence of such prior rights, the state does not use force in instituting an alternative ownership structure, and hence it does not destroy ownership when that structure is, perhaps, bifurcated in the way I am suggesting.

My main reply to all these objections will have to wait until chapter 9, where I use the notion of individual autonomy to make the distinction between control and income rights even clearer. First, however, I want to underscore the importance of this new understanding of ownership as I have described it so far by indicating various areas where certain confusions can be alleviated when we take the distinction between control and income properly into account.

III. Illustrations

Before turning to specific examples, let us consider how ownership has been characterized at the conceptual level. George Mavrodes, for instance, defines ownership this way: a person "owns a certain object if and only if he has the right to decide upon the disposition to be made of that object." This entails: "(1) the fact that the owner has disposed of the object in a way contrary to some other agent's preference is not, *per se*, evidence that the owner has done something which he ought not, and (2) the fact that some other human agent has disposed of the object in a way contrary to the owner's preferences is, *per se*, evidence that this other agent has done what he ought not."[21]

As Mavrodes admits, this definition is not complete as it stands. For example, the terms "object" and "disposition" must be construed loosely to accommodate ownership of intangible assets. But the two implications Mavrodes draws concerning property rights and *prima facie* wrongs is a provocative way of capturing what I am arguing is *control ownership*. For notice that Mavrodes's account does not even mention the right (*prima facie* or otherwise) to benefit from the trade of an object in a competitive setting. So while Mavrodes thought he was defining ownership, he was defining only control ownership.

Now others will often characterize ownership in the opposite manner, defining ownership as the receipt of income flows *alone*. This definition is common among economists, and I discuss it specifically (see pp. 141–43). And as we will see, this neglects the component of ownership having to do with control.

This kind of narrowness can be seen in many theoretical discussions of property rights. At a more practical level, let us discuss some other examples that help illuminate the usefulness of the distinction between control and income rights to property.

Privacy

One general human interest that is often said to be protected by property institutions is the interest in one's own privacy. What "privacy" or the "right to privacy" turns out to mean is not a settled issue,[22] but it may well be thought that an effective way to protect one's privacy is to have property rights over—to own—various items that comprise the arena where one's privacy is manifested. Let us look more closely at this claim.

In the various debates over the proper meaning of privacy (and over whether it even has a unified meaning), there do appear to be two strains to the concept as it is usually discussed. These are "informational privacy" and "intrusional privacy."[23] The former is the interest we have that certain facts about us, personal or intimate information for the most part, not be freely disseminated to others without our knowledge or permission. This sort of privacy is violated when other people come to have this information or it is made public, and such revelations are objectionable, for the most part, independent of how the information came to be revealed. The second construal of privacy is the interest in having certain physical *areas* closed off to other people—to control access to certain areas of physical space. One might want people to stay out of one's house (or bedroom or bathroom) whether or not their entering those places would reveal any sensitive information about oneself.

In both cases, an argument could be constructed that having private property rights over the relevant pieces of information (the physical manifestations of the information) or over the physical space in question, would contribute to, or even be necessary for, the protection of privacy. The conclusion would be that the protection of privacy is an interest whose importance provides *prima facie* support for the institution of private property.

Whether or not an argument along these lines will have force,[24] notice that the elements of ownership that accomplish the tasks mentioned (controlling access to information or space) are the exclusive use and possession rights included in control ownership. In fact, it is the very *excludability* in these rights that achieves the desired protection. Privacy interests provide argument for *only* the general protection of control ownership, not transfer and income rights. It certainly cannot be claimed that my gaining certain market returns on trades is constitutive of my privacy, since that would make privacy an indeterminate, unpredictable, and fluctuating aspect of my life. So insofar as privacy considerations are relevant to a defense of ownership, it is only so in the case of control ownership.

Now it is certainly true that income rights, and income, will make a contribution to a person's ability to maintain her privacy. This is because, trivially, income can have an instrumental role in the purchase of just about anything in a free exchange economy. But that is to say that the interest a person has in privacy has no direct bearing on her desire for income rights over any particular piece of property. For what she would then be trying to purchase are those goods the *control* of which affords her a degree of privacy.

The Psychology of Ownership

The distinction I defend here also has application to some of the empirical literature on property. In various social psychological studies, questions have been pursued about whether the concept of ownership—and the social norms it embodies—is an innate, cross-cultural, or otherwise universal human idea.[25] What is often asked is whether the impulses toward acquisitiveness, possessiveness, and perhaps reciprocity are to be found everywhere or at every stage of human development (even in non-humans).[26] For example, in a series of studies, Lita Furby has investigated possessive behavior, language patterns, and other indications of a general concept of property in humans.[27] This research has led to the conclusion that "possessive behavior, in one form or another, appears to be universal in all human societies."[28] This conclusion could quite easily be understood to imply that some form of *ownership* was thereby universal. But when Furby's work is scrutinized, it is clear that it is exclusive possession that she has in mind. In fact, in setting the groundwork for studying the possessive behavior of *non*-humans, Lee Ellis refers directly to Furby's conclusion and builds his model on it. In spelling out the "human concept of property," Ellis defines property "as a special type of possession," namely, "those possessions toward which no counter-claims are generally recognized."[29]

Similarly, in another survey of empirical work on the question of whether there are universal innate norms of property-related behavior, Kate Loewental cites the conclusion that "the property institution, although subject to great cross-cultural variation, is ubiquitous."[30] But when the operative term (property) is defined, the proposal for a general meaning of the verb "to have" is used as a model, and this involves the idea that "it is permissible for X to use O, and if X consents, it is permissible for others to use O."[31]

In all of these studies, the question that is really being investigated is, in effect, whether *control ownership* is to be found universally (or at every stage of an agent's cognitive development). It is a very different question whether a system of private exchange (individual income ownership) is to be found everywhere. The latter question seems obviously answerable in the negative. But in all of these studies, the aspect of property that is focused on is control ownership alone. None of these studies produce evidence that the claim of income (or private benefit from traded goods generally) is universally or cross-culturally observed.

I am not suggesting that these psychologists have confused their terms, or that they have substituted reference to possessive behavior for a full-fledged legal concept of ownership. In fact, most explicitly acknowledge the obvious fact that *private* property is not co-extensive with "property." But as I explained in chapter 1, the qualifier "private" merely refers to the number of persons in whom the ownership rights vest. This distinction can easily be confused with the idea that ownership with income as well as control rights is the structure that is at issue (whether the bearer of those rights is one person or a whole community). My principal claim here is that failure to understand the deep differences between control ownership and income ownership allows these scientists to produce evidence for what they label "property" but which is only one kind of property, which is associated with control rights alone.[32]

The Economic Perspective

What these examples so far all show is that it is control ownership at issue, though perhaps implicitly so, in questions about the relation between ownership and other phenomena. This is ironic in one sense, since according to one very influential approach to the notion of property rights, that of economists, the essence of ownership is the receipt of income flows.[33] This suggests a deep confusion. Bruce Ackerman understands this confusion and introduces what he describes as two incompatible perspectives from which to view questions of the nature of ownership: that of the Ordinary Observer and that of the Scientific Policymaker.[34]

Ackerman's distinction is not parallel to the income ownership/control ownership split being examined here, though his discussion is relevant to it. Ackerman is principally interested in the takings clause of the Fifth Amendment and in reconciling what he sees as the "chaos" in its interpretation. On his view, there are two separable viewpoints from which to approach the question of property rights. The Scientific Policymaker is one who attempts to utilize a technical legal language and construct a comprehensive normative view to decide takings questions. The Ordinary Observer, on the other hand, uses concepts in ordinary language in order to illuminate questions from *within* the existing social and legal order. The Scientific Policymaker's view of property, which Ackerman claims is common in any first-year property class in law school, is tantamount to what I labelled the "full disaggregation view" in chapter 1. It is the view that "ownership" is itself meaningless, and that property rights are nothing but an infinitely variable bundle of rights that describe the "legally sanctioned uses" of some thing.[35]

The view of ownership of the Ordinary Observer is closer to what I have been calling control ownership. It is the idea that an owner may, "(a) without negative social sanction, use the thing in lots more ways than others can; and (b) others need a specially compelling reason if they hope to escape the negative social sanctions that are normally visited upon those who use another's thing without . . . permission."[36]

Whether or not the distinction between these two perspectives will stand scrutiny,[37] the split is instructive in the present context because each approach emphasizes, in different ways, the two kinds of ownership I am distinguishing. Ackerman's gloss of contemporary legal language, which he thinks a current Scientific Policymaker would adopt, gives centrality of place to the economic approach to legal questions, which has close ties to a utilitarian comprehensive moral view.[38] Thus, Ackerman's view of Scientific ownership is tied to a theory that views wealth maximization and efficiency as the primary goals of social institutions (including the private law). As I have been arguing, this scheme elides the important interests that controlling property expresses (interests that cannot meaningfully be captured by, for example, "willingness to pay" measures of benefit).[39] The Scientific Policymaker of Ackerman's theory of property fails to see the difference between rights alterations affecting control and rights alterations affecting income flows. The latter encompasses a much broader range of cases, including, for instance, the case where lowering the speed limit lowers the resale value of one's Ferrari.

In this way, I think that the two perspectives that Ackerman describes cannot be thought of as incompatible perspectives from which to view ownership. Rather, each emphasizes one or another of the two *kinds* of ownership that I am here distinguishing. If lawyers in contemporary America tend to presuppose the income flows aspect of property, then this merely means that income ownership is their focus.[40] The common view of ownership focuses on control rights. Since these two kinds of ownership protect such different interests and have such different structures, it is no surprise that they occupy such separate roles in the language of property. And so they should not be thought of as being two complete and incompatible views of the same phenomenon, but rather as emphasizing different *modes* of ownership.

In all these examples, the arguments advanced are better understood as providing support for only one type of property ownership.[41] One could add to this list and mention similar arguments culled from other quarters: consider traditional arguments, for example, linking property with virtue, or autonomy, the extension of personality onto material things, alienation, individuality, or economic efficiency. In all cases, simply ask yourself how the argument would go if one took only one of the kinds of ownership I distinguish as the construal of property in the conclusions. In every case, I think, you will find that it is not ownership per se that is supported (certainly not ownership in the liberal sense), but merely *either* control ownership or income ownership.

Control, Income, and the Structure of Corporations

As a final illustration of the usefulness of the distinction, I want to discuss the claim many have made that the separation of income rights from control rights has become a *fait accompli* in the developing structure of corporations. In a seminal work in 1932, Adolf Berle and Gardiner Means argued that for the modern corporation, operating control had become effectively separated from what they called "ownership."[42] In fact, they argued that the prerogatives of private property can be divided functionally into the roles of supplying capital, having power over its use, and actually initiating operations of capital use.[43] The first and second of these functions, according to Berle and Means, are performed by the owners of the modern corporation, while the third is performed by the managers.

Managers, they point out, have a very different motivational structure than do the residual claimants who hold the company's stock. Managers might be moved to direct the firm's resources toward the comfort, safety, or luxury of the workplace, for example, rather than to uses that maximize the profit of the firm. These differential motives, it is argued, create conflicts in the organizational structure of the firm. More to our purposes, it embodies a rights structure where the different interests protected by control rights and income rights respectively are distinguished.

If Berle and Means are essentially correct, the thesis I am defending here is difficult to reject. For if the separation of control rights and income rights is already a fact of life in modern corporate society, it is hardly controversial to claim that ownership should be considered, not as a single notion, but as either control ownership or income ownership.

There has been much discussion, however, of the Berle and Means thesis as a descriptive claim about the structure of corporations (and of the corollary claim that efficiency suffers from the diverging incentive structures of managers and owners). Relevant to the present discussion are various subtleties concerning the kinds of control and residual ownership exhibited in corporate settings that have been introduced. For example, Eugene Fama and Michael Jensen further complicate the notion of managerial control, introducing the distinction between "decision management" and "decision control." The former refers to the formulation of policy and the latter to the implementation of that policy.[44] The functional roles of various individuals who carry out these tasks can be described in terms of the limited property rights that each has over the factors of the firm.

Similarly, distinctions have been introduced from a different quarter concerning the various functions that might be relevant to *capital* investment. For example, Robert Clark suggests that in modern capitalism, capital investment involves not simply the income maximization function that income ownership makes possible. There must also be room for investment portfolio management and savings planning in the modern corporate structure. This arrangement demands that some people will need use as well as income rights to carry out these functions.[45]

But these subtleties should not complicate the basic distinction being defended here. For my claim is that control rights and income rights are sufficiently different, in the interests they promote and are based on, that these should be considered as two kinds of ownership. The distinctions concerning degrees of control introduced by Fama and Jensen still manifest rights to exercise judgmental control over the thing owned. In the case of both decision management and decision control, those who have these functions (and hence the rights to carry them out) are given the opportunity to express their judgment over how the object of ownership is to be developed, altered, and utilized. In both cases, this activity is sufficiently different from the right to the residual income from that activity that the distinction I defend here remains meaningful.

Similarly, portfolio managers and savings planners are using the financial resources over which they have rights only in the sense that they are choosing optimal ways to maximize their income. The interests protected by these rights are income-related interests, not autonomy, desires for privacy, or any of the interests that control rights protect. So insofar as they are acting as agents for someone else, it is the income rights on the part of the beneficiaries of these services that are being exercised.

Another response to the Berle and Means claims that is of interest here is from those economists who claim that since a firm is nothing but a collection of contracts, the distinction between control and ownership is wholly without substance. For on their view, individual members making up a firm are all trying to maximize their own utility in a competitive setting.[46] So if an office manager chooses to order more comfortable furniture (that is, control the assets of the firm so as to maximize her own utility rather than the profits of the firm), then either that function is written into her employment contract or it is not. If it is, and the contract is efficient, then those decisions are indeed maximizing the overall efficiency of the firm. If this control is exercised without explicit contractual permission, then that merely means that the contracts in question were not complete in their specification and function. We assume that all these contracts are made by rational utility-maximizing individuals, with full information and facing no transaction costs. So by definition the firm is efficient if those contracts are obeyed.

Of more relevance to our purposes is the overall outlook presented here by the "nexus of contracts" view concerning the interests represented by the various elements of a firm. On the contracts view, the only interest that is ever manifested in such relationships is the all-pervasive interest in maximizing one's own utility. On this view of things, the control that one person is in a position to exercise is no different from the residual claims of another person, since both are doing what is in their rational self-interest to do. It makes no difference whether we describe one sort of thing as "controlling" and the other as "gaining income." As Harold Demsetz puts it, having an interest in the actual operation of one's workplace is like having a preference for leisure that one exercises at one's job.[47]

But as I argued in chapter 1 and will argue in greater detail in chapter 9, there is a crucial difference between being in a position to control an arena of activity and simply being eligible for full compensation if someone decides to interfere with such an arena. With Demsetz's arguments, the assumption is that the difference is only in the total amount of utility I receive from each standpoint (including the difference in income since one will likely be cheaper than the other). This assumption blurs the distinction between control-related interests and income-related interests.

But rather than show that the distinction is blurred, I think this line of thinking merely reveals the paucity of the value categories in the models upon which these theorists rely. Being in a position to intentionally carry out one's plans, to make decisions, and control areas of one's life, are fundamentally different interests from the well-being that such decisions may or may not produce. Mere well-being (no matter what level) without the capacity or opportunity to make one's own decisions is, on the view I defend, a morally impoverished state of affairs.

This point reverberates throughout the present discussion since I am arguing that property rights cannot be bundled into one big utility-maximizing package. Those rights that protect the independent decision-making opportunities of individuals (or groups who share their rights) cannot be measured on the same linear scale laid out by welfarist measures. Similarly, such agency interests cannot be fully captured by the right to income (or residuals) that income ownership protects. This point will be reprised in the next two chapters.

Conclusion

The distinction concerning the nature of property I am describing is certainly not new. The view was influential in the ancient world, for example. Along with the biblical prohibition explicitly denouncing usurious activity (at least with those of one's own kind),[48] these ancient attitudes developed into a general mistrust of trade for income that lasted throughout the Middle Ages.[49] The claim that those aspects of ownership which allow the pursuit of income in trades are not the most noble or essential components of property has deep and pervasive roots.

The recognition of the distinction between private use and public trade also surfaces later when the liberal emphasis on individual liberty and independence emerges. John Stuart Mill, for example, stresses the difference between possession and use, on the one hand, and trade on the other, in *On Liberty*. Mill argues that the private use of property (or private transactions between individuals) is fundamentally different from the public sale of a thing for profit. In discussing several examples, Mill distinguishes those activities that are self-regarding and private and hence outside the scope of legitimate interference from those that can be regulated or restricted. On his view, "trade is a social act. Whoever undertakes to sell any description of goods to the public does what affects the interest of other persons, and of society in general."[50]

More recent writers, from liberal thinkers such as Stanley Benn and R. S. Peters to leftists of various stripes, suggest making the distinction between (what amounts to) control and income rights in discussing property.

The conclusions one can draw from this emphasis on the control-income distinction are several, as I will draw out as we proceed. For example, writers who have attempted to argue about property rights but have failed to see this distinction have misdescribed whatever clash there appears to be between institutions of private property and concerns for distributive justice. As I have argued, the income-rights component of ownership is connected with resource distribution, and control rights comprise the element of ownership most intimately related to the individual decisions of use and consumption (in chapter 9 I show its relation to autonomy). In addition, this distinction suggests that instead of asking whether private property per se can be justified, we should ask whether, on the one hand, control rights can be justified (and what scope they should have and what objects they should cover), and, on the other, whether and what sort of income rights can be defended. The latter are of most concern to leftists who think that distributive considerations motivate sharp curtailment of individual property rights, with the state being the rightful holder or regulator of these rights. The former are most stressed by liberals (and conservatives), who are concerned with the importance of individual liberty and autonomy. Since these two elements of ownership are justified with reference to different values, and one does not entail or necessitate the other, they should be dealt with separately.[51]

8

Self-Ownership

I now put the new understanding of ownership sketched in the last chapter to use. Here I show how the bifurcated conception of ownership, the understanding that control ownership and income ownership are two separable rights bundles, will aid in the analysis of the principle of self-ownership. That principle embodies what some have seen as one of the most basic rights to be protected in a free society, namely, the view that a person should enjoy those rights, liberties, and powers associated with the ownership of property over her own body, talents, and labor. The bifurcated view helps in the understanding of self-ownership, especially in the relation between that principle and egalitarianism. The aspect of that relation which I discuss here concerns the alleged conflict between the principle of self-ownership and egalitarian principles of distributive justice. This analysis sets the stage for a more detailed discussion of principles of equality in the next chapter.

The principle of self-ownership has been a difficult sticking point for egalitarians because, while they must acknowledge the force of this principle, they also see that individuals are born with different talents and skills. Hence, allowing individuals to exercise their talents freely—an implication of self-ownership—implies under most conditions severe material inequalities will arise. Some egalitarians, in pointing out the moral arbitrariness of differential talents, simply deny self-ownership by assuming the *public* ownership of skills.[1] Others in the tradition are more troubled by the conflict between equality and the undeniable intuitive force of the self-ownership postulate.[2] However, this conflict is diminished, if not eliminated, when control ownership and income ownership are properly relegated to their separate normative spheres.

The plan in what follows is this: first, I discuss briefly the principles of economic egalitarianism (a subject expanded upon in the next chapter). In section II I take up an analysis of the notion of self-ownership, attempting to localize the central intuitions behind that idea. Then, in section III, I argue that self-ownership does not conflict with principles of economic equality in the way some have claimed when ownership is properly understood.

I. Egalitarian Principles

Egalitarianism, to put it most simply (and least helpfully), demands that political institutions operate so as to treat everyone in society equally. More precisely, this equal regard must be manifested independently of arbitrary facts about the individiduals, such as their race, gender, or natural talents. In chapter 9 I elaborate on the various issues concerning the structure of these egalitarian principles. For present purposes, let us define economic egalitarianism as the principle that a major component of the economic structure of the state must be policies which attempt to direct the distribution of all goods and welfare toward equality; that is, all goods produced in the economy should be distributed as equally as possible.[3] For reasons I bring out below it is necessary to state the principle in this somewhat qualified form, for exact equality may be neither possible nor required by the principles upon which egalitarianism rests.

One way to envision the instantiation of such egalitarianism is to imagine a kind of market socialism.[4] The details of such a system are complex, but the core goal of the structure is the equality of condition of citizens. This goal implies that equality of income, say, is not of *intrinsic* value, as many critics of egalitarianism assume.[5] Such a goal is derivative from the more basic ideal of the equal moral status of persons. Only when citizens are able to pursue valuable lives to an equal degree of success (independent of gender, race, luck, and natural talent) is their equal status respected. Hence, the collective benefits of social cooperation must be distributed to all in a way that is consistent with those goals.

For now we will at least assume that such a goal demands that profits from production and sales of goods must be distributed equally. This is a simplification, since unequal distribution of income will in many cases be *required* by the equal respect principle, when, for example, extreme shortages would render such equal distributions equally disastrous. There are many criticisms of this kind of egalitarianism, but here we are concerned to discuss the particular criticism that such an ideal is incompatible with the self-ownership of citizens.

II. Self-Ownership

In chapter 4 we saw how difficult it is to separate the principle of protecting negative liberty from the need to promote individuals' rights to be "enabled" in the pursuit of their purposes. The issues discussed there included whether, for example, the state fully meets its obligation to protect citizens' liberty when it merely leaves them alone, or whether such a principle demands more of an active role by the state in the empowerment of people in relation to their self-development and self-control. I argued there that something akin to these latter considerations inevitably arises in the context of a principle protecting liberty, and we will see here that under the rubric of self-ownership the same implications emerge.

A powerful way of expressing the principle of individual liberty, then, is to claim that every individual has full property rights over her body, skills, and labor. The view is that those rights, liberties, and powers associated with the ownership of property comprise the rightful sovereignty that each person has over herself. In short, people own themselves.

This claim is part of the very principle that critics of egalitarianism claim is denied by strict equality. I illuminate this problem by applying the analysis of ownership introduced in chapter 7. The distinction between control ownership and income ownership has direct application here. Moreover, self-ownership itself should be understood as a manifestation of control ownership (of oneself), and this understanding will do much to alleviate the supposed conflict that this principle is thought to have with egalitarianism.

The Nature and Value of Self-Ownership

Before describing this conflict, I must articulate what it is about self-ownership that seems so compelling. If decisions about whether and how to use my skills and talents are made by people other than me, even if such decisions are made for the public good, I have been denied one of the basic conditions of independence and self-determination—something of fundamental value to me. I have lost an essential aspect of my autonomy in that I cannot, under these conditions, control and plan my own life. The basic intuition is that no one should be able to force me to act in any way but that which I choose, except in the enforcement of others' previously established rights. Hence, insofar as my body moves or acts, *I* should be the one who has the ultimate say over what it does or where it goes. "To say that I own myself is to say that nobody but me has the right to dispose of me or to direct my actions."[6]

We should separate, however, two distinct construals of the postulate of self-ownership. One can be called Lockean and the other Hegelian, referring to the bodies of thought that these positions most closely resemble. The Lockean defense of self-ownership expresses the idea that self-ownership is necessary as a kind of protection, in particular against invasions by the state into the private and personal aspects of one's life. The Hegelian view is that self-ownership is more than a mere negative barrier against intrusion, but rather a positive good that manifests a person's extension of her personality and will into the world. Self-ownership, on this view, is an expression of the person's embodiment in her own body and talents, and it is valuable because it is necessary for the self-expression that is constitutive of a truly human life.

It is debatable whether Locke himself held to the Lockean view of self-ownership. Recall that Locke's theology committed him to the view that God created human beings, and in doing so (like all creators of things) He retains rights in them. In particular, God's partial ownership of people restricts the uses to which individuals can put their bodies or selves. For example, His partial ownership bars the liberty to "alienate" oneself, that is, to destroy oneself.[7]

The basis of this view is that what is wrong with denying the rights involved in self-ownership are the intrusions themselves, the manipulation of another person's sovereignty over her own person. We can call this approach to self-ownership "self ownership as non-interference." Richard Arneson has given an analysis of this concept where he says that self-ownership amounts to the principle that "people should be left free to do whatever they choose unless their actions cause (or threaten to cause) harm, in specified ways, to non-consenting others."[8] This principle is not based on a direct positive evaluation of the lives that sovereign individuals lead. In the tradition of liberalism, this version of self-ownership is neutral concerning the good or bad that self-owning individuals pursue within their protected spheres.

The contrasting principle of self-ownership, which I am all too loosely connecting with Hegel, envisions self-ownership as self-*control*. On that view, one is self-owning when only oneself, acting in a way that is free and autonomous, decides where and how one's talents and body are used, within the parameters set by others' enjoying similar control. This principle is different from the Lockean view in both its implications and its basis. In the Hegelian view, there is a positive specification of the internal characteristics of the self-owning person. This perspective presupposes that there is a proper developmental process that a truly human life can be said to manifest, for which the ownership of the self is a necessary condition. In short, self-ownership is a kind of self-control. Hegel's own view, of course, is embedded in a dialectical form of argumentation and, in particular, a specific view of historical development of which self-development is a part.[9] The distilled view mentioned here can be thought of as emerging from the tradition of political principle in which autonomy and positive liberty are given pride of place.[10]

Let us consider some of the contrasting implications of these two versions of self-ownership. One of the most glaring differences echoes the difference in the traditions that prize positive and negative liberty respectively. That is, if one sees self-ownership as self-control, and one thinks this should be granted and protected, then one must favor directing resources in such a way that allows the conditions of such control to manifest themselves. For example, if one thinks that rational self-reflection is a necessary condition for self-control, and one thinks (what is surely plausible) that certain resources (such as education, housing, and perhaps counselling) are necessary to exercise such reflection, then one must favor the equal and wide distribution of these resources. Seeing the value of self-control as the basis for the postulate of self-ownership entails (with the other premises) a positive duty on the part of society to supply people with those resources necessary for the *establishment* of such self-control.

Now self-ownership as non-interference has no such implication. Arneson's principle, that "people should be left free to do whatever they choose unless their actions cause (or threaten to cause) harm, in specified ways, to non-consenting others" lacks any such directive concerning the duties of others. In fact, it is silent on what to do when the capacity for choice is lacking in people whose self-ownership is being protected.[11] The metaphor that captures this version of the principle is that of a fence, where self-ownership provides an argument that a kind of fence be built around people to keep other people out. The questions that arise about the principle then are where to put the fence (that is, what counts as harm or interference) but with no evaluation of what goes on inside it.

Another important difference between the two interpretations of self-ownership concerns the derivation of rights to transfer, and (perhaps) gain income from the use of, one's talents and labor. In the Lockean mode, the right to make bargains concerning the use of one's skills follows logically from the rights involved in self-ownership whenever such bargains do not violate the legitimate concerns of others. For this reason, focus must be placed on the possibility of "externalities" that trades might visit upon others. In chapters 2 and 6, I placed great emphasis on this eventuality, arguing that those agents put at a competitive disadvantage as a result of trades (of external goods) were the victims of externalities. Those considerations apply here as well, where it could be argued that differential access to potential trading partners affects the legitimate expectations of non-traders in a way that is not reflected in the terms of contract of the bargaining partners.

But my real aim here is to draw a contrast between such questions and the ones that concern self-ownership construed as self-control. In particular, we must examine that contrast with regard to the right to bargain with others over one's body and labor. In fact, rights to bargain and trade are much more difficult to justify when self-ownership is understood as self-control, because it is always questionable whether such activities, which include the accidental and unpredictable outcomes of market-induced trades, are truly an extension of one's autonomy or positive freedom. It may be, for example, an important part of my self-understanding, and hence a component of my self-control, to exercise and develop certain talents, personality traits, or emotional tendencies, but it can hardly be seen as comparable to want to lend my skills to others for the purposes of mutually satisfactory remuneration. Exchange of one's labor for pay is certainly not always or obviously an extension of one's self-concept. Such an activity is much too malleable, unpredictable, and world-dependent to be thought of as constitutive of such a self-concept.[12]

This is not to say, of course, that connections with others, family members, loved ones, or co-members of communities, will not be constitutive in this way. But here is the crucial contrast: when I am connected to others in a way that manifests a self-constituting relation, I must in some important manner *identify* with that relation (or a component of it). That identification must be of the sort that is also true of my relation to (those non-relational aspects of) myself.[13] For this reason, these relations must be in some way *fixed*, or at least stable and consistent. Otherwise, the self-concept that these relations help to constitute will not itself have sufficiently stable content.

This speaks to the important contrast between such person-constituting relations and market interactions perpetrated with an eye toward increased income. The latter project, no matter how passionately executed and deeply rooted in a person's life plans, cannot achieve the stability or consistency that would justify inclusion under the rubric of self-control. This is a point I make much of shortly. For now it serves to underscore a different point, namely, that rights to trade one's talents are more difficult to justify on the basis of self-ownership when that principle is understood as the manifestation of a person's interest in self-control than they are when viewed through the lens of the Lockean version of that idea.

Support for these competing interpretations must be provided, of course, by moral principle. Self-ownership is expressed in juridical terms—the language of rights and privileges whose structure is borrowed from the legal contexts in which they are also operative. But to understand the true contours of such rights, it is necessary to probe the moral considerations that make them important, to utilize concepts which, while admittedly more vague, are closer to the root ideas that principles such as self-ownership express. In order to better understand the contrasting notions of self-ownership, it is necessary, then, to take a look at the property of autonomy.

Autonomy

Much has been written about the conditions of individual autonomy.[14] The physical and psychological circumstances under which a person undergoes preference changes should be, I would argue, the central focus of any model of autonomy. Autonomy must at least involve the authenticity of those preferences, the competence (or minimal rationality) of the agent, and some degree of self-control.[15] There is, however, much disagreement about what these or related conditions might mean and what the value of autonomy, however it is conceived, amounts to.

Most who develop a notion of autonomy stress the importance of the condition of authenticity, saying, for example, that what is crucial about an agent's welfare or integrity is that her values and preferences are "her own" in a special sense. Some have argued, however, that greater attention must be given to the property of independence. To be autonomous is not only to be moved by authentic desires, they argue, but to be free from oppressive conditions that make one's actions external to oneself. To lack autonomy, in this sense, is to lack sufficient separation between oneself and others to pursue one's purposes freely.[16]

I think, however, that the condition of independence will *collapse* back into the condition of authenticity as I expressed it. It is important to see how this collapse occurs in order to see the connection between autonomy and the principle of self-ownership. The conditions of autonomy that I have elsewhere defended are, loosely, that one is autonomous when one is moved by desires which were formed under conditions that allowed one to reflect on and resist those changes—that is, one was able to be self-reflective. Also, it must be the case that these changes do not produce manifest conflicts in the agent, whether such changes amount to processes not under the agent's direct control or to steps in reasoning (which ostensibly are). Autonomy requires that the agent does not resist the development of these desires in light of the factors that direct and determine them. An autonomous agent must also be minimally rational and not be self-deceived both in this (perhaps hypothetical) process of self-evaluation and in the resulting desire set.[17]

So one's desires must have been formed in a "transparent" manner or have been justified by reasons that one was in a position to evaluate in a clear-headed and rational way. The disjunction is necessary since desires often arise from the practical conditions that one finds oneself in while at other times they arise as a result of a process of inference and reasoning. In both cases, one is autonomous only when these factors do not operate in a way that cannot be evaluated and resisted. The characteristics of minimal rationality and lack of self-deception are also necessary concomitants to these conditions.

But what of independence? Joseph Raz has argued, for example, that in addition to the conditions of authenticity of desires, there must be a realm of "significant choice" available to an agent for her to be autonomous. He argues for this conclusion by way of examples which ask us to imagine sorts of people that he thinks lack autonomy because they lack an arena of significant choice. One sort of person exists completely inside a small enclosed area and is so confined physically that his action choices are limited to when to eat the little food that is given to him. The other is a "hounded woman" who spends her days on a desert island constantly being chased by a wild animal. In both cases, the individuals described lack autonomy, according to Raz, specifically because "neither has an adequate range of options to choose from."[18] The one has trivial options and the other has options which, while they are numerous (which way to run), all have disastrous consequences. Raz argues that autonomy must include conditions which guarantee that the options one faces allow one to engage in "activities which, taken together, exercise all the capacities human beings have an innate drive to exercise, as well as to decline to develop any of them."[19]

For these reasons, Raz argues that independence is a separate condition of autonomy and must be understood as the adequacy of one's range of options.

Let us consider this conclusion, for it bears on the question of the correct understanding of self-ownership. What is it, we may ask, that makes an area of choice *significant*? Raz mentions capacities that human beings have an innate drive to exercise, but what are these? In the film *Woman in the Dunes*, for example, a woman spends her entire life removing the sand from her small hut, and one of the points of the film is to show that this lifestyle of simplicity and regimen contains real value and meaning. The opportunities to do other things, like travel to a nearby village or to change her habits in a radical way, might be completely removed from her realm of choice, yet the meaning that the activity she engages in would not, I submit, be lessened because these other opportunities have no significance to *her*, given her values and desires.[20]

Now if we imagine that the desires and values she is moved by are authentic—that they meet the conditions I set out for autonomy—then can we not conclude that any other choices that she might or might not face are irrelevant to her autonomy? If she does not care that she can do nothing else, and her not caring is itself authentic, then her actual choices (limited though they are) meet a plausible level of significance. What this example shows is that unless we can say objectively that this or that activity is necessary for autonomy independent of the person's viewpoint and values, then the question of what is a significant realm of choice for a person will depend on the person's other desires and the authenticity of those desires. This is especially true if the conception of autonomy we are trying to articulate is content neutral, that is, does not specify in advance the content of the desires and values an autonomous person should have.[21] For content neutrality demands that the conditions of the significance of opportunities are not objectively fixed.

Therefore, significance of choice is ultimately derivative from the notion of authenticity. For if it is a person's desire set that determines whether the choices she faces are of a significant range, that set must meet conditions that make it her own. Certainly, if the level of significance that a person adopts for her opportunities is fixed by manipulation and oppressive conditioning, we would not say that she is independent in the way necessary for autonomy. I am not independent (and hence not autonomous) when I am in constrained circumstances only because I would resist (feel internal conflict with) the paltry desires and values that such constraints allow me to have and pursue.[22]

What this argument shows is that, in a parallel manner, self-control is more *basic* as a value to be protected than non-interference. What counts as interference will inevitably be derivative, in the same manner just discussed for autonomy, from the conditions of the authentic control of one's talents, skills, and tastes. What *counts* as an intrusion into the realm of my personal sovereignty cannot be specified without understanding the realm of authentic desires and values that constitute my true self. These desires, in turn, are those that manifest my self-expression and self-control. For these reasons self-control should be seen as the basic value to be protected by self-ownership, not non-interference.

Of course, the two conceptions of self-ownership may well be co-extensive: the Lockean view prohibits the same intrusions that the Hegelian, self-control model prohibits. But as we saw, the two conceptions differ in what they imply about others' positive duties toward each other and about the distribution of resources. A person who is not autonomous (self-controlling) but who is being left alone is self-owning in the Lockean sense but not in the sense favored here. So a society that is committed to the value of self-ownership must respond to such a person's condition on the self-control view of self-ownership, but not under the Lockean understanding of that concept.

So protecting self-ownership as "control ownership of the self" implies that persons have such rights as "possession" and "use" over their bodies, talents, and labor. They will, in other words, have all of the rights included in control ownership over themselves. Among these is the right to modify and destroy their bodies and talents. It also implies a right of non-interference with such control, since, as I pointed out in chapter 1, the rights involved in ownership are assumed to be exclusive rights. Such rights involve, then, rights to decide whether or not to work, what talents to exercise and develop, and rights against any intrusions into bodily integrity.

The implications this claim has for the question of the conflict between equality and self-ownership will be drawn out presently. What I have not yet argued, except by implication, is that self-ownership (understood as control ownership of oneself) *should* be protected in an egalitarian society. Such a protection amounts to allowing individual citizens to use or withhold their labor and talent as they will. We should now turn to the implications for egalitarian justice of protecting the ownership of one's self in the sense I have outlined.

III. The Conflict between Self-Ownership and Equality

The distinction defended in chapter 7, between control ownership and income ownership, was meant as a general claim about the ownership of property and its justification. These conclusions can, however, be extended to all areas of ownership, since the claim is that control of a good is fundamentally different, in structure and value, from the rights to benefit from the trade or development of that good. This last point is more crucial and poignant when what is owned is not external goods but one's own body and talents.

G. A. Cohen has considered the question of whether "substantive self-ownership," a version of self-ownership that allows a person to lead her life relatively independently and which is a value that underlies basic regard for individual liberty, is in conflict with strict equality of condition.[23] Consider that in owning oneself one owns one's talents. Cohen imagines a world of people with unequal talents who enjoy the rights associated with self-ownership. He argues that to enforce a system of equality in the distribution of external resources in such a world would inevitably conflict with that self-ownership, if the latter is construed in more than a merely formal manner. (A strictly formal sense of self-ownership is one where individuals retain rights over their bodies and talents but have no rights over those things that enable them to lead a meaningful life—external resources.)

Strict equality of resources is interpreted by Cohen as *joint* ownership of all resources by the individuals in the population. So we imagine a society of just two such people, Able and Infirm, who are granted ownership rights over themselves (though Able is far more skilled than Infirm), and they are given joint ownership of all external resources as a way of enforcing equality of condition. But, Cohen argues, joint ownership implies that each person will need the permission of the other to utilize any external good, a situation that dilutes the self-ownership of each actor to a mere formal right. No one could be considered as having control over a meaningful life if no action was independently permissible (no action, that is, that required any physical resources or even space). So in this way, equality of condition seems to conflict unavoidably with self-ownership. On the other hand, self-ownership could be allowed in a substantive sense, and, say, Able and Infirm might each be given equal amounts of external goods and allowed to develop them independently. What would result from this initial scenario, of course, is severe *in*equality of condition, since Able will produce much more than Infirm over a period of time.

Let us now focus on the apparent conflict between self-ownership and equality. Imagine a world where all inhabitants are awarded a per capita (equal) share of external resources, assuming that all bundles are of uniform value. Imagine also that all production is private; that is, all persons can initially, at least, produce improved goods from their original store by virtue of their skills. And imagine that the people have differential levels of talent for this activity, so the level of production of new goods varies from person to person. There are no other resources (except space, which is not scarce), and all goods are created with differing ability by the individuals in the state of nature. Now the inevitable result of this situation will be that the talented will be able to lavish upon themselves tremendous riches, and the underendowed will barely subsist. (Assume that all put equal effort into the process.) Massive inequalities would certainly result, and all the attendant evils that egalitarians are wont to decry would evolve. The rich elite would be moved to hire the less talented and could enjoy increased leisure time as well as the political power that comes from greater resources.

But it is here that the control rights/income rights distinction would be most useful. What matters in self-ownership, I have suggested, is self-control. The kinds of rights that protect self-ownership in this sense will be full control rights over one's body and talents. The specific motivation behind self-ownership involves the strong interest I have in running my own life. If the state or other entity tells me when and where I must utilize my abilities—forcing me to produce this, or preventing me from producing that—something deep and fundamental is sacrificed.

But to say that I alone possess the right to dispose of me and direct my actions does not entail that I thereby have also the right to benefit from the *exchange* of my skills in any way available. To say that I have the right to control myself cannot entail that I have a right to make or benefit from bargains involving others. This would entail that self-control implies "other-control" since such bargains depend on others' tastes and decisions. But it is the right to increased benefit—the right to trade and retain income from those trades—that causes inequalities. So the interests outlined as the core of self-ownership are not the components of property rights that generate the horrific inequalities of unrestrained capitalism. For only if I am able to reap the *increased* benefits from the production of what I own (my talents to create goods) will I become richer and more powerful than my compatriots. But preventing me from reaping these increased benefits does not *ipso facto* prevent me from controlling my life. As long as the store of goods I enjoy is stable and predictable, I can pursue the goals and projects essential to my liberty and autonomy.

For example, let us consider the case of owning one's body parts. Imagine some population that contains a minority of blind people for whom eye transplants (even for a single eye) would be simple and effective. The egalitarian impulse to redistribute eyes from the sighted to the blind in order to promote the most equal distribution of sightedness seems to offend directly the bodily integrity that self-ownership protects. Here the intuition behind self-ownership is quite strong. But then imagine that the sighted people began bargaining with the blind and sold one of their functioning eyes at huge profits, creating a class of very rich, one-eyed people. I think that our intuitions concerning self-ownership become seriously weakened here, in that although the belief that self-*control* should not be trumped in favor of distributive purposes, benefiting from one's endowments via the happenstance of the surrounding distribution is not so intuitively supported.[24] (I made a similar point about ownership of one's body parts in chapter 3.)

As a further illustration of how the new theory of ownership I describe here connects with self-ownership, let us consider a conflict of intuitions concerning the autonomy of women and their rights pertaining to their bodies. In the debate over the legalization of abortion, a powerful way to express the principle that women's right to access to abortion should be protected is to focus on their rights to their bodies. Those defending this position might well use the language of self-ownership to express this view, to say that since all people are self-owning, making abortions illegal violates the rights pregnant women have over their bodies; therefore legal abortions must be maintained. The view here is that making it illegal for women to terminate their pregnancies violates the aspect of their self-ownership under which they can control their body functions as they wish.

Also bearing on the issue of women's self-ownership is the controversial question of the legitimacy of surrogate parenting and the question of whether people should be allowed to sign contracts under the terms of which a woman will bear a child and another couple (usually) will then take and raise the child.[25] All this is done for monetary remuneration at a level deemed acceptable by all parties. Many of the same voices, however, who defend abortion rights on the basis of the rights women have over their bodies are highly critical of these types of contracts. The argument goes that allowing such contracts can result in the exploitation of poor women, whose dire economic straits might induce them to bargain away their rights to their bodies for this temporary economic respite.

But how can these two positions be reconciled within the terminological structure of self-ownership? On the one hand, it is claimed that women are self-owning and therefore have the rights of exclusive control of their bodies and bodily functions, of which the right to abortion is an extension. On the other, however, it is denied that women should have the right to barter away these very rights in the marketplace. How are these claims consistent?

They are consistent because the two positions are focusing on different aspects of women's self-ownership in statements of the positions, and (in a theme that should be familiar at this point) it is the two concepts of ownership that are facilitating these positions. Abortion rights are said to be secured by virtue of the control rights that women have over their bodies. So it is self-ownership as control ownership that is being claimed there. In the case of surrogate mothering, it is transfer and income rights that are at stake. And just as in the case of selling body parts, the considerations that bear on the granting of self-ownership of that sort connect with the larger distributive considerations that income ownership raises. So if one keeps these conceptions of ownership separate with a clear understanding of the different considerations that are relevant to their respective justifications, then this inconsistency evaporates.

This discussion reveals how the value of control rights for people is independent of the distribution of goods. This value is grounded in the individual need for autonomy and independent existence, given some allotment of goods. The value of income rights, on the other hand, is purely conditional upon the contingencies of the market, in particular, others' endowments.

Now let us return to the state-of-nature scenario involving Able and Infirm described above and the clash of principles it seems to evince. I suggest here a solution to the conflict between self-ownership and equality, one which shows that it is possible to protect the essentials of self-ownership and also promote equality. The proposal is this: The state must sever its protection of control rights from the structuring of income rights that it institutes to equalize resources. In this scenario, there would be a redistributive tax on all goods produced, the proceeds from which would be used to distribute to those who are comparatively worse off, in order to maintain equality. These tax policies would not extend to the decisions by individuals about *whether or not* to actually produce anything (decisions on use of talents) but rather amount to restrictions on benefit. Insofar, then, as the core of self-ownership is control rights (and these remain untouched in this scheme), self-ownership is preserved along with the promotion of equality. (In the next chapter I discuss a model such as this in more detail.)

The suggestion is that individuals would be allowed to exercise their talents freely, but all the profit from this exercise would be redistributed on a per capita egalitarian basis. So in a population of n people, I would produce whatever I wish and receive $1/n$ over my original store of goods. The incentive structure would remain for me to produce at maximum output since $1/n$ increases uniformly with my productivity.[26] This principle, which could be labelled "equality of product," is similar to the public ownership of talents when that is considered as public income ownership, though as I have argued it retains the essential elements of self-ownership.

Notice that the mechanism suggested here differs crucially from Cohen's joint ownership scheme. In that system each person needed the permission of all others to exercise her abilities and carry out her plans. On my view, no such permission is needed to produce goods. The regulations and redistributive structures that determine how much everyone benefits from any activity are external to the agent's preferences and plans. Since these regulatory structures can in principle be stable and predictable, the agent will be fully able to plan strategies, construct projects, and pursue goals.

To illustrate the scheme let us model an economy populated by our friends Able and Infirm. Imagine that Able can produce 10 units of (uniformly valuable) goods per economic cycle. Infirm, on the other hand, is able to produce 2, which is the subsistence level. If left unchecked (that is with full individual income rights), Able will soon amass wealth enough to hire Infirm and exercise all the prerogatives and differential power attendant on unequal wealth. On the egalitarian view I am proposing, the total product (12 units) would be subject to redistribution (assuming subsistence is the baseline of preproduction holdings). This means that Able and Infirm would each receive 6 units per cycle, preserving equality of condition. And since Able's share increases proportionally to the final share, she has an incentive to produce all 10 units each cycle.

The central egalitarian planner, though, cannot force Able to produce at any rate, nor can it prohibit the production of goods. All it does is redistribute what is produced.[27] In this way control rights (to utilize one's talents) remain individual and private, and income rights are held collectively. This may suggest that Able will be in a position to bargain for greater shares in that she can threaten to withhold production unless Infirm pays her part of his share (up to 3.9 units on this model); indeed Infirm will have an incentive to pay since he is better off than when Able produces only her own subsistence. But in our constitution it will simply be against the law to bargain for kickbacks that will upset the redistributive pattern, just as would be the case for any other black market operation. (This argument assumes that no individuals have any information about talents that the state doesn't have, so Able cannot secretly tell Infirm that she is underproducing and will put out more for some side payment.) This constraint on private contracts is similar to restrictions like a minimum wage.

In the private production case I have described, the use of market mechanisms for the development of income is artificially excised, at least for the initial rounds of production (after this, individuals can trade goods for prices yielded by the market and regulated by the tax policies of the state). This excision means that the rights that are to be publicly controlled do not precisely have the same structure as the income rights we have been discussing. But the arguments are analogous, since the increase in benefits from the creation of goods emanates from factors which are as closely connected to artificial scarcities as the market and natural factors that determine prices are. Able's and Infirm's differential positions in the production of goods result from their technical inability to compete for and trade talents, and hence their positions are a direct product of the distribution of skills. The unequal distribution of skills is equivalent economically to artificial monopolies or barriers to market entrance. These differential positions produce what we have referred to as economic rent. My lack of access to your talents functions the same way as do natural barriers that let proximity to resources determine distribution. The talented gain from the lack of competition for their skills in the same way that the price of an asset reflects the relative inability of potential competitors to undercut a producer's offer to consumers. Thus, the intuitions that motivate the distinction between income and control rights for external (transferable) goods apply here as well.

Two qualifications, however, are in order for this argument. First, this scheme may not be able to generate exact equality of goods if the total talent pool in the economy is not enough to generate a sufficient surplus, whose redistribution equalizes shares. In these cases, like cases calling for enforced samaritanism, there remains a direct conflict between self-ownership and the public good. I have not argued here in great detail that self-ownership should *in the end* be protected, but only that the considerations that make that principle initially quite compelling do not have the distributive implications that many have thought they have. Under such conditions of scarcity, the distinction I invoke will not eradicate all conflict between self-ownership and distributive goals; nevertheless, the conflict that remains between the control of one's talents and others' needs is of a different order than the conflict that was thought to exist between self-ownership (in the full sense) and distributive concerns. This is especially so if one assumes that skills are not as scarce as this objection presupposes.[28] But if they are, such extreme shortages pose a problem for virtually *any* theory of distributive justice. (What if a single unfortunate person needs all of society's resources to survive?)

Second, I have artificially assumed in the Able and Infirm story that labor is costless, thereby supporting the claim that the redistribution scheme I describe is not inefficient. But this assumption may well be false, of course.[29] People have varying preferences over labor and leisure such that marginal decreases in income will have an effect on their total output. So it must be admitted that *any* redistributive taxation will have some negative effects on the productive efficiency of the economy.

What is at issue here of course is the problem of maintaining an incentive structure necessary to produce optimal outcomes while insisting on continuous equality. One response that egalitarians have traditionally made here is that the question of efficiency is just a *different problem* from the (more basic) question of distributive equality. The claim that distributions that maintain equality may result in Pareto suboptimal outcomes will strike some egalitarians as simply beside the point. It may turn out, for example, that *slave* economies in some places will produce more efficient outcomes given a particular initial distribution of goods, but this efficiency provides no reason to suppose that maximizing utility should outweigh the more basic moral principle that no one can own another person. What this view shows is that maximizing the total productive output is merely one value among other, more basic, moral principles. Egalitarians drawn to this line argue that the unequal distribution of wealth, and the exploitation, degradation, and oppression that this inequality involves, is an evil that should be avoided even at the cost of sub-optimal outcomes (which are, after all, measured in the narrow fashion of Pareto Optimality).

On the other hand, egalitarians might respond to the efficiency objection by giving ground in the other direction. The conception of equality that is, in the end, adopted by the egalitarian principles guiding the economy may be complex and flexible enough to allow some degree of *in*equality of income into the picture. That is, the metric by virtue of which equality of condition is defined may not be confined to the single vector of external resources. Egalitarianism is a complex doctrine. It sees equality of condition as a manifestation of a more basic moral principle by which the state must show equal respect for the value of every individual in society independent of arbitrary aspects of that person's circumstance. This principle may well be consistent with some inequality of income, especially if this inequality is supported by all involved in order to maintain a pattern of incentives that benefits everyone.

It is clear that no egalitarian worthy of the name will support too great a departure from income equality. Egalitarianism is certainly inconsistent with a degree of inequality that would allow the exploitation of one class by another, or would limit access to resources necessary to pursue an autonomous life plan, or that would underwrite social relations that are hierarchical and degrading. Such levels of inequality are in sharp conflict with the basic value of equal respect that provides the foundation for egalitarian theory. I am suggesting here only that the degree of inequality of resources that may be thought necessary to secure maximum productive levels is not necessarily in direct conflict with egalitarian principle. All of these points will be rehearsed in the next chapter.

What is at issue here comes to this: protecting "control self-ownership" (self-ownership understood as the right to use, and thus to withhold, one's talents) implies a right to opt out of the economy with one's individual skills intact. This right of secession may conflict with the overall productivity of the economy.[30] One solution may be to allow the talented to earn extra income as a "bribe" to remain and produce at maximum levels. What could not be allowed, though, is a kind of individual bargaining (between the talented and particular less talented people) that might secure an unequal income for the skilled. These bilateral bargains would be ruled out (as a kind of black market) based on the consideration of overall equity: allowing them opens the way for free riding on the stability of the overall distributive mechanism by those who strike such bargains.

I say more about the details of egalitarian policy in the next chapter. Here I merely want to point out that the potential conflict between the goals of productive efficiency and those of egalitarian income rights structures does not comprise a fatal objection to a robust egalitarian theory based on the bifurcation of (self-)ownership I suggest.

9

Toward an Egalitarian Theory of Ownership

> [People who are] equal in the dignity of their persons and equal before the law, should be equal in their conditions.
>
> P.-J. Proudhon

I hope to have accomplished, to some extent, the dual tasks of rejecting the liberal conception of ownership and of suggesting an alternative picture. I now show the usefulness of this alternative model of ownership more directly, specifically, how it makes a contribution to the development of egalitarian principles of social and economic justice. The entire task of working out an acceptable egalitarian theory would include, of course, providing a blueprint for the legal and economic institutions of a society. This cannot be done here, and certainly not by me. All I can contribute to this project is a discussion of ways that the control ownership/income ownership distinction should be utilized in the development of such a picture of society.

In chapters 3 and 8 I showed that the natural right to one's body and labor, one's self-ownership, amounts to the right to (authentically) control access to and use of one's body and labor. Self-ownership, I argued in both chapters, does not extend to a right to the income from trade of these things. Also, in chapter 4 we saw how negative liberty (in the sense of the absence of constraints *simpliciter*) had value only insofar as it connected with other valuable states of the agent, which have to do with the agent's ability to successfully carry out her authentic desires and plans. Finally, in my discussion of utilitarianism, I raised questions about the value of the satisfaction of preferences that were not formed in an authentic manner, a manner that expresses the agent's autonomous self. Hence, in all of these discussions, there is a repeated emphasis on the condition of agents whereby they can act on authentically formed values and preferences. Autonomy, broadly considered, captures this requirement, and in this chapter I give that notion further treatment.

This chapter proceeds by elaborating on and extending ideas introduced earlier and putting them more directly to work. In section I, I extend the discussion of the last chapter about the nature of individual autonomy in order to further clarify the basic distinction between control rights and income rights. I follow this with an argument, in section II, that the control ownership of property is uniquely connected with the autonomy interests of the person. I then devote the remainder of my discussion to the implications of these conclusions, in particular of the new model of property, for the broad structure of social policy. I turn first, in section III, to welfare-state liberalism and make some brief comments about the relation between the structure of ownership and programs for the provision of basic welfare goods. I then consider the application of my conclusions to the structure of egalitarian principles (section IV). I first argue that egalitarian principles must contain a commitment to granting first priority to the autonomy of citizens, and then I show how market socialism can embody this priority by making use of the control ownership/income ownership distinction I am describing. In this way I draw the general outlines of an egalitarian theory of ownership.

I. Autonomy, Continued

As I said in the last chapter, autonomy is achieved when one is moved by desires formed under certain conditions, which allowed self-awareness and reflection and did not result in manifest conflicts within the person. This, it will be noticed, is an open-ended trait, which can be achieved to a greater or lesser degree depending on how many of one's desires meet the test. What the trait involves are the capacities of the agent to be authentic, minimally competent (rational), and self-controlling. The minimal capacity for these things is, I think, a necessary condition for basic well-being. But one must distinguish the concept of minimal autonomy from the more fully developed trait, a point to which I will return.

Autonomy *interests* are simply those interests functionally connected to one's autonomy. I have an interest in securing, maintaining, and (if this is the correct way to speak) increasing my autonomy.[1] The material conditions I face—my access to technology, resources, and the cooperative labor of others—carve out the network within which I can plan and pursue my life's projects. This means that those projects are truly "my own"—they are authentic in the way necessary for my autonomy—only if I face material conditions that in some minimal way make reflection upon and development of them possible. This point will become relevant when the connection between autonomy and property is made more explicit.

Autonomy is *exercised* when a person is able to deliberate and choose according to the aspects of her character—including her desires and values as well as her passions and impulses—that have been shaped by processes that meet the conditions of authenticity. Autonomy is *established* when the conditions for authenticity are met, when the person's changing character is shaped by conditions that allow self-reflection and do not produce manifest conflicts within the person. In other words, a person is autonomous when she would not resist the processes of her character development were she to reflect upon them.

To make these claims clearer, however, I want now to extend comments made in the last chapter and to draw some finer distinctions concerning the characteristic of autonomy.

Minimal and Full Autonomy

As a background assumption to the model of autonomy being discussed here, I consider the person not as a static and settled entity but as continually changing, adapting, and fluid. As I discussed in chapter 6, while it may be the case that many of our preferences and values are fairly settled, it is clear that our characters, tastes, and desires are also in constant flux. In many situations of choice, we often do not *have* a clear preference for one state of affairs over some alternative at any one point in time. In many cases, for example, we need to deliberate with others and interact with our immediate environment in order to come upon a settled idea of what we want. And this is not to say that we engage in this interaction in order to *negotiate* with these other people, to bargain with them in a way that assumes an existing ranking on all our parts for which the aggregation of desires might be possible.[2] The observation I am making is that in a wide variety of situations, we need to interact with others and with institutions in order to *develop* the preference in question in the first place.

What this assumption implies is that autonomy, both minimal and full autonomy, relates to the conditions under which this process takes place. As I have already claimed, having the minimal ability to consider options, gather information, and reason normally will be necessary to maintain autonomy under those conditions. Therefore, one must have access to education, health care, and welfare conditions (such as housing), which are necessary for this ability to be developed. It will also mean, in the ideal case, having full control over the conditions under which one's character is formed and one's decisions are made.

Although autonomy requires the capacity for self-reflection, self-control, and cognitive competence (rationality), the distinction between minimal autonomy and full autonomy has most to do with the requirements of competence. In the specification of the trait of autonomy I gave above, I mentioned briefly the necessity of minimal rationality. While I cannot argue for it here, I would defend the claim that only minimal "internal" conditions for rationality, such as consistency of beliefs and desires, are plausible as conditions for minimal autonomy.[3] What this requirement for consistency entails, though, is that the autonomous agent does not act on the basis of mistaken inferences or violations of logical laws. If I believe *p* and I believe "if *p* then *q*," but I desire something X which is based on the belief that "not-*q*," then the desire for X is not autonomous.

Internal rationality, then, requires that the agent have the cognitive capacity to make settled and consistent reflective judgments about the world, about herself, and about the manner in which she has developed the values she has. For all this, it is necessary that a person have had access to particular nutritional, medical, and educational resources which are necessary for the development of these capacities. In addition, it must be the case that a person's living conditions are such that she is able to turn her attention to the variety of choices and opportunities that are relevant to her self-development.[4] One must be in a position to tend to one's own life plan, which means, in effect, that one is not constantly straining with other elements of one's survival so that one can engage in the process of self-reflection and self-development that autonomy demands. I am referring here to minimal housing and welfare needs that are necessary for a person to formulate and pursue a life plan of her own choosing.[5] I return to this point below, where I have more to say about these material requirements for minimal autonomy.

When individuals are minimally autonomous, they are then able to make basic life decisions and develop individual values and preferences. Full autonomy, on the other hand, is an ideal. It is a character trait which consists of variables that vary along two vectors. On the one hand, we can be more or less autonomous depending on how many of our values and preferences—how much of our characters—have been formed under conditions that manifest autonomy. On the other, we can be more or less autonomous depending on how much we are able to become aware of the changes we are undergoing and how approving we are of the process as we perceive it. This second variable can be summarized by saying that we are more autonomous the more we control our immediate environment. The more direct the relation is between our decisions and the aspects of the surroundings that constrain us the closer we are to full autonomy.

Full autonomy would mean having *only* desires (and values and the like) that were formed under ideal conditions, which allowed full reflection and awareness by the agent. A fully autonomous person is never conflicted, is never moved by urges or desires that are not in full accordance with her other desires and with her judgments about self-development. Although a desirable trait, and one toward which a just society must allow its citizens to move, such a state is never fully achieved. For it implies that a person has stopped changing, or at least that she has full control over her environment in ways that shape that change, and this level of control is simply not possible.

But it still functions, I submit, as an ideal. And as such it motivates commitment to other principles and values, for example, that persons ought to be given the fullest possible control over the conditions under which they develop and change, consistent with like control on others' parts.[6] Therefore, autonomy is most fully realized when individuals are given maximum control over the aspects of their lives that shape their development.

This approach to the concept is based on the assumption that autonomy is a value for persons and that this value is not reducible simply to some function of the extant desires that a person has. That is, the value of autonomy is not a subjective, desire-based value but a more objective presupposition of the value of persons and their choices. This claim (to the objective value of autonomy) would be resisted in many corners. One could, for example, give a purely subjective, "welfarist" account of autonomy. Such a view would mean, in effect, that it is useless to make pronouncements, up front, about the value implications of social institutions (such as the structure of property), for if all values reduced to subjective preferences, we should merely arrange institutions so that individuals could bargain over and trade the rights packages that satisfied their particular preferences.[7] This stance on the nature of values would thus cast doubt on the bifurcated conception of ownership I am defending here. It is necessary, therefore, to digress a moment to consider this view.

Recall that "welfarism" refers to the claim that the only normatively important aspect of states of affairs is the utility of the agents in that state. The subjectivist version of this position is that all values reduce to the satisfaction of (actual) individual preferences. Welfarism can attempt to accommodate the supposed value of autonomy in a number of ways. One is to characterize autonomy as the object of a higher order *preference*. Autonomy, on this view, is a "consumer good," something some people have a taste for, and the preference for autonomy is counted as one desire among the others. Autonomy is a good for a person only when she *wants* to have the capacities which comprise that trait.

The problem with this view, though, is that when people lack autonomy they often also lack the ability to develop the preference for autonomy. First, consider a paradigmatically non-autonomous person, one forced, say, to take drugs and submit to reprogramming psychotherapy until she willingly submits to every whim of her masters. After such a program is successfully completed, such a person would, presumably, not have a *desire* to break free of such conditions, since no self-respecting cult leader would leave her with such a lingering wish. The conclusion a welfarist must come to in this case is that such a person does not lack anything of basic value. This conclusion, however, amounts to abandoning autonomy as a value altogether, even a subjective one. I would submit that such a position should be rejected out of hand.[8]

If a welfarist tried to respond to this criticism by imposing other conditions on the concept of welfare—for example, that higher order preferences for autonomy must not be "manipulated"—then either the account has stepped outside the bounds of welfarism or it has introduced a regress. It does the former if the conditions amount to non-desire-based conditions of autonomy, for under this qualified sense of welfare something is of value to a person independently of her actual desires or potential for pleasure. On the other hand, if the welfarist claimed that the manipulated person lacked something of value because some higher order preference of hers (a preference not to be manipulated) was ignored, then a regress of conditions ensues, for we would then ask whether *that* desire (or, more likely, the lack of such a desire) was manipulated or authentic. And this moves the question back to another level, and the same inquiry begins again.

Moreover, the value of autonomy is not typically well defined or consistent under the welfarist analysis. There is much evidence that people's taste for "internal control" (arguably an analogue to a component of autonomy) varies with the circumstances within which the person develops. It appears that people change their preference for control of their environment depending on how much territory they control and occupy.[9] The welfarist account of autonomy, however, would necessarily ignore the significance of this tendency. On the welfarist account, autonomy is a preference and its value resides in the satisfaction of that preference, no matter how manipulated and adaptive that preference turns out to be. But surely we think that the value of autonomy for people remains constant independently of the (perhaps oppressive) environment they face, even if that environment diminishes the person's taste for autonomy. The phenomenon of adaptive preference formation poses a general problem for welfarists, and this is a particularly egregious example of it.[10]

A final approach that welfarists might make to autonomy is to claim that the capacities which comprise autonomy have *instrumental* value for the agent. That is, agents who are autonomous in this sense have a higher capacity for personal satisfaction and pleasure than do less self-aware, self-governing, and competent individuals. While it is not obvious that self-awareness, competence, and the like are traits which successfully produce happiness in a general manner (and there is some evidence to the contrary),[11] it is not clear that such an account captures what is valuable about autonomy. If the view is that autonomy *contingently* (and hence only some or most of the time) contributes to happiness, then this account will not do justice to the different reactions we have to autonomous and non-autonomous people. When an obviously non-autonomous individual is addressing us (say a person who is very drunk), we do not merely sympathize with her based on goods that she will likely miss out on. Rather we do not take her ramblings at all *seriously* (no matter how polite we might be to her). Such cases show that autonomy is a basic presupposition of interpersonal respect and individual dignity, not merely a contingent good connected with eventual happiness.

Nevertheless, the instrumental view of autonomy is not a position that I need to reject, for it is not inconsistent with the general program outlined here that puts a basic value on autonomy interests. Such welfarists will agree with such value pronouncements, though they will do so on different grounds.

This extended aside concerning welfarism and autonomy was necessary to properly support the arguments to follow connecting property with the value of autonomy. To reject these welfarist accounts is to claim that the capacity to choose for oneself is a value that is separably identifiable from the outcomes, good or bad, of those choices. As Amartya Sen and others have argued, this is to distinguish well-being, which welfarism measures and which is a function of the success a person has in satisfying her preferences, from agency, which refers to a person's ability to form goals, commitments, and values.[12] I call these interests "autonomy interests." Such interests are served when a person is able to make decisions that are reflective of her settled character and that emerge from those authentic values and preferences the development of which she has been able to reflect upon or directly control. And such interests are fundamentally different from the well-being that such decisions may or may not produce.

II. Autonomy and Property

In chapter 7 and further in chapter 8, I brought out the many differences between control ownership and income ownership. Here I add to the compendium of contrasts. In particular I focus on the differences in the interests those sets of rights tend to protect. I am particularly concerned with what I am calling autonomy interests and with the relation between these needs and the control of goods.

As I have said, autonomy is the condition of being moved by desires that are part of a person's authentic character. An authentic character (desires, projects, values, and the like) is that which a person develops in an autonomous manner. So if the material conditions a person faces are such that the desires she develops are not authentic (since she resists the constricted manner in which they develop), then those conditions subvert her autonomy.

Now there is an appearance, perhaps, of this account's being overly broad. All of us, one might point out, face disappointments in our conditions (we would all like more stuff), but it seems wrong to say that none of us are autonomous. My claim, however, applies to only those of us who harbor, in a settled and considered manner, a resistant attitude toward the conditions under which we become who we are. To lack autonomy, one has to really wish that one could pursue the impossible project, in a way that makes one disgruntled with the alternative values and desires one's conditions leave one with, so as to feel that what one is doing is not "really oneself." This, I would claim, is not so widespread a phenomenon that it dilutes the force of claims for the importance of autonomy.

The material conditions of one's life have a direct effect on the opportunities and options which, in turn, constrain the development of one's tastes and character. If there is no television around me, for example, or if the books I can read are all Zane Grey westerns, then these conditions will affect directly the values and attitudes that I will come to have. One's immediate living environment, of course, has the most direct affect on this process, but other conditions of one's life such as social arrangements, leisure activities, work setting, and access to political life, will all play a basic role in the lifestyle that one must adopt as one's own.[13]

What is necessary for minimal autonomy, then, is that individuals have a degree of control over, or approval of, the general aspects of these material conditions. As I mentioned above, certain social programs, such as those providing education and health resources, will be necessary for these goals. However, insofar as it may be objectively determinable just which such programs guarantee minimal competence, autonomy may not require that a person has direct individual control over the resources themselves for their contribution to autonomy to be felt. On the other hand, the basic provisions of life—one's house, mode of transportation, access to social life, and family arrangement—must be such that one can exercise that degree of control over them necessary for autonomy-producing approval. Such basic goods are intrinsic to the lifestyle and social structure within which one grows and changes, and in order to maintain the degree of approval (lack of resistance) that authenticity requires, one must at least be able to consider their structure and alter them to the extent that one can plan one's life. Minimal control over such things as one's dwelling, mode of transport, clothes, and access to social life will ensure this approval. A person who must adapt begrudgingly to constrained living conditions over which she has no say will not very likely be autonomous.

It is not the case, however, that having actual occurrent control over the immediate aspects of one's environment is crucial for the development of autonomy. Control can be active or passive. Active control is not directly necessary, for all that autonomy requires is the lack of resistance to (that is, approval of) the processes of change. But certainly control is a sufficient condition for approval, and hence insofar as control can be granted, approval is assured. Now the aspects of one's environment over which one must have control to be autonomous are difficult to pinpoint generally, for different people have different relations to their situation. The general rule is that those aspects of one's material conditions that bear the closest relation to one's (changing) character will be such that control over them, or ability to approvingly reflect upon them, will be required by the conditions of autonomy. The decisions one makes in one's private life, for example, have much to do with the characteristics of one's immediate surroundings (one's dwelling). Some control over such things as one's home, personal effects, mode of transportation, and leisure activities will be directly relevant to the general control one has over oneself.

It follows that having control *rights* over those material conditions upon which one's plans and projects are contingent contributes directly to one's autonomy. In this way, control rights serve autonomy interests. How directly such interests are served varies, of course, according to the differing projects people have, the material necessities that facilitate them, and the like. But it is control over those resources—the ability to manipulate, develop, perhaps destroy, and consume such resources—that constitutes the requirement of autonomy.

Or so it is my claim, and it is admittedly a contingent one. It is contingent because the effect that having the right to use and possess goods will have on the development of one's character will vary with the good in question and the surrounding environment. But as I have argued, control over the basic goods that comprise one's immediate environment—housing, clothes, mode of transport (which in turn affords access to social and political interchange), and material components of daily activities—will be most closely tied to autonomy. My argument here is that this connection will be systemic and pervasive and, more important, will be true uniquely of control ownership.

"Control" is not a term without negative connotations. It brings to mind, among other things, the desire to control other *people*, or to be (or feel) superior to others, to be manipulative of both other people and the conditions one faces. The other source of negative connotation in the notion of control is its overly individualist slant. To want control is, it is thought, to want control for *oneself*, irrespective of the needs and desires of others, and to conduct one's life and one's projects in total isolation from one's community.

But the autonomy interests that control rights protect need not include, and certainly need not be limited to, desires and values characterized this way. As I have been claiming, the central characteristic of individual autonomy is authenticity. Whatever account one gives of this notion, no plausible reading of it will have the implication that close ties with others, with one's family, lover(s), community, or children, will mitigate or preclude authentically embracing values collectively shared. If the common goals or values that I share with family members are ones that I can reflect upon (in light of how I came to have them), then, even if such shared values are intrinsic to the composition of my self-concept, I will be autonomous in expressing and acting on them. Similarly for individuality: autonomy demands that a person act alone (be "self-made") only in the sense that it is her *point of view* (somehow described) that is the locus of evaluation of her involvements and connections. This position in no way implies that the particular values or projects that she autonomously embraces will exclude others in their execution. Autonomy is self-government, but the strategy and composition of that "government" may well involve deep and abiding ties to other human beings and institutions.

So the autonomy interests that control rights protect need not be atomistic or isolationist. The interests being adumbrated here can, in any one instance, be collectively shared. Control rights protect interests that either individuals have (*qua* individuals) or groups of people have. For example, a co-op will have an interest in controlling the nature of the development of its assets while no individual member of the co-op has that interest for himself or herself. The locus of the autonomy interests I am describing here varies according to the nexus of connections that are constitutive of the values and projects of the individuals involved. Although I continue to use individualist language here, this is merely a simplified way of referring to the person or persons to whom the characteristics and conditions of autonomy are attached.

This connection between autonomy and control rights further highlights the differences between control ownership and income ownership. For the autonomy interests protected by control rights are not equally served by income rights. As I mentioned in chapter 7, psychologists have done much work measuring and defining personality traits that are linked to autonomy. Similarly, there is much empirical evidence linking the ownership of property to "internal attribution," "effectance," and other psychological characteristics connected with autonomy.[14] Although the research is complex and incomplete, there is much indication of a close link between the possession of goods (control rights) and the sense of personal control an agent experiences, both over herself and her immediate environment. Lita Furby, for example, summarizes the evidence she and others have gathered by pointing out that "the central feature of possession—its principal defining characteristic, as well as the major motivational force behind it—is causal efficacy or control over aspects of one's environment. . . . The significance of possession seems to lie in the very high degree of personal control it entails."[15] She and others have also pointed out the direct connection between the personal control of items of ownership and one's self-concept.[16]

One of the main points of my argument, however, is to underscore a basic difference between control rights and income rights. For while trading and gaining income will affect a person's changing character, the rights to these things cannot be seen as pervasively connected with the interest in autonomy. This is because, as I argued, the outcome of the exercise of income rights is too indeterminate and varying (even in a relatively *fixed* economic environment) for such rights to be functionally tied to autonomy in a systematic way.

If securing one's autonomy depended on the outcomes of market transactions, that trait would consequently be as fluid, unpredictable, and shifting as are one's prospects in market competition. George Brenkert, for example, makes a similar point in the context of discussing what he calls "radical freedom": "[A] person's rational self-determination [in a private property economy] is contingent upon the antagonistic actions and hostile interests of other people. Radicals contend that people cannot rationally determine their lives when their fate, income, security, family life, etc., are dependent on the vagaries of the market; when one day they might have sufficient funds to live and another day not; when their source of income may flourish one day but be destroyed the next day by fire, storm, crowds, or the market; when they might be fired for no reason at all from their jobs or injured on the job with little or no compensation."[17] Whether or not my view is "radical," my point is that the lack of predictability of the benefits derivable from income rights makes such benefits a poor and unstable source of the conditions of autonomy. Minimal autonomy requires more predictability than the market can provide.

Gaining income serves a wide variety of interests, and while it can also serve autonomy interests indirectly, it need not. Income rights are connected only with welfare interests more broadly considered and not necessarily autonomy interests. Or if they do increase autonomy indirectly (through purchases), their value will be parasitic on the control rights one then comes to have. Only if one gets to *use* the items will they contribute to one's autonomy.[18]

That is not to say that *exchange* may not have this effect. Robert Lane argues that exchange actually contributes significantly to a person's "self-attribution" or feeling of effectiveness and control (something Lane argues is constitutive of autonomy).[19] Such evidence is surely relevant, though it is not clear that it shows any comparative relation between rights to exchange goods and rights to control them (with regard to self-attribution), for Lane only cites evidence concerning the former. More crucially, the right to exchange goods (alienation) is not equivalent to full income rights as I am conceiving them. For the latter include not only rights to alienate one's holdings but also rights to all of the economic rent that is available to those trading. So while it might be claimed that the right to exchange one's goods (with someone for some price that one was able to determine oneself) has a positive effect, this effect is not diluted if all of the surplus goods due to artificial scarcities that produce rent were confiscated, say, by the state. Lane's evidence says nothing about cases where exchange is allowed but income flows are regulated (through taxes, price controls, and the like).

The arguments I am making here are not at all inconsistent with claims that the opportunity to engage in market exchange is important for autonomy. Indeed, the ability to choose from among an array of other items offered for sale, and to express the value of one's own goods through a price mechanism, may well be crucial to the sense that one's life is under one's control. And the outline of egalitarian economic policy I refer to below gives a central place to retail and labor markets. My only point here is that income rights, which include the right to capture economic rent, will not be essential for such an effect.

What, then, should be the guiding principles for the structuring of income rights? That depends, of course, on the distributive principles operative in the state. For the major function of income rights is to direct the distribution of goods. No matter what those distributive goals are, however, it will be relevant to consider the various effects that income rights packages have on production, investment, and consumption patterns. Consideration of these incentive effects should be combined, as well, with attention to the ways in which people come to depend upon and expect certain flows of incomes from market interactions. These "reliance interests" in property may well block certain radical (or overly frequent) government restructuring of settled income rights packages. In general, however, and this is the central point, the considerations governing the shape of income rights should be consequentialist and, in particular, should concern the distributive consequences of those rights packages.

The relevance of this to egalitarianism will be sketched presently. It will concern the necessity of separating the goal of distributing control ownership over goods from that of equalizing incomes. As we just saw, autonomy interests are served by control rights, but those rights should extend to many things other than one's personal possessions for such interests to be properly served. Equalizing the satisfaction of those interests, insofar as that is a central egalitarian goal, will require different social policies than simply equalizing income and wealth.

However, independently of the development of plausible egalitarian principles of justice, the distinction I have been arguing for should be of use to any theory that takes autonomy (or some correlate) to be a basic value. Insofar as autonomy is a fundamental value to be protected and promoted in a society—whether that society is egalitarian, traditionally liberal, or guided by some other set of principles—the bifurcation of ownership I have suggested must, in some form, be considered.

III. Applications of the New Model: The Welfare State

As I have said from the beginning, my interest here goes beyond defending this all-purpose conclusion about property. I very much want to contribute to the development of economic policies that reflect a basic commitment to the deep equality of persons. But as I also said, the distinction between control and income claims is relevant to any view that takes the autonomy of individuals seriously. As I understand it, welfare state liberalism, in many of its various guises, does this. So I now want to explore briefly how the new model of property I have developed helps in clarifying the basic goals and principles of that view.

Welfare state liberalism, in general, is the view that while markets and individual ownership should be utilized as a central economic mechanism in society, the state must also take positive action to secure for every citizen the basic goods necessary to an adequate life. The market must be supplemented, then, by various state-sponsored programs that supply all citizens with whatever resources are considered fundamental for a minimally decent life. In the terminology I am using here, we could say that the welfare state is committed to supplying, through non-market means, the resources necessary to secure minimal autonomy for all citizens.

In referring to markets above, I used the term "individual ownership," but as I argued in chapter 2 and indirectly in chapter 6, the kind of ownership structures protected by the state need not be equivalent to liberal ownership for markets to operate. So even within the arena of resource allocation that welfare states allow the market to govern, ownership structures need not be full liberal ownership. Indeed, they *must* not be, if tax revenue and other resource-generating mechanisms are used to fund the programs that comprise the provision of basic welfare.

As Brian Barry has pointed out, however, welfare states can be characterized either as systems that "prevent poverty" (through the general supply of basic welfare goods to all citizens) or as systems designed only to "relieve poverty" (by supplying means-tested benefits to those citizens who have fallen below a poverty threshold).[20] This latter arrangement, which is basically a holdover from the days of the Poor Laws, rests on the assumption that the market should be the *principal* vehicle for the distribution of goods in a society, and only those citizens whose failures in the market leave them with little or no access to basic resources are eligible for the state's supply of basic welfare provisions.

I have already cast much doubt on the moral standing of the market itself, arguing that markets distribute goods neither according to what people morally deserve nor in a way that maximizes either utility or liberty. This is not to say, of course, that the use of limited and constrained markets will not be a central part of any just political structure, but only that the use of markets as the main determinant of the life prospects of citizens has no moral importance in itself.[21] For this reason, I would not support the Poor Law approach to welfare provisions, since it presupposes that the market should be the principal mechanism for the allocation of resources, even resources basic to an autonomous life. (This approach, I might add, generally characterizes the structure of welfare programs in the United States.)

Although I cannot argue for it here, I would defend the view that any just state must not only supplement the market-generated incomes of those citizens who fall below the poverty threshold, it must also directly provide those resources required for individuals to be autonomous participants in their own society. The very participation in markets themselves has value for individuals (or expresses their true preferences) only if it can be presupposed that those people have the resources necessary to make informed, authentic decisions about their lives. Hence, whatever resources are necessary for the establishment of minimal autonomy must be provided directly and universally by the state.[22]

The relevance of the bifurcated conception of ownership to this conclusion emerges when we remind ourselves of the connection between control rights and autonomy. For insofar as autonomy must be a basic priority for the policies of the welfare state, and insofar as control rights connect more directly with autonomy than do income rights, it follows that the supply of control ownership over those goods requisite for autonomous living must be a priority of the state's economic policies. Furthermore, curtailing the *income* rights of some, through taxation and other measures, in order to redistribute resources, control over which is necessary to secure autonomy for others, is required by justice. I will return to this point later.

It follows further that people need not own, in the traditional (liberal) sense, those resources that play the role of securing minimal autonomy. What is necessary is that they have control ownership over those resources. This means that they are allowed access to, and decision authority over, aspects of those resources which they need to be autonomous. Such provisions as adequate health care, education, food, and housing must be available to individuals to secure their minimal autonomy. These provisions can be publicly provided (through such things as national health insurance, public hospitals, public education systems, and the like) without granting individuals more than access to and control over the relevant aspects of the resource.

The relevance of the control-income split for the structure of the welfare state will be made more clear if we consider a proposal made some years ago for the restructuring of welfare provisions, a proposal that dealt directly with property. The argument was first introduced by Charles Reich, who urged that such grants should be considered a kind of "new property."[23] The traditional approach to the distribution of welfare provisions had been to understand these grants as a legal privilege for their recipients. A privilege is a weaker legal claim than a (claim) right, and hence weaker than a property right, so that the government protection of a mere privilege is considered provisional upon the general social and economic goals of the state.

Reich discussed various examples of government "largess"—from the granting of licenses and permits to the distribution of welfare and health provisions—and warned that if these provisions were understood as merely the granting of a legal privilege, people's rights to them would be subject to the unpredictable and intrusive happenstance of government action (undertaken in the name of the public interest). Courts have repeatedly circumscribed or limited the availability of these provisions on the basis of the enforcement of state policy, often by demanding of these recipients things that they otherwise have a perfect right to avoid or refuse. In the name of such things as fighting communism, drug use, drunk driving, and abortion, courts have repeatedly allowed the government to curtail and restrict rights to state-supplied provisions. In the words of one court, "in accepting charity, the appellant has consented to the provisions of the law under which the charity is bestowed."[24]

On Reich's view, this kind of overreaching into the private lives of individuals on behalf of the public interest denies such recipients the prerogatives of privacy and individual autonomy that other citizens can depend upon. Reich's answer to this overintrusiveness into an individual's private domain was to urge that these provisions of government largess be newly construed as property, the "new property" of his title, rather than "charity," which is a mere legal privilege. Only then, he argued, will the protections and immunities of exclusive property ownership be extended to these areas and stem the tide of government intervention into the otherwise protected domain of autonomous living. Such a move would bar many of the restrictions often placed on welfare recipients as a condition of their receiving support.

I have much sympathy, of course, with Reich's proposals, but I do not think that the considerations he advances support the conclusion that these entitlements should be thought of simply as property. Indeed, failure to recognize the control-income distinction gives Reich's view certain untoward implications that it need not have. Imagine, for example, that we adopt his proposal and treat the welfare provisions he mentions as private property. But then imagine that the recipients in question begin taking their licenses and food stamps and *selling* them to others in the area. If these things are treated as private property, the right to transfer for value would presumably be attached to those rights. But this eventuality is clearly not what Reich had in mind or what his arguments supported. What the considerations of protecting privacy and autonomy help to support are that individuals have *control* rights over these provisions, that they have exclusive rights to use and possess them, along with the immunity against expropriation that attaches to such exclusive rights. It is the exclusive use and possession of such things (or related elements of control) that matter to autonomy, not the right to sell and profit from such resources.

So what Reich's arguments actually support, and indeed what I would argue should be the general structure of welfare provisions, is that individuals should be given universal and relatively unrestricted control rights over those basic goods. Now having "control" over such things as health care and education may have a paradoxical ring to it, especially if one thinks of this control as a kind of ownership. (What control do I exercise in being allowed access to a public hospital or national health insurance?) But remember that control ownership amounts to a package of rights over resources which include, chiefly, rights of possession and use. In contexts such as publicly provided health and education resources, rights of possession amount to rights of free access (which have the status of property rights). Hence, such rights cannot be curtailed or revoked in the same manner that legal privileges might (for the purposes of advancing some other public goal, for example).

As I have said, the connection between control ownership and autonomy will vary in degree and character depending on the nature of the resource over which the rights have scope as well as the particular aspect of autonomy to which the resources may be contributing. What matters in the relation between health resources and autonomy, for example, is that specific kinds of medical care are provided whose absence would take from a person the basic ability to make informed and authentic life choices (in particular the prevention of premature mortality and morbidity). Added to this list of autonomy-related resources must be other health-supporting provisions whose features are more flexible, so that individuals can express some decision authority over them and tailor the resources to their particular needs. Allowing patients to choose their own physician may be an example. Such decision-making authority is also important for autonomy.

A more important point should also be made here. As I have tried to show in several ways, the redistributive mechanisms needed to fund these provisions, which will involve curtailing the income rights packages of some citizens in order to provide these goods to others, do not offend any basic principles of political morality.

Since liberal ownership (which, if justified, would have blocked such mechanisms) was not found to be generally defensible, then citizens have no claim on their income rights that is not trumped by the need to supply autonomy-supporting resources to all individuals. Insofar as autonomy interests should have priority over more general welfare interests (and I submit that they do), then curtailing income rights for the sake of control rights over goods required for autonomy is called for by sound principles of political morality.

Now I certainly would argue that justice demands that state economic policy go beyond the provision of basic welfare goods. And I will say in a moment what the stronger principles would look like. My point here is to show how the bifurcation of ownership is useful in contexts governed by other than strictly egalitarian principles. Isolating the interests that are served by differing aspects of ownership claims helps to clarify the issues which are at stake in debates over such economic policies.

IV. Applications Continued: The Egalitarian Theory of Ownership

Traditional types of economic egalitarianism—various sorts of socialism—have typically implied that private property of any kind is anathema to the goals and principles of social justice. Proudhon claimed that property was theft, after all. But I finesse this position by attempting to identify and isolate the differing interests that property ownership protects. Having done so, I now claim that not only must egalitarianism turn a more friendly eye toward certain kinds of individual ownership (as Proudhon himself did), but it must also embrace it, once its structure is properly understood.

As I explained in the last chapter, egalitarianism rests on the abstract principle that equals must be treated equally, combined with a substantive view about what it means to be counted as equals. In particular, egalitarians argue that economic inequality, relations of exploitation and domination, and disparate positions of personal, economic, and political power, all conflict with this basic abstract equality. This notion of equality builds upon the basic intuition that the relative success with which citizens attain their life goals should not depend on factors for which the agents are not responsible, such as their race, gender, prejudice they face, and other personal misfortunes. This intuition is extended to reach the conclusion that, as much as possible, *no* accidental or arbitrary factors which vary among people should determine such relative success. Therefore, the basic institutions of the state, in particular its property structure, must not exacerbate and legitimize inequality of prospects caused by arbitrary and unchosen factors.

Moreover, as I described in chapter 7, we must view the state's property structure as essentially its distributive mechanism. In short, the ownership structure of the state, whatever it turns out to be, mediates between the preferences and plans of individual citizens and those factors that determine relative well-being (such as the availability of natural resources, opportunities to circumvent extant transaction costs, access to information, and the like).

So the state, by its nature, regulates the relative well-being of its citizens. As a background condition of the principles of justice, then, one must assume this interrelation between individual wants and state control. Hence, the central egalitarian principle should be understood to read, *given* the role the state must play in directing the relative well-being of its citizens, the state must be guided by principles that show equal concern and respect for them all. This principle entails (by way of much intervening argument left out here) that in so mediating between citizens' preferences and the factors that figure in their achieving well-being, the state's ownership structure must include the aim of equalizing that well-being. Hence, the state must adopt a defensible way to distribute (mediate access to) certain goods that will translate into the well-being of their recipients. The state does this by adopting some property scheme or other.

I pursue some of the details of this picture in this section, in particular by showing the relevance to it of the new theory of property I have advanced. The structure of the argument I am relying on here is this: the most plausible egalitarian principles must give priority to the establishment and protection of individual autonomy; control rights are distinguished from income rights by virtue of their closer connection with autonomy; therefore, egalitarianism must give priority to control rights in the economic policies derived from those principles. I turn shortly to a discussion of how such egalitarian principles will give this priority to control ownership, and hence make use of the control-income rights split. First, however, it is necessary for me to defend the first premise in the argument, the claim that egalitarianism must give priority to the autonomy of individuals being guided by those policies.

Egalitarianism and Autonomy

The bedrock of egalitarian principles is that substantive equality of well-being is a basic goal of social and economic policy. This goal presupposes, however, that it is uncontroversial what realizing equal well-being would actually mean. There has been a complex internecine debate among egalitarians in recent years over what should be used as a yardstick for the achievement of the equal outcomes that are demanded by the principles. Some claim that it is welfare that must be equalized, others that it is resources, or primary goods, or opportunity for welfare, or capabilities.[25] One way to look at the problem is simply to say that egalitarians want to equalize the condition of people in a society. Whatever turns out to be the best account of a person's condition—her welfare level or her resource level or whatever—should be "distributed" equally.

The problem of defining the metric for measuring equality, however, begins when it is realized that some people have expensive tastes. Imagine, for example, that there was just one person living alone somewhere, and it was your job to make this person as well off as possible, given the resources available at the time. (Imagine you have no other motivation concerning your own good.) What metric would you use to determine this level? An obvious criterion, of course, is welfare. Assuming she is an autonomous person, you could give the person the amount of resources that would satisfy as many of her desires as possible. Now she may well have preferences that we could regard as expensive, which she has cultivated and could reform but which demand high levels of resources to satisfy. If that were the case, would you have reason to balk at satisfying her expensive tastes? If these preferences were not otherwise evil or self-destructive (say that she cultivates appreciation of live performances of Wagnerian operas), then there is no reason to ignore or reform that preference set.

If that is what makes her happy, it is plausible to say that you advance her good when you give her resources that satisfy that and related preferences to the highest degree possible.[26]

But add another person to this scenario. Imagine now that your job is to make *both* people as well off as possible and that you must again decide on a metric of well-being. Here your attitude toward the first person's expensive tastes may well change. For now if you pick welfare as the metric, then the second person (who has no unusual tastes) will be less well off than if you had picked simply resources, for the Wagnerian's costly preferences will drain resources from the pool to be distributed. On the other hand, if resources become the standard of well-being, the Wagner lover would have to bear the cost of her expensive taste herself, choosing her own pattern of internal trade-offs between opera companies and other goods.

This is, of course, an intuitive question, namely, whether there is something wrong with allowing a person to consume an unequal amount of resources simply because she chose to adopt less efficient tastes (less efficient in turning resources into satisfaction). But many would claim that it is unacceptable, as equality of welfare would demand, that the distribution be skewed so that those with voluntarily adopted expensive tastes would receive more resources than those who have contented themselves with cheaper and more everyday preferences.[27]

The problem of expensive tastes concerns those in the population who *voluntarily* develop tastes that cost more of society's resources to satisfy. For example, G. A. Cohen argues that what differentiates those welfare deficiencies that egalitarianism should compensate for and those (like expensive tastes) that it should ignore is the quality of being voluntarily chosen by the people in question, in light of the effect it may have on the rest of the community.[28] The cut between compensable and non-compensable welfare deficiencies should occur between those detriments that the agent simply is saddled with, referred to as handicaps, and those that are developed freely, expensive tastes.

The problem of expensive tastes is that it is unfair for some to adopt a life plan the pursuit of which demands resources that others, with more mundane tastes, could use. To reject equality of welfare is to treat people as autonomous beings who must take responsibility for their own character. I would suggest, then, that the measure of well-being adopted should forthrightly embrace what is being adumbrated in these standards: the intrinsic value of autonomous voluntary choice. What matters, or at least a crucial part of what matters in a person's well-being, is that she *chose* to be in the condition she is in or to lead the life that she leads. She is responsible for her choices and for the effect that her choices will have on her fellow citizens.

This view suggests that egalitarians should be directly interested in the *autonomy* of the individuals who populate the landscape of the distribution. Unless these individuals are minimally autonomous, one cannot regard their choices (and hence the satisfaction of their desires) as true reflections of their well-being. Moreover, when people are minimally autonomous, the distribution should be sensitive to the responsibility they then bear for the choices they make. If one autonomous person chooses a life of Wagnerian opera watching, the distribution can hold her responsible for that choice by making her pay the costs of it herself (at least not compensating her with extra unequal amounts of resources to satisfy this taste).

But not all expensive tastes result from autonomous choice. If a person finds himself addicted to a very expensive drug, and this addiction is in no way an outgrowth of autonomous choices he himself has made, then the egalitarian distribution must contribute extra resources to him to alleviate the dearth of welfare that he is experiencing from this addictive taste. (This contribution may take the form of state-supported clinics that would restore his capacity for autonomous choice.)[29]

These arguments are based on the view that basic to the value theory of egalitarianism is the claim that society should be structured so that people are able to lead equally flourishing lives. Insofar as being an autonomous chooser—and hence being responsible for both one's tastes and one's choices—is part of what it means to lead a flourishing life, then egalitarianism must give priority to supplying the goods that are necessary for this autonomy to be established and maintained. Distinguishing between expensive tastes that one finds oneself with—handicaps and addictions—and ones that one freely develops indicates that responsibility for oneself is part of the theory of value relied upon by egalitarians. The directive to treat autonomous people equally, because they are autonomous, entails a commitment to promote and protect that autonomy.[30]

How, then, should we characterize the general metric that is to be used for the measurement of equality? The answer, I think, is that such a metric must be *complex* and *lexically structured*.[31] For there is no single vector along which a person's well-being can be measured. At some levels, what is necessary for well-being is resources to establish the conditions of autonomous agency. This includes access to, and the ability to utilize, resources that ensure basic abilities of reflective rational choice. At other levels, what contributes to well-being is simply increased welfare. At still other levels, it might be access to resources (of any sort). So goods, the distribution of which is directed by the state, must be lexically ordered to capture adequately the value of lives being promoted by the distributive principles. For this reason, egalitarian society might, for example, put greater resources into educational structure—access to which is necessary to develop conditions of autonomous agency—before directing the distribution of other goods.

The basic contours of complex lexical equality must be worked out elsewhere. The main point is that there is a basic commitment to the lexical priority of securing minimal autonomy for all citizens. Thereafter, social goods can be ranked and combined in any number of ways according to a public conception of social goods.[32] This ranking implies that there is room for the political definition of these goods. Hence, following the provision of those goods necessary for all to lead a minimally autonomous life, the populace can utilize democratic institutions in order to define the nature of goods that are constitutive of the publicly accepted conception of well-being. These goods, however, must be distributed equally.

This suggestion leaves a great deal up to the expressed will of the populace as voiced through their democratic procedures. Actually, however, it leaves less up to the will of the populace than at first appears, since the claim also is that the material and political bases of minimal autonomy must *first* be provided (equally) to all before directives for other distributive programs are defined. This priority implies that the basic liberties—freedom of speech, press, and religion; freedom from arbitrary arrest, search, and seizure; and the right to privacy—must be protected equally for basic autonomy to be secured. This conclusion rests on an intervening premise, not fully articulated or defended here, that such freedoms are crucial for the enjoyment of minimal autonomy.[33]

Nevertheless, the use of democratic institutions to make such decisions remains egalitarian only insofar as such institutions themselves embody equality of status and political power. Therefore, if social decision procedures are used to determine the structure of public expenditure (to the constrained extent here described), those institutions must be strictly egalitarian in their foundational structure and in their outcomes.

This notion of complex lexical equality also leaves much room for trade-offs between various social goals other than achieving strict equality of income. Hence, when it is the case that productive efficiency, for example, can be promoted only by virtue of some deviation from strictly equal income and wealth, and efficiency is determined by fair democratic procedures to be a dominant social good, then income inequality to the degree necessary to secure such efficiency is not inconsistent with the overall egalitarian program outlined here. That must be qualified, however, with the claim that no degree of inequality will be allowed that would engender political and social power shifts which, in turn, could disrupt the ability of some in the population to enjoy minimal autonomy and basic freedom. This restriction effectively limits the parameters of trade-offs between strict income equality and efficiency, though it does not prevent them.

In addition, provisions for securing the conditions of minimal autonomy for all must be sensitive to the differential needs of different members of the population. For example, an important manner in which special resources must be earmarked and given special distributive priority involves the undue burden that childbirth (and in most cases child rearing) places on the lives of women. Families may receive equal annual incomes while the people in those families face very different and unjust life prospects as a result of gender-based differences. Therefore, in the complex formula for equal shares of society's resources, there must be room for institutional support of women bearing children and people (men and women) raising and educating them. Social institutions that guarantee true autonomy in the choice of life plan must include such things as obstetric and gynecological resources, child care, hospital services, and time release/parental leave policies as part of the background conditions necessary for the establishment of autonomous conditions of choice.[34]

These theoretical conclusions must now be connected to the theory of property I have developed here. Insofar as the rights to control one's property have a closer connection to the establishment and protection of individual autonomy, and insofar as egalitarian principles have a commitment to the autonomy of citizens, then egalitarian principles must give special weight to the control rights that people have over their property. This connection entails that allowing citizens to enjoy control rights over goods—an equal share of goods—should get first priority in the economic policies of the egalitarian state. Income rights, on the other hand, do not have this connection with autonomy and hence should be reshaped and regulated in whatever manner is necessary to achieve economic goals of the society, in particular equalizing shares (politically defined). (The shaping of income rights must be done in a consistent and public manner, so that individuals who come to rely on particular income flows will not have their lives unduly disrupted.)

Of course, a full development of this view would demand a more detailed account of the central concepts involved, in particular the relation between the different levels of the lexical conception of well-being that I have presented. I cannot provide that here. What I want to do now, however, is to tie the strands of the argument together and to model these conclusions by virtue of a description of egalitarian economic policies. Doing so will show how such an egalitarian program makes crucial use of the control-income rights split that I have developed.

Egalitarian Property Rights

To help to illustrate the usefulness of the property theory I have discussed, I adopt the schema of market socialism outlined by others and to show how this schema can be made to instantiate the egalitarian principles I describe here. More important, I want to use such models to show how the bifurcation of ownership aids in the clarification and plausibility of egalitarian social principles.

John Roemer and others have recently worked out the general guidelines of an efficient and feasible market socialist plan of economic justice. Such plans are not exactly seen as the wave of the future these days, given the political shifts in traditionally central-state socialist economies (Eastern Europe) as well as welfare-state socialist countries (Sweden). But there is no reason to believe that the regimes of the former Soviet bloc exemplified anything much like the egalitarianism described here. Nor is it the case that the adoption of market systems of distribution and private property of some kind is inconsistent with such an egalitarianism. Indeed both, when properly understood, are central to it.

Recall that private property is not a simple notion, and its vagaries prevent an easy equation between such an ownership structure and traditional capitalist free markets. If private property means liberal ownership, then not only does that not exist (and certainly not what defenders of market reforms in Europe are adopting), it is also not a plausible option on grounds of justice, as I have argued. Indeed, the market systems of the new regimes in Eastern Europe contain countless restrictions on the full package of traditional liberal ownership rights, not the least of which is heavy and progressive taxation on income and profits. The recommendations here, which I present only in general form, will depart from such market systems only in degree, in particular, the degree to which income rights for all productive goods are publicly held.

Roemer's plan, which follows in general form the work of Alec Nove and other market socialists,[35] involves several major components. First, firms "will be managed by managers whose goal will be to maximize profits, at going prices."[36] Managers would act very much as they do now in capitalist economies, at least those managers who do not also own the firms for which they work. Second, labor will be supplied according to a market, where supply and demand will direct the relative wages. Third, goods will be allocated by market mechanisms, which means that prices for goods are set by the competitive workings of those markets. Finally, governments will have the claim to direct all income from those ventures, that is, governments, which must operate by virtue of robust democratic institutions, will collect profits and direct investment. The government will also supply public goods such as public parks, public education, health care, and a national defense, financed by those profits and taxation on wages. All profit generated by the firms (defined as the total receipts minus total outlays for operating costs, interest on debt, resource inputs, and the wage bill) is collected by the state.

Public investment can be undertaken, according to this model, by virtue of manipulating interest rates in state-controlled banks. Market forces will signal managers to expand or curtail production through borrowing state funds at the announced interest rates. Rates of interest that are lower than the rate the state banks pay to savings accounts will cost the state money, which is also supplied by capital generated by firms and taxation of wages. Profit collected by the state, which is not used for special projects (supplying basic services and other public goods) and which is not needed to subsidize investment programs, will be distributed equally to citizens as a "social dividend."[37]

The feasibility of this model depends, of course, on the motivating factors inducing managers to maximize profits that neither they nor others to whom they owe their jobs get to keep. Roemer argues that the motivation to do this can be achieved by adopting a system of public finance modeled on the Japanese *keiretsu*: various firms of similar natures will be organized around, and financed by, a particular bank, and each firm will own shares of the other firms in the group. The board of directors of each firm will be comprised of its own managers as well as the shareholders from other firms and from the bank. The network of shared interest (in the profitability of each firm) would supply pressure on a particular firm to maximize profits or to face reorganization by directive from the other shareholders. Hence, managers have a structural incentive to do their jobs well or to face losing them in the wake of such a reorganization. The threat of hostile takeovers in present-day capitalist America serves the same purpose though with much less predictable and more brutal results.

Could such a system work? There are certainly those who do not think so.[38] As I said, I cannot engage in a defense of it here, though I do think that many criticisms of this kind of approach can indeed be answered. My purpose here is to explain how this model exemplifies the principles of egalitarianism and property that I have articulated. Let me explain.

The main difference between this market socialist model and a traditional capitalist economy is that there do not exist, in the egalitarian model, individuals who have private income rights to the profits of firms. Moreover, since there is neither a stock market nor private financing of ventures, there are no individual private income rights (from productive capital) at all. The public holds the income rights to all productive resources.

But private individuals retain control rights. Although the plan contains many incentive structures for managers to act a certain way—for workers to pursue the lines of work demanded most by society and for consumers to buy their most valued products at the cheapest price—all of these actions are *up to the people involved*. These individuals retain the constitutional right to opt out of all such economic interactions and to consume whatever goods (or talents) with which they opt out.

By "opt out" here, I mean only that they can opt out of the market—they can stay home. (This does not mean that they can emigrate with all their resources; that is a different matter which I don't comment on here.) What it does mean is that individuals retain control rights over their private resources: they can decide how much to save and how much to spend; and over their talents: they decide how much and where to work. Also, since wages are subject to taxation, it is not the case that individuals have (full) income rights to their labor. Insofar as at least some wage income is due to economic rent (lack of perfect competition from others and differential natural talents), and tax levels do not exceed this level, then only income rights are touched by the taxes on wages, not control rights. This policy follows the suggestion I made in chapter 8.

It must be made explicit, however, that the first priority for public expenditures in this model is the provision of goods necessary for citizens' basic autonomy. Those resources, access to which manifests the degree of control over one's material conditions that autonomy demands, must be fully provided by the state. This priority implies, of course, that medical, educational, (minimal) nutritional, and basic housing resources will be guaranteed to all citizens. Furthermore, those resources that are needed to correct for gender inequities—childbirth- and childcare-related resources, for example—must also be provided.

The direction of investment subsequent to the provision of basic goods can be determined by political means. This means that public spending is directed by democratic action, much in line with the suggestion I made in the last section that beyond the provision of basic autonomy-producing goods, the question of how to define and to direct the primary goods of society can be determined by political means.

So in these ways this model of market socialism embraces the principles I have developed, in particular the new model of ownership based on the control-income rights distinction. In general, complex lexical equality is instantiated here also. This is because, first, priority is given to provision of those goods necessary to ensure minimal autonomy, second, priority is given to control rights over income rights to goods and labor (and hence priority is given to autonomy interests), and finally the distribution of the social surplus follows the political conception of primary goods that I endorsed (this last point I added as a consistent amendment to the Roemer model).

There is, however, an alteration in this model that the principles I am defending would strongly recommend: my view of autonomy had much to say about the ways that one's immediate material conditions affect that trait. I would argue also that the conditions of one's paid employment (or unpaid employment if one works in an informal setting such as one's own household) are directly connected to one's autonomy interests. The job that I have (if paid employment is my source of income) is directly connected to the plans and projects I can authentically develop. If that job is unstable, or the conditions under which I work are demeaning and debilitating, or if I have no say in important management decisions, then my autonomy interests are not being served by such employment.

Indeed, I will go further in suggesting that control (direct or indirect) of the general character of one's workplace is crucial to the advancement of one's autonomy interests.[39] I cannot be autonomous, or as autonomous as I might be, if the firm for which I work pursues production strategies that (unpredictably) result in my being laid off, or in my being forced into a retraining program, or in my relocating. Only when I have direct input into the decision mechanisms that govern strategies of this sort, which directly affect my plans and projects, can I achieve full autonomy in relation to the material conditions (which underpin my expectations and plans) that my employment provides. For this reason, I argue, autonomy interests are directly served only when there is some measure of worker control or worker democracy in the employment setting.

On Roemer's model it is left open whether firms would be organized such as to give workers collective managerial control. There may be very good reason for this open endedness, since worker democracy may well conflict directly with the other structural features of the system, in particular the linchpin component of directing managers to maximize profits. It is not clear, however, that worker-run firms are indeed less profitable than the more centralized alternative authority structure.[40] Nevertheless, I would argue that autonomy interests are served by having direct input into the decision-making mechanism whose outcomes shape and regulate the direction of one's life.

For reasons that I have been developing throughout this work, it is clear that worker ownership (*simpliciter*) is not the goal I want to consider. There are many forms of worker ownership, and each instantiates a different combination of control and income rights. ESOPs (Employee Stock Option Programs) grant income ownership to workers, whereby part of their wages flow from stock in the company and profit-sharing programs. This type of program is not the form of worker ownership that I would claim is called for by the considerations I have advanced. For such rights do not, I have argued, have the connection with autonomy interests that ownership, in this context, should have. It is at least some measure of worker *control* that matters for autonomy, for only then can it be at all claimed that workers have significant input into the material and financial conditions that shape their lives.

I am presenting this point largely as if one's workplace is outside one's home. The analogous point for those individuals who pursue their livelihoods at home is that particular control rights must be secured in that space for autonomy to be maintained. This requirement implies that conditions of domination, oppression and, in the extreme case, battering, must be eradicated by the enforcement of such rights. Ensuring such control also implies that the state must be cautious in its endorsement of particular family structures, since many such arrangements have traditionally served to deny basic autonomy and lifestyle choices to large classes of people (women, for example, and homosexuals). Having control rights over one's home is a way of expressing the prohibition of such conditions.

Now is such a vision of economic policy purely utopian? Notice, first, that such a system differs only in (a kind of) degree from the capitalist property systems we are familiar with. In chapter 2 I discussed the difference between the property structure of capitalism and that of socialism. It is necessary now to reiterate those points.

Under real-world capitalism (as opposed to ideal, fully free market versions), managers generally do not own the firms they work for and are directed to maximize that firm's profits by others. Also while workers can choose their jobs, they cannot keep all of their wage income. That is, they are taxed. In addition, the government engages in much directing of investment patterns through tax incentives and other measures. In fact, as things now stand, tax rates on profits could increase in a stepwise fashion until there would be no sense to the private ownership (privately held income rights) of firms at all. Add the elimination of the stock market and development of central banking, and you've virtually arrived at market socialism.

As I argued in chapter 2, present-day capitalist economies cannot be distinguished from such socialist plans as the one I described on the basis of the presence or absence of private ownership (of the means of production, say). Under both systems individuals have some limited rights to use and trade their goods, and the state plays a direct role in directing and controlling income flows. The major difference between the two systems rests in the *point* of these income-directing policies. The egalitarianism that I recommend rests on the claim that only if property structures are shaped by the basic equality of persons, understood in the robust way I have described, can justice be achieved by such property structures.

We can assume that a central tenet, if not *the* central tenet, of socialism is the prohibition of individuals' owning capital. "Owning" here means specifically the right to transfer and gain income from capital goods (goods other than labor). The presence of a stock market, where such trading occurs, can be seen, then, as a more or less sufficient condition that such rights exist. Hence, the eradication of such institutions would mean that the state holds all rights to such income.

But what if the state, through democratic vote, decides that certain individuals, who have rare and valuable technical skills in entrepreneurial areas, could only be motivated effectively if they are allowed to trade shares of companies and to keep the proceeds? And, say, the state has an interest (perhaps only a short-term one) in utilizing such trades in order to better fix the value of the assets of some previously state-owned firms. Now imagine further that the prospective outcome of this program is the greater productivity of that sector of the economy, which, it is reliably predicted, will in turn allow the state to provide expanded employment opportunities for sections of the population at present unemployed or underemployed. In this scenario, despite the greater income received by these entrepreneur-owners, such a program actually increases overall equality of well-being in the society. Now would we say that such a program amounted to the development of capitalism and a move toward a private property economy?

As I have set this case up, the state *grants* such income ownership for the specific purpose of equalizing resources in the society, and the income rights granted to the new "owners" are expressly structured to bring about this end. If the underlying normative principle of socialism is egalitarianism, then I think such economic restructuring is not obviously a rejection of socialism.

So the difference between the market socialism that I have described and traditional capitalism concerns the structuring, and the point of the structuring, of income rights (since individual control rights are afforded in both economies). That difference in income rights structure can, in addition, be understood as a function of at least two factors: the degree to which income rights on all exchanged goods (including labor) are granted to individuals or confiscated by the state (the nature and rate of taxation); and the degree to which *parts* of firms (securities such as stocks and bonds) are owned by private individuals who have a claim on the flows from those securities. (Technically, income rights flow only from stocks, since bonds confer rights to fixed premiums only.) And the second variable is subject to variations of the first. The version of such structuring that I favor here is distinguished from liberal ownership capitalism by virtue of this one key element: property structures in the egalitarian economy are specifically fashioned so as to accomplish the goals of equality.

Conclusion

I have made numerous and disparate claims in this book. And although I have tried to bring many of them together into a coherent picture in these last pages, I fear that several of them will remain free-floating conclusions. Indeed, the blueprint for egalitarian distributive justice just described will not likely convince skeptics nor fully satisfy supporters. But I hope that it at least indicates the usefulness of the conclusions concerning ownership I had earlier reached for the development of a plausible egalitarian program for justice.

I would like to think that I have accomplished four general things in this book: (1) I have given a rather complex and far-reaching exploration of the concept of ownership and the implications of its structure; (2) I have provided a battery of arguments for the conclusion that the liberal conception of ownership should be discarded as the paradigm of individual ownership in any society; (3) I have shown that control of the things one owns is sufficiently different from the right to profit from those things that these concepts should be understood as occupying different locales in the landscape of political principle; and (4) I have sketched some of the ways that this new understanding of ownership would aid in the development of a program for justice based on robust egalitarian principles.

This last claim received a relatively cursory treatment, though in many ways it is the principal motivation for the whole of the project. For it is my view that justice demands that social and economic institutions—such as the institution of property ownership—serve to ensure that individuals' life prospects truly manifest their equal dignity and equal moral status. And this demand can be met only by seeing through the myth of property, at least the myth of liberal ownership. At the same time, however, we must appreciate the particular aspects of that myth that express powerful moral ideas which no adequate theory of social justice can ignore.

Notes

Introduction

1. *Private Property and the Limits of American Constitutionalism*, p. 260.

2. Indeed, it is ironic that this is the phrase for which Proudhon is most remembered, for he also claimed that property was *homicide*. See *What Is Property?*, p. 177.

3. This income takes the form of land rent, interest, and profit, what Proudhon referred to as the "aubaines." See *Selected Writings of P.-J. Proudhon*, p. 69.

4. In his posthumously published work *Théorie du Propriété*, Proudhon argues that not only is private property *not* the root of all evil, but in fact it is a necessary component of a just society. See *Selected Writings*, pp. 131–143.

5. This is what Lawrence Becker calls a "special" justification, namely consideration of whether a particular *kind* of property institution can be justified. See *Property Rights*, pp. 3–4.

6. Some no doubt see recent events in Eastern Europe and the former Soviet Union as providing powerful arguments against egalitarian economic principles of the sort I defend. As I say elsewhere in the text, I understand the fall of Communist regimes since 1989 as manifesting the fact that a certain kind of centrally planned authoritarian (and militaristic) socialism is not efficient in, among other things, the production and delivery of consumer goods. Anyone who thinks that recent world events have destroyed the credibility of egalitarianism generally understands neither those events nor egalitarianism very well, I think.

7. For a general discussion, see David Lyons, ed., *Rights*, pp. 1–13. For a discussion of these issues and their bearing on property, see Stephen Munzer, *A Theory of Property*, pp. 47–49.

8. Cf. Joel Feinberg, "The Nature and Value of Rights," pp. 143–58.

9. For comparison, see Jeremy Waldron's treatment of what he calls "general rights based" strategies for justifying private property: *The Right to Private Property*, pp. 106–26.

10. For an argument of this general sort, see Jan Narveson, *The Libertarian Idea*.

Chapter 1

1. The idea of liberal ownership is similar to what A.M.A. Honoré calls "full liberal ownership": see "Ownership," p. 107.

2. Subsequently I will use the shorthand "rights" or "property rights" in place of this complete list of the various legal and moral modalities associated with ownership.

3. See, e.g., Jeremy Waldron, *The Right to Private Property*, pp. 26–61; Stephen R. Munzer, *A Theory of Property*, pp. 15–27; Lawrence Becker, *Property Rights: Philosophical Foundations*, pp. 7–21; and Andrew Reeve, *Property*, pp. 9–37.

4. C. B. Macpherson has argued that the shift from understanding the term "property" as the thing that is owned to understanding it as referring to the rights comprising ownership is a politically and philosophically important transition in history, dating from the later seventeenth century. See *The Political Theory of Possessive Individualism*. See Andrew Reeve, *Property*, chap. 1, for a critical discussion.

5. See John Austin, *Lectures on Jurisprudence*, lec. 48. For a discussion of Austin's view, see G. P. Wilson, "Jurisprudence and the Discussion of Ownership."

6. I follow the lead of Jeremy Waldron here. See *The Right to Private Property*, pp. 33–37.

7. Stephen Munzer, for example, focuses on the thing-relation confusion rather than the simple-complex confusion in the concept of property. See *A Theory of Property*, chap. 2.

8. Scholarship that has been put under the heading "history of property" can be divided into two kinds: the history of the legal institution of property ownership (and its distribution) and history of philosophical *theories* about such institutions. An example of the latter is Richard Schlatter's *Private Property: The History of an Idea*, though for Schlatter, the "idea" of property refers to ideas concerning the distribution of property, not what it means to own something. See also Alan Ryan, *Property and Political Theory* and *Property*.

9. The question of what ownership means arises even before we get to Rome of course. For discussion of the Greek law of property, for example, see A. R. W. Harrison, *The Law of Athens*. Consider also claims concerning "primitive communism" made by Engels and other Marxists in order to bolster the argument for historical materialism. For analysis, see Henry Maine, *Ancient Law*. For critical discussion of the issue, see Irving Hallowell, *Culture and Experience*, chap. 12, and Lawrence Becker, "The Moral Basis of Property Rights," pp. 198ff.

10. See Charles Donahue, Jr., "The Future of the Concept of Property Predicted from Its Past," p. 35. This notion of ownership remains influential into the modern period in the civil law jurisdictions of the Continent which, unlike common law systems, remained guided by the classical law codes. See J. H. Merryman, "Ownership and Estate," pp. 918–23.

11. As Richard Duncan-Jones puts it, in Roman society there were "heavy ostensible prejudices against trade and traders. A society in which senators were forbidden to own ships, and shopkeepers were admitted to the town council only if *honesti viri* were in short supply, was one which tried hard to separate involvement in trade from social position" (*Structure and Scale of the Roman Economy*, p. 46). See also Barry Nicholas, *An Introduction to Roman Law*.

12. Some tax rates went as high as one-fifth of the yield of a crop: see Duncan-Jones, *Structure and Scale in the Roman Economy*, chap. 12, esp. p. 187.

13. See Henry Maine, *Ancient Law*, for a by now dated analysis of Roman social structure. More recently, Charles Donahue, Jr., claimed that "[w]e might argue that the tendency toward absolute rights in Roman law was more apparent than real" ("The Future of the Concept of Property Predicted from Its Past," pp. 35–36.) Similarly, R. W. M. Dias traces out some of the connections between laws specifying ownership in ancient Rome and those defining political status as *pater familias*; see *Jurisprudence*, p. 406, n. 2.

14. Blackstone, *Commentaries*, Bk. 2, p. 2; Austin, *Lectures on Jurisprudence*, Vol. 2, pp. 817–18.

15. Patrick Atiyah, *The Rise and Fall of Freedom of Contract*, pp. 335–58; see also Henry Maine, *Ancient Law*.

16. Honoré, "Ownership," p. 107. Some have been critical of this conceptualization since it allows that *any* economy will have an institution of ownership, even common property regimes. This is because there will always be a "greatest interest allowed" in the economy (cf. Jeremy Waldron, *The Right to Private Property*, p. 48). For general analyses of the concept of ownership, see also Lawrence Becker, *Property Rights*: *Philosophic Foundations*; Andrew Reeve, *Property*; and Frank Snare, "The Concept of Property."

17. I follow Lawrence Becker here ("The Moral Basis of Property Rights," p. 191 and n. 10). Also, the power to transfer title—even under the terms of a sale—should not be confused with the right to income described below (though they are related). The former merely amounts to the owner's privilege to alienate the property while appointing title to someone else.

18. Other elements include the right to security, which is an immunity against uncompensated expropriation by the state (which can be seen as an adjunct to the non-interference provision of the *exclusive* rights of possession and use); transmissibility and absence of term, which concern the "duration" of the owner's interest in the thing owned (transmissibility refers to the determination of ownership after the death of the present owner; absence of term describes the temporally indeterminate interest during an owner's lifetime). Transmissibility is an extension of transfer rights (after death), and absence of term is merely a temporal indexical added to the other ownership rights protected in the system.

Commentators also mention the prohibition of harmful use and the "residuary character" of ownership. The first of these is controversial (my duty not to hit Fred over the head with a baseball bat is just the same whether I happen to *own* the bat or not), and the second is a structural necessity of the legal system that protects ownership, not an element of ownership itself. For discussion, see Honoré, "Ownership," pp. 119–24, and Waldron, *The Right to Private Property*, p. 49. (See also chap. 7, n. 5.)

19. For example, Lawrence Becker (*Property Rights*, p. 20) claims that any subset from these rights would comprise ownership if coupled with the right to security and absence of term.

20. Thomas Grey, "The Disintegration of Property," p. 73. For critical discussion, see Richard Epstein, *Takings: Private Property and the Power of Eminent Domain*, pp. 20–24, and Munzer, *A Theory*, pp. 31–36.

21. Grey, "The Disintegration of Property," p. 81.

22. Guido Calabresi and A. Douglas Melamed, "Property Rules, Liability Rules and Inalienability: One View of the Cathedral."

23. See Grey, "The Disintegration of Property," pp. 72–73. The difference between being protected by the two kinds of rules may become blurred when, despite being protected by property rules, prohibitions are so ineffective that owners see themselves as basically protected only by private insurance policies. In such cases, *ex poste* compensation is one's only protection.

24. Jeremy Waldron uses a similar argument concerning the necessity of a settled concept of property to make sense of an "allocation." See *The Right to Private Property*, pp. 26–31.

25. Like many economic theorists, Grey could accept these implications but claim that the idea of a distribution involves the assumption of the possibility of interpersonal comparisons of well-being, and that idea should be rejected on other grounds. I discuss the defense of a different version of the full disaggregation view and the use of this kind of subjective value theory in its defense in chapters 7 and 9.

26. See, e.g., Stephen Munzer, *A Theory of Property*, pp. 31–36.

27. Epstein writes, "through all the doctrinal murkiness, the settled legal rules make perfectly clear, more that 99.9 percent of the time, who, if anyone, possesses and owns anything" (*Takings*, p. 24).

28. See Reeve, *Property*, pp. 39–45, who also provides a "framework" that can be contrasted with this one. Also, for a more detailed study of the structure of ownership and property systems, see Frederic L. Pryor, *Property and Industrial Organization in Communist and Capitalist Nations*, chap. 1 and Appendix A.

29. James Grunebaum ("Property Rules and Property Rights") also gives a separate characterization of background rules of a system of property. He makes this separation, however, differently from the one presented here. See also his *Private Ownership*, chap. 1.

30. Waldron, *The Right to Private Property*, p. 40.

31. For a discussion of this point and the idea of ownership "systems," see Waldron, pp. 31–33 and 42–46.

32. This is to ignore the major pattern of the development of English law, where the ownership of one sort of thing (land and estates) developed earlier and entirely separate from law pertaining to the ownership of "chattels." See Dias, *Jurisprudence*, chap. 13 for discussion.

33. Cf. Waldron, *The Right to Private Property*, p. 56, who makes a similar point.

34. Those who identify themselves with "the new property rights literature" are of particular interest here. See Harold Demsetz, "Toward a Theory of Property Rights," pp. 31–42. I discuss this view in chapter 6.

35. Pryor, *Property and Industrial Organization in Communist and Capitalist Nations*, p. 2 (emphasis added). For a comment on Pryor's insistence on the "economic value" of ownership, see Reeve, *Property*, p. 25.

36. Note the use of a similar distinction by G. P. Wilson ("Jurisprudence and the Discussion of Ownership," p. 225) between "internal" and "external" powers of disposition (which he argues are included in ownership). Internal powers are rights of use and consumption, while external powers are those that involve interaction with others and are conditional on their cooperation.

Chapter 2

1. Liberal ownership is what some have referred to as "full ownership" or "full liberal ownership." I prefer the term liberal ownership since (as James Grunebaum pointed out to me) the word "full" seems to imply that any deviation from this would grant only "limited" rights to owners of goods—that it is a bundle that is more restricted than it could otherwise be. The connotations of this are that one's potential rights are limited (and hence one's freedom is also limited) by anything less than the "full" package. However, rejecting that view is one of the central themes of this work. See also Margaret Jane Radin, "The Liberal Conception of Property: Currents in the Jurisprudence of Takings."

2. Robert Nozick, *Anarchy, State, and Utopia*, p. 156.

3. As I mentioned in chapter 1, Honoré includes the "prohibition of harmful use" in the elements of ownership. I also mentioned the problems with this inclusion. The provision nevertheless leaves open the question of the scope of "harm" to be considered (especially given the ambiguities of "externalities" that will be introduced shortly).

4. These are the so-called direct and indirect theorems, respectively. The latter holds only when other conditions are added, such as the assumption that there are no economies of scale. There are many discussions of this of course; see, e.g., Jules Coleman, *Markets, Morals and the Law*, pp. 246ff.

5. The parenthetical phrases indicate an ambiguity in the usual definitions of Pareto efficiency. Some refer to preferences over the allocation and others to preferences over goods. These are of course quite different.

6. This is essentially the limitation of using the indirect theorem as a solution to distributive problems. For discussion, see Amartya Sen, *On Ethics and Economics*, p. 36.

7. There is much work among economic theorists to provide models that deviate from perfect markets. For an example of a theory that relaxes the condition of zero transaction costs, see Yoram Barzel, *Economic Analysis of Property Rights*.

8. For a discussion that parallels much of what is said here, see Andrew Levine, *Arguing for Socialism*, pp. 5–11.

9. C. B. Macpherson, *The Political Theory of Possessive Individualism*, pp. 53–54. The conditions I list here are compressed from those given by Macpherson.

10. For a discussion of economic rent that bears on distributive issues, see David Gauthier, *Morals by Agreement*, pp. 98f.

11. This is not to say that in informal settings, ownership could be voluntarily respected by the possessors and traders. Such a convention would be stable, however, only in closely knit groups with little or no contestation of holdings. If this were not the case, a central enforcement mechanism would be needed to define and protect rights.

12. For a similar point, see R. H. Tawney, *Equality*, p. 46.

13. Jules Coleman defines a perfect market in such a way as to specify liberal ownership structures, since one of his conditions is that all consumption and trade is "private" (see *Markets*, p. 244).

14. Cf. Macpherson, *The Political Theory*, p. 54, who also adds this condition.

15. See Joseph Carens, *Equality, Moral Incentives, and the Market*, for a development of this idea.

16. Cf. Levine, *Arguing for Socialism*, p. 6.

17. See Sen, *On Ethics and Economics*, p. 80.

18. This point is made forcefully by Frank Michelman in "Ethics, Economics, and the Law of Property."

19. Whether it is equivalent will depend for the most part on whether one treats labor as a capital good. Labor (or more precisely, labor power) is certainly part of the means of production, but some theorists define capital as any *non-labor* input factor in production (e.g., Levine, *Arguing for Socialism*, p. 5, n. 2).

20. One could argue here, of course, that the adult population of the area has indirect control rights over the asset since it is their elected representatives who exercise the power in question. But this stretches virtually out of existence the idea of "primary functional control" that I discussed in chapter 1. In most cases, as Andrew Reeve points out, the title to goods like public parks and the like is held by the representative body of the municipality. See Reeve, *Property*, p. 32.

Chapter 3

1. In chapter 8 I will subject the idea of self-ownership to detailed scrutiny.

2. See John Bogart, "Lockean Provisos and State of Nature Theories."

3. H.L.A. Hart, "Are There Any Natural Rights?"

4. Hart, "Are There Any Natural Rights?," p. 15.

5. Hillel Steiner, "The Natural Right to the Means of Production," p. 41.

6. Steiner, "The Natural Right to the Means of Production." See also Jeremy Waldron's distinction between "special" and "general" rights in *The Right to Private Property*, chaps. 3–4.

7. This is similar to John Rawls's definition: *A Theory of Justice*, p. 505n.

8. Several have argued for this recently. For example, Waldron, *The Right to Private Property*, chap. 6. I do, however, emphasize different aspects of Locke's view here.

9. *Two Treatises of Government*. Paragraph numbers in the text refer to this work.

10. See C. B. Macpherson, *Political Theory of Possessive Individualism*, pp. 197–220.

11. There has been much debate concerning the extent to which Locke's views can be understood outside the context of his theological vision. In particular, it has been argued that there is a crucial connection between the claim in (a) and the duties that human beings have to work and develop the resources given to them. On this reading, Locke sees the develop-

ment of property (making "use of [the fruits of the earth] to the best advantage of life and convenience" [26]) as the fulfillment of an *obligation to God* as a condition for the receipt of these gifts. See James Tully, *A Discourse on Property: John Locke and His Adversaries*. See also Alan Ryan, *Property and Political Theory*, pp. 14–48.

12. See Lawrence Becker, *Property Rights*, chap. 4.

13. See David Snyder, who sees the argument this way ("Locke on Natural Law and Property Rights"). Snyder's understanding of Locke's conception of natural law is such that all things which contribute to the preservation of humanity are justified by the natural law. Nevertheless, this view of natural law theory may be hard pressed to make room for Locke's emphasis on the non-instrumental status of natural *rights*.

14. For convincing criticisms of first occupation arguments for property, see Becker, *Property Rights*, pp. 24–31.

15. He writes, "'The rich,' exclaims Jean Jacques, 'have the arrogance to say, "I built this wall; I earned this land by my labor." Who set you the task? we may reply, and by what right do you demand payment from us for labor which we did not impose on you?' All sophistry falls to the ground in the presence of this argument" (*What Is Property?*, pp. 84ff.). For discussion, see Becker, *Property Rights*, chap. 4, and Waldron, *The Right to Private Property*, chap. 6.

16. Becker, *Property Rights*, chap. 4.

17. Becker, *Property Rights*, p. 35.

18. Becker, *Property Rights*, p. 36. This was a claim made also by Mill; see *Principles of Political Economy*, bk. 3, sec. 1.

19. See John Christman, "Can Full Ownership Be Justified by Natural Rights?"

20. *Second Treatise of Government*, paragraph 37 (emphasis added). As Marjorie Grene made clear to me, the first half of this quotation, the non-spoilage proviso, is logically independent of the second half, the claim that one invades one's neighbor's share. On Locke's view, one offends against the commands of God if one lets one's goods spoil no matter how much one has.

21. This was the view defended by Hugo Grotius and Samuel Pufendorf. For a discussion, see Richard Schlatter, *Private Property: The History of an Idea*, pp. 130–47.

22. Locke, *First Treatise of Government*, chap. 11.

23. This interpretation is implied by Macpherson's view. See *The Political Theory of Possessive Individualism*.

24. See, however, John Simmons, "Inalienable Rights and Locke's Treatises."

25. The argument also assumes that the idea of "mixing" labor with something, such that the new something "contains" that labor, is a coherent thing to say. For an argument that it probably is not, see Waldron, *The Right to Private Property*, pp. 180–91.

26. J. R. Kearl, "Do Entitlements Imply That Taxation Is Theft?," and Cheyney Ryan, "Yours, Mine and Ours: Property Rights and Individual Liberty," also make similar points.

27. Becker, *Property Rights*, p. 49.

28. Sam Wheeler, "Natural Property Rights as Body Rights."

29. See *The Philosophy of Right*, secs. 41–65. For discussion of Hegel's political views, see Charles Taylor, *Hegel and Modern Society*, and Waldron, *The Right to Private Property*, chap. 10.

30. Cf. Tully, *A Discourse on Property*, pp. 116ff. For a critical view of such rights, see Richard Arneson, "Property Rights in Persons."

31. For an organizing overview that pertains to theories of property, see Ryan, *Property and Political Theory*.

32. For a battery of arguments against the claim that labor is a disutility, see Robert Lane, *The Market Experience*, chaps. 13–16.

33. This is basically Bogart's argument in "Lockean Provisos and State of Nature Theories." See also Richard Arneson, "Property Rights in Persons." For a contrastingly optimistic approach to the success of labor-based arguments (though not for liberal ownership), see Stephen Munzer, *A Theory of Property*, chap. 10.

34. Robert Nozick, *Anarchy, State, and Utopia*, chap. 7.

35. Nozick, *Anarchy, State, and Utopia*, p. 176.

36. For a similar line of argument, see G. A. Cohen, "Self Ownership, World Ownership and Equality."

37. See Murray Rothbard, *For a New Liberty*, p. 34. Cf. also J. J. Rousseau, "Discourse on the Origin of Inequality," p. 60.

38. Nozick, *Anarchy, State, and Utopia*, pp. 151 and 230–31.

39. I make these comments about the history of the United States by way of example. In Britain, I need only point out that ownership claims connected with the ancient manorial estates must reconcile themselves with the fact that William I established all those estates by conquest (declaring all the land of England as property of the Crown), just following the invasion of 1088.

40. Nozick, *Anarchy, State, and Utopia*, p. 231.

41. See Murray Rothbard, *For a New Liberty*, pp. 23–26, and "Justice and Property Rights," pp. 115–21.

42. This is what Kant and Hume both thought Locke's view reduced to. Their criticism was that either prior permission was needed to occupy the resource (in order to labor upon it), in which case the labor theory was unnecessary, or it was not, in which case it was in violation of the common rights assumption. Cf. Waldron's discussion in *The Right to Private Property*, pp. 173ff.

43. Blackstone, *Commentaries*, Bk. 2, chap. 1, p. 471.

Chapter 4

1. This naturally leads many to conclude that "freedom" is simply not a concept that can be given a definition apart from the particular normative conclusions one intends to draw with it. For a recent discussion of this issue, see George Brenkert, *Political Freedom*, chap. 1.

2. The locus classicus for this distinction is Isaiah Berlin's "Two Concepts of Liberty." See also his Introduction to *Four Essays on Liberty* for later refinements on the issues raised by his arguments.

3. For similar lists of such a gradation, see Richard Flathman, *The Philosophy and Politics of Freedom*, appendix, and Andrew Levine, *Arguing for Socialism*, p. 21.

4. See Gerald MacCallum, "Negative and Positive Freedom." On his view, the predicate "is free" is a triadic relation that holds among agents, acts (or conditions of character), and restraints. It was MacCallum's point, however, that the supposed distinction between so-called negative liberty and positive liberty disappeared when the schema was utilized. I have been critical of this claim: see John Christman, "Liberalism and Individual Positive Freedom."

5. For a thorough discussion, see W. A. Parent, "Recent Work on the Concept of Liberty."

6. See Joel Feinberg, *Social Philosophy*, chap. 1.

7. To be boringly precise, an account of restraints can vary along at least two dimensions, their source and their effect on the unfree person. I deal with source here. Theories about effect range from thinking that only if the agent's actions are made impossible is the agent unfree, to thinking that when the proposed action is made more costly it is unfree. The

former position is defended by both Hillel Steiner, "Individual Liberty," and G. A. Cohen, "Capitalism, Freedom and the Proletariate." For a general discussion, see George Brenkert, *Political Freedom*, pp. 65–100.

8. For example, Hobbes saw freedom as simply the range of *movement* allowed to the agent. Whether the acts prevented or allowed were by some standard moral or in accordance with the law was irrelevant to the freedom the agent enjoyed. See *Leviathan*, Part 1, chapter 14. Locke, on the other hand, distinguished liberty from license: on his view, freedom referred to that area where agents could "order their Actions, and dispose of their Possessions, and Persons as they think fit, within the bounds of the Law of Nature" (*Second Treatise of Government*, p. 309).

9. Cohen, "Capitalism, Freedom and the Proletariate," and Feinberg, *Social Philosophy*, p. 13, make a similar distinction.

10. Robert Nozick, *Anarchy, State, and Utopia*, chap. 7. Cohen ("Capitalism, Freedom and the Proletariate") and David Zimmerman ("Coercive Wage Offers") interpret him this way.

11. Nozick, *Anarchy, State, and Utopia*, p. 245 (emphasis mine).

12. See Gerald Dworkin, "Compulsion and Moral Concepts," pp. 227–33, and Robert Nozick, "Coercion." Jan Narveson slips into a moralized conception in his account of coercion in "Equality vs. Liberty: Advantage Liberty," p. 50.

13. See H.L.A. Hart, "Are There Any Natural Rights?," p. 21; see also Jeremy Waldron, *The Right to Private Property*, pp 106–26.

14. Nozick, *Anarchy, State, and Utopia*, pp. 160–74.

15. Nozick, *Anarchy, State, and Utopia*, p. 151. G. A. Cohen discusses this principle in "Robert Nozick and Wilt Chamberlain: How Patterns Preserve Liberty" and levels somewhat similar criticisms.

16. Nozick, *Anarchy, State, and Utopia*, p. 171.

17. Many defenders of free markets based on liberty make this claim. See, for example, Jan Narveson, "Equality vs. Liberty: Advantage Liberty," p. 55. Cf. also his *The Libertarian Idea*, chaps. 7–8.

18. These range from J. S. Mill, *Principles of Political Economy*, to, more recently, T. M. Scanlon, "Nozick on Rights, Liberty and Justice."

19. For an argument that in any supposed contest between, say, equality and liberty, "liberty must lose," see Ronald Dworkin, "What Is Equality? Part 3: The Place of Liberty."

20. Isaiah Berlin and others have made this move in different guises in order to give content to the idea that a greater quantity of freedom is gained or lost according to how important the acts considered are to the agent or to society. See Berlin, *Four Essays*, p. 130, and Lawrence Crocker, *Positive Liberty*, pp. 61ff. Charles Taylor, in "What Is Wrong with Negative Liberty?," considers these questions and concludes that there is no way to make other than "qualitative" judgments about the degree of liberty a person enjoys.

21. A perspicuous version of the argument being discussed here can be found in Andrew Levine, *Arguing for Socialism*, chap. 2.

22. See John Rawls, *A Theory of Justice*, p. 61, and "The Basic Liberties and Their Priority."

23. Milton Friedman, *Capitalism and Freedom*, pp. 7–21. Friedman also confuses incentive with obligation, in that he thinks a profit motive will ensure that people will always act in that narrow economically self-interested way. But as I pointed out in chapter 2, the market itself can in no way guarantee such outcomes.

24. One might argue that socialism, as instantiated in China, for example, requires unwieldy restraints on civil liberties and other non-economic actions in order to enforce an extreme egalitarianism: see John Hospers, "Socialism and Liberty," pp. 231–38. Since I don't take that legal structure to be the "purest form" of socialism, as Hospers does, nor Marxist socialism as the only alternative to liberal ownership of property, I do not discuss this claim.

25. Cf. David Zimmerman, "Coercive Wage Offers," and G. A. Cohen, "The Structure of Proletarian Unfreedom."

26. This is what Richard Arneson calls "the desire thesis" in "Freedom and Desire." Cf. also Isaiah Berlin, *Four Essays*, p. xx.

27. For a defense of free markets based on maximum equal liberty, see Jan Narveson, "Equality vs. Liberty: Advantage Liberty," p. 48, and his *The Libertarian Idea*, pp. 13–101.

28. Of course other intentional human actions aimed at restricting people's range of behavior (e.g., criminal behavior) will also count as a restraint, but these thinkers would certainly say that measures aimed at the prevention of these acts apply equally to all.

29. Narveson, "Equality vs. Liberty: Advantage Liberty," p. 49. See also *The Libertarian Idea*, pp. 26–27.

30. Narveson, "Equality vs. Liberty: Advantage Liberty," pp. 49–57, and Michael Levin, "Negative Liberty."

31. See, for example, Narveson, *The Libertarian Idea*, pp. 38–40.

32. David Miller, "Constraints on Freedom," p. 74.

33. See William Connolly, *The Terms of Political Discourse*, pp. 166–70, who argues this way.

34. This can also be used to show that costliness of removing the restraint is irrelevant (within some degree of feasibility), since the judgment that the valleyites are unfree does not need to be *postponed* until the cost of blasting through the blocked road is determined.

35. This is basically a reprise of a point I made in chapter 2 showing that liberal ownership and free markets could clash with each other.

36. See Alan Gibbard, "What Is Morally Special about Free Exchange?"

37. Presently in the United States, only about 12 percent of the work force is unionized, and this ignores the numerous legal and institutional restrictions on union bargaining and strikes that prevent the power of workers from approaching that of owners. For arguments similar to those developed in this section, see Cohen, "The Structure of Proletarian Unfreedom," and Miller, "Constraints on Freedom."

Chapter 5

1. Lawrence Becker, *Property Rights*, pp. 53–56.

2. Becker, *Property Rights*, p. 49.

3. Becker, *Property Rights*, pp. 53–54.

4. For further argument for this point, see John Christman, "Can Full Ownership Be Justified by Natural Rights?," pp. 166–68. Gerald Gauss has criticized my argument, however. His view is that Becker plausibly suggests that "our morality presupposes the sensibility of moral statements of the sort . . . Alf deserves X because of some act A that Alf has performed" and that "classifying people as deserving or undeserving because of some previous act of theirs" is a notion that all moral perspectives must include. See *Value and Justification*, pp. 411–15. I don't disagree. What I claim here is that all that is established by this observation is that a moral theory needs to include criteria of personal responsibility that affix treatment to people based on what they have done. It nevertheless is left open what such treatment should be in any given case.

5. Stephen Munzer defends a labor-desert argument that attempts to avoid these problems by presenting an "idealized" version of the argument (in a state of nature of abundant resources) and utilizing parallel reasoning to apply it to the real world. These arguments cannot, however, be used to defend liberal ownership (Munzer argues, for example, that the power to transfer is not justified by this strategy). See *A Theory of Property*, pp. 254–91.

6. Allen Buchanan, in *Ethics, Efficiency and the Market*, pp. 51–53, makes this point.

7. See John Rawls, *A Theory of Justice*, pp. 15, 310–15; and Joel Feinberg, "Justice and Personal Desert," pp. 88–94. For a sympathetic account of "desert defenses" of markets, see John Hospers, *Human Conduct: An Introduction to the Problems of Ethics*, pp. 433–46.

8. The view that markets provide this benefit rests on the claim that preferences revealed by market behavior are true reflections of an agent's welfare. This view has been widely criticized; see, for example, Amartya Sen, "Rational Fools: A Critique of the Behavioral Foundations of Economic Theory," pp. 317–44. Also, see section IV.

9. See Paul Samuelson, *Economics*, chap. 31; Frank Knight, *Risk, Uncertainty and Profit*, chap. 9; and Hal Varian, *Microeconomic Analysis*, p. 6. For a revision of the "standard account," see Israel Kirzner, *Competition and Entrepreneurship*, chap. 2. For an explanation of the role of the entrepreneur and the emergence of profit that parallels the present account (though his specification of entrepreneur is narrower than mine), see Joseph Schumpeter, *The Theory of Economic Development*, chap. 4.

10. I simplify here by talking only of starting a firm. An entrepreneur can also redirect production in an already existing firm in a variety of ways. The arguments I make should apply in those cases as well, though.

11. See Samuelson, *Economics*, pp. 592ff. See also Knight, *Risk, Uncertainty and Profit*, chap. 2.

12. See Knight, *Risk, Uncertainty and Profit*, p. 280, where he speaks of the "residual income" of entrepreneurs.

13. Feinberg, "Justice and Personal Desert," p. 61.

14. This judgment is distinct from saying that a person is (simply) undeserving. She may, for example, deserve praise but not the particular praise offered. This claim is important for the conclusion I eventually reach. If, for example, an institutional arrangement systematically distributes benefits and burdens, we can ask whether the recipients deserve those outcomes, *given that institutional arrangement*. If our answer to this is negative, it leaves open what they may deserve or if moral desert has any application to the situation at all.

15. See N. Scott Arnold, "Why Profits Are Deserved." My criticisms here are expanded in John Christman, "Entrepreneurs, Profits and Deserving Market Shares," pp. 6–10.

16. Feinberg, "Justice and Personal Desert," pp. 81ff, also makes this point. Scott Arnold considers an objection such as this but claims that since the justification is not *utilitarian*, it does not disqualify the claim from the realm of moral desert ("Why Profits Are Deserved," p. 393). But this rejoinder misses the point of the objection, for desert is not just a non-utilitarian concept; it is a non-consequentialist one.

17. Rawls, *A Theory of Justice*, p. 310.

18. See Robert Nozick, *Anarchy, State, and Utopia*, pp. 213–15.

19. See Alan Zaitchick, "On Deserving to Deserve."

20. Arnold, "Why Profits Are Deserved," p. 395, makes points similar to these.

21. Knight, *Risk, Uncertainty and Profit*, p. xx.

22. Rawls, *A Theory of Justice*, p. 311.

23. See Buchanan, *Ethics, Efficiency and the Market*, p. 52, for a point similar to this.

24. For elaboration on this point, see Edward Nell, "On Deserving Profits," pp. 408ff.

25. David Miller, *Market, State and Community*, pp. 158–67. Miller argues that a sense of personal deservingness is an essential component of the justification of markets (though what he defends is market socialism, not a system of liberal ownership).

26. Miller, *Market, State and Community*, p. 166.

27. Miller considers this reply also (pp. 170–72) but responds that market *socialism*, which diminishes the effect of luck by continually equalizing incomes, will not be vulnerable to this charge. Liberal ownership regimes, however, remain so.

28. Some may balk at the thought that retribution in penal institutions is strictly conventional. But the claim here is merely that such desert-driven institutions as the penal sys-

tem have irreducibly conventional elements. How else could it be settled upon that criminals are put into jails for their crimes rather than, for example, made to run in place for so many hours? After all, if we take the principle that the punishment should literally fit the crime, the only crime for which a jail term is strictly appropriate is kidnapping!

Chapter 6

1. See Amartya Sen, "Utilitarianism and Welfarism."

2. Bentham lists other attributes of pleasure that define its degree, though only intensity and duration are intrinsic to pleasure itself. Others, such as certainty, are separate. See *The Principles of Morals and Legislation*, chap. 4.

3. It is often unclear whether these choices are meant as evidence for the preferences (utility) of the agents or whether they actually *define* them. For discussion, see Amartya Sen, "Well Being, Agency and Freedom," pp. 187–92.

4. Nicholas Kaldor, "Welfare Propositions in Economics and Interpersonal Comparisons of Utility"; J. Hicks, *Value and Capital.*

5. This may not be surreptitious. See, for example, the way Allan Buchanan defines Kaldor efficiency in *Ethics, Efficiency and the Market*, p. 4, n. 1.

6. See T. Scitovsky, "A Note on Welfare Propositions in Economics."

7. *The Works of Jeremy Bentham*, p. 305 (*Principles of the Civil Code*, Part 1, chap. 6). Notice of course that this claim can be made only if interpersonal comparisons of utility are meaningful.

8. "If all property were to be equally divided . . . [e]verything would be speedily destroyed" (Bentham, *Works*, p. 303).

9. Bentham, *Works*, pp. 158ff.

10. Bentham, *Works*, p. 310.

11. Bentham, *Works*, p. 311.

12. See *Works*, pp. 313ff where Bentham lists the legitimate purposes for which the state may tax, limit, or even appropriate property. Admittedly, his argument is that the aims listed all involve direct or indirect maintenance of the general security of the state, which in turn protects property. But if some security in individual possession survives these encroachments, why won't it in the case of others?

13. Lawrence Becker, in *Property Rights*, pp. 57–67, discusses similar arguments.

14. For a similar argument, see R. H. Tawney, *The Acquisitive Society*, pp. 73–74.

15. See Daniel Hausman, "When Jack and Jill Make a Deal," for a discussion of externalities that emphasizes this.

16. See, e.g., Yoram Barzel, *Economic Analysis of Property Rights*.

17. See Harold Demsetz, "Toward a Theory of Property Rights"; see also Eric Furubotn and Svetozar Pejovich, eds., *The Economics of Property Rights*. For a critical appraisal, see Thrainn Eggertsson, *Economic Behavior and Institutions*. The approach has much in common with the economic analysis of law movement, although the latter promotes the maximization of "wealth" in its theories rather than simply utility. See Richard Posner, *The Economic Analysis of Law*; for discussion, see Jules Coleman, *Markets, Morals and the Law*.

18. Demsetz's claim is partly descriptive: Property rights will arise whenever the benefits of internalization outweigh the costs, that is, when the costs of non-negotiated effects of exchanges or production (externalities) are greater than the transaction and policing costs of extending full property rights over those effects; see "Toward a Theory," p. 34.

19. Ronald Coase, "The Problem of Social Costs." The theorem is meant to show that in any conflict over resource use, in the absence of transaction costs, the efficient solution will be the same no matter what the distribution of initial rights to the conflicting factors is.

This has been widely (and critically) discussed. See, e.g., Jules Coleman, *Markets, Morals and the Law*, chap. 3.

20. See Demsetz, "Toward a Theory of Property Rights."

21. See Frank Michelman, "Ethics, Economics, and the Law of Property." Demsetz admits this much when he mentions the conditions under which it would be optimal to separate the ownership of land from ownership of its product (crops): see "Professor Michelman's Unnecessary and Futile Search for the Philosopher's Touchstone," p. 37, n. 3.

22. Demsetz, "Toward a Theory of Property Rights," p. 38.

23. For an argument about some of these other distribution-sensitive alternatives, see Svetozar Pejovich, "Towards a General Theory of Property Rights," pp. 347–50. Pejovich considers specifically "attenuated state ownership" and advances various criticisms against the efficiency of the tax structure that this involves. His argument, however, concerns macroeconomic considerations such as optimal interest and savings rates rather than microefficiency.

24. For a similar argument, see Lawrence Becker, *Property Rights*, p. 73.

25. In *Poverty and Famines*, Amartya Sen explains how some of the most severe famines in our century have been caused by the external effects of certain distributions of entitlements (rather than a shortage of food). See also Hausman, "When Jack and Jill Make a Deal," who is skeptical about ignoring pecuniary externalities.

26. Michelman, "Ethics, Economics and the Law of Property," pp. 21–34.

27. See Russell Hardin, *Collective Action*, pp. 16–20, for discussion.

28. See Buchanan, *Ethics, Efficiency and the Market*, pp. 22–26.

29. There is much criticism of the view that market behavior mirrors a person's good. See, for example, Amartya Sen, "Rational Fools: A Critique of the Behavioral Foundations of Economic Theory." For a discussion that is critical of the line I take here, see David Miller, *Market, State and Community*, pp. 130–50.

30. Attempts have been made to apply market models to these very interactions; see, for example, Gary Becker, *A Treatise on the Family*.

31. See Elizabeth Anderson, "The Ethical Limitations of the Market."

32. For skepticism that such comparisons can be made, see Buchanan, *Ethics, Efficiency and the Market*, and Alec Nove, "Some Observations on Intersystemic Comparisons."

33. As Allan Buchanan notes, if the product in question is, say, nuclear weapons, the productive efficiency of its production hardly can be said to be directly related to well-being. See *Ethics, Efficiency and the Market*, pp. 5–6. See also Edward Saraydar, "The Conflation of Productivity and Efficiency in Economics and Economic History."

34. See E. Barone, "The Ministry of Production in the Collectivist State." I follow Deborah Duff Milenkovitch here in her discussion of this debate in "Is Market Socialism Efficient?"

35. See Ludwig von Mises, "Economic Calculation and the Socialist Commonwealth." Actually, the original claim by von Mises was that the calculations were impossible, which runs afoul of the Barone argument. It was F. A. Hayek who put the argument in terms of the practical possibility of calculation. See Hayek's contributions to a volume he edited, *Collectivist Economic Planning*.

36. See Oskar Lange and Fred M. Taylor, *On the Economic Theory of Socialism*.

37. See Buchanan, *Ethics, Efficiency and the Market*, pp. 17f. For an explanation of how egalitarian economic systems can be efficient if one assumes the "moral" motive of wanting to do what is best for society, see Joseph Carens, *Equality, Moral Incentives, and the Market*.

38. Another such system, though different from the Lange plan, is the worker-controlled competitive framework which was found in, say, what used to be Yugoslavia. In that system, firms competed among themselves though each particular firm was owned by its employees.

For discussion of this and other systems, see Jon Elster and Karl Ove Moene, *Alternatives to Capitalism*. See, also David Miller, *Market, State and Community*.

39. See Joseph Schumpeter, *Capitalism, Socialism, and Democracy*, p. 83. The argument concerning entrepreneurs and productive efficiency is in Schumpeter, *Theory of Economic Development*, esp. chapter 4. For discussion, see Jon Elster, *Explaining Technical Change*.

40. Schumpeter, *Theory*, pp. 90–94.

41. See Giovanni Dosi, *Technical Change and Industrial Transformation*. "Demand-pull" indicates a perceived market demand for a new product or technology. This theory will not, however, explain why *major* breakthroughs occur when they do, since presumably there is always an infinite demand for such things. "Technology-push" refers to the ongoing R&D work that constantly produces innovations. This theory won't explain the particularly economically sensitive nature of innovation, however.

42. See Morton Kamien and Nancy Schwartz, "Market Structure and Innovation: A Survey." See also Richard Nelson, "Research on Productivity Growth and Productivity Differences: Dead Ends and New Departures."

43. Jon Elster, in *Explaining Technical Change*, critically discusses both of these approaches.

44. See L. Putterman, "Some Behavioral Perspectives on the Dominance of Hierarchical Over Democratic Forms of Enterprise"; these points are summarized in Jon Elster and Karl Ove Moene's introduction to *Alternatives to Capitalism*, p. 31.

45. Little, but certainly not none. There are many reasons to believe that maximization of any but the most abstract sort is a poor description of what people are motivated to do. See, for example, Amos Tversky and Daniel Kahneman, "Rational Choice and the Framing of Decisions," for empirical evidence against wholesale maximization.

46. The latter term is from Andrew Zimbalist in his introduction to *Comparative Economic Systems: Present Views*, p. 4.

47. See Putterman, "Some Behavioral Perspectives on the Dominance of Hierarchical over Democratic Forms of Enterprise."

48. According to Graef S. Crystal (*In Search of Excess*), the typical chief executive of an American company makes 160 times what an average American worker makes, while in Japan, that ratio is 20 to 1. (This was brought to my attention by an op-ed piece by Richard Cohen, *Washington Post*, December 24, 1991.) The points in this paragraph follow closely the observations of John Baker in *Arguing for Equality*, pp. 94–102.

49. See A. Allen Schmidd, *Property, Power and Public Choice*.

50. The evidence is summarized in Elster and Moene, Introduction, *Alternatives to Capitalism*, p. 30.

51. See Richard Brandt, *A Theory of the Good and the Right*, pp. 306–16, for discussion. For criticism of this line of defense of egalitarianism, see Harry Frankfurt, "Equality as a Moral Ideal."

52. Also, many economists who have noted that perfect competition and ideal markets do not exist anywhere in the real world have nevertheless relied on the so-called theory of the second best, by which is meant the theory that real-world markets are the best approximation to the ideal (or allow for the greatest possibility that movement toward the ideal will occur), and hence the conclusions reached in the ideal models have application in the real world. This theory, however, has been much criticized. The classic statement of the view is R. G. Lipsey and K. Lancaster, "The General Theory of Second Best" (though their specification of the view differs from what I have here). For discussion, see S. K. Nath, *A Reappraisal of Welfare Economics*, chapter 3.

53. Buchanan, in *Ethics, Efficiency and the Market*, pp. 36–46, argues that the comparisons cannot really be done. There have, however, been numerous attempts, in particular

comparing the growth patterns of Western capitalist economies with those of the (pre-1989) East European economies of the Soviet block. See, e.g., Frederic L. Pryor, *Property and Industrial Organization in Communist and Capitalist Nations.*

Chapter 7

1. Hume defends something close to this view; see *A Treatise of Human Nature*, Book 3, Part 2, chaps. 1–4. Also, John Rawls makes barely any mention of property rights in *A Theory of Justice*, the implication being that the structure of ownership will be determined, in a purely derivative way, by the Difference Principle.

2. Some theorists make this point by referring to "effective commodities" (the combination of a physical asset *and* the property rights bundle that an owner enjoys in relation to it). See Eric Furubotn and Svetozar Pejovich, eds., *The Economics of Property Rights*, pp. 4–5.

3. C. Edwin Baker, in "Property and Its Relation to Constitutionally Protected Liberty," also discusses the disaggregation of ownership and defends distinctions similar to these. Baker distinguishes six separable functions that property rules perform: protecting use, ensuring basic welfare, protecting the conditions of personhood, protecting against exploitation, allocating resources, and securing interpersonal sovereignty. For reasons made clear in the text (and to avoid some additional complications raised by the increased number of categories), I reduce these to two. There is a great deal in Baker's important discussion, however, which is mirrored in the present analysis.

Other recent writers who have utilized or mentioned a similar bifurcation concerning property rights include Carol Gould, *Rethinking Democracy*, ch. 6; Jeremy Waldron, *The Right to Private Property*, chaps. 11–12; and Edwin Hettinger "Justifying Intellectual Property," p. 38.

4. A word about terminology: some have made a distinction that is similar to this one but is called the separation of "ownership and control." This terminology stems from the view that the essence of ownership is what I am here calling income ownership. Since I reject that claim, I describe what amounts to a similar distinction in different terms.

5. I have dropped reference to the ancillary elements (absence of term, residuary character of ownership, and the prohibition of harmful use). As C. Edwin Baker puts it, these rules concern *when* one owns a thing rather than *what* it means to own it (see "Property and Its Relation to Constitutionally Protected Liberty," p. 742 n. 3).

6. This will not be true for so-called positional goods, which require for their optimal use that others have certain resources. See also Fred Hirsch, *The Social Limits to Growth*, chap. 2. My point is that cooperation is not essential for use *qua* use.

7. See Baker, "Property and Its Relation to Constitutionally Protected Liberty," pp. 742–43, who puts it this way; see also George Mavrodes, "Property," whom I later discuss in more detail.

8. This distinction must be recognized in practice quite often, in the collection of taxes at different rates for income and gifts, for example.

9. Lawrence Becker describes the right to income as being a right "to the benefits derived from forgoing personal use of a thing and allowing others to use it" (*Property Rights*, p. 19).

10. This connection will not hold for all taxes: a lump sum tax on total holdings would not amount to a limitation of income rights. Only taxes on traded goods involve such an attenuation.

11. This variability has led Yoram Barzel to argue that, in fact, property rights are never fully *defined*, since rights are defined only when their true value is known. See *Economic Analysis of Property Rights*, pp. 2–4.

12. I follow here Russell Hardin's concise discussion of these points in *Morality within*

the Limits of Reason, pp. 84–89. See also Jules Coleman, *Markets, Morals and the Law*, chap. 10.

13. See Baker, "Property and Its Relation to Constitutionally Protected Liberty," pp. 748–51, who discusses the allocative function of property.

14. For discussion, see Jules Coleman, *Markets, Morals and the Law*, chap. 10.

15. See, for example, John Roemer, "A Challenge to Neo-Lockeanism."

16. Richard Epstein, *Takings: Private Property and the Power of Eminent Domain.*

17. Epstein, *Takings*, pp. 57–62.

18. Epstein, *Takings*, pp. 59–61.

19. This line of reply also applies to Epstein's strategy of arguing from an analogy from tort law. He claims that since any partial taking by a private citizen of the property of another is grounds for an action, the government should be subject to the same provision (*Takings*, pp. 74–92). But as I have just indicated, there are many things that private citizens can do to affect the property rights of other private citizens that Epstein wants to claim are illegitimate for governments to do. The argument works both ways.

20. Epstein, *Takings*, chap. 7.

21. Mavrodes, "Property," p. 184.

22. For a survey of views on the nature of the right to privacy, see W. A. Parent, "Recent Work on the Concept of Privacy." For discussion of privacy and property, see Stephen Munzer, *A Theory of Property*, chap. 5.

23. The distinction is mentioned by Munzer, *A Theory of Property*, p. 92 n. 4, and p. 95.

24. Munzer, who discusses such arguments, does not think that a plausible case can be made that private property is a necessary condition for privacy. See Munzer, *A Theory of Property*, pp. 90–96.

25. For a survey of social psychological studies, see Kate Loewental, "Property." For anthropological evidence, see Lawrence Becker, "The Moral Basis of Property Rights."

26. See Lee Ellis, "On the Rudiments of Possessions and Property."

27. See Lita Furby, "Possessions in Humans: An Exploratory Study of Its Meaning and Motivation."

28. The conclusion is noted by Ellis in "On the Rudiments of Possession and Property," p. 121.

29. Ellis, "On the Rudiments of Possession and Property," p. 117.

30. Loewental, "Property," p. 344.

31. Quoted in Loewental, "Property," p. 344.

32. Ellis cites Furby's conclusion that "the most salient feature of what 'ownership' means to humans, at least as they are able to report it verbally, roughly is 'the power to control and/or use an object however they choose'" ("On the Rudiments of Possession and Property," p. 122).

33. Often economists presuppose, for example, that the "owner" of a corporation is the "residual claimant," or in our terms the person who holds income rights to the property.

34. Bruce Ackerman, *Private Property and the Constitution.*

35. See Ackerman, *Private Property*, pp. 26ff.

36. Ackerman, *Private Property*, pp. 99–100.

37. It may well not. See T. M. Scanlon, "Comments on Ackerman's *Private Property and the Constitution.*" For elaboration and defense of the distinction, see Ackerman, "Four Questions for Legal Theory."

38. "Probably the most popular [approach to law] today is the distinctive vocabulary deployed by the practitioners of the so-called economic approach to law" (Ackerman, *Private Property*, p. 26 n. 1; though Ackerman does mention other perspectives, his sympathies are clearly with this approach).

39. This measure assumes that the value of things can be measured by hypothetical

inquiry into what people would be willing to pay for the thing in question. This technique has been widely criticized. See, for example, Mark Sagoff, "Ethics and Economics in Environmental Law."

40. The affinity of lawyers in the Anglo-American common law tradition to the "full disaggregation" view of ownership may in some ways result from the accidents of cultural history, in particular, from using the complex property rules of the feudal law as the institutional backdrop of legal doctrine. Continental law, by contrast, places much more emphasis on "ownership" as a meaningful concept. See Ackerman, *Private Property*, p. 27 n. 3. For a general discussion, see J. H. Merryman, "Ownership and Estate."

41. Consider again Jeremy Bentham's claim, discussed in the previous chapter, that in the interest of the security and reasonable expectations of owners, property rights ought to be private and unattenuated. We saw the weakness of this line as an argument for the liberal conception of ownership. But the conclusion that Bentham should have reached in that argument was that the interests of security in possession and reasonable expectations about holdings provide some *prima facie* support for stable *control rights* over property.

42. Adolf Berle and Gardiner Means, *The Modern Corporation and Private Property*. Recall the terminological difference that I have with those who equate ownership with income rights (and hence distinguish "ownership" from control). In our terms, the claim is that control rights vest in different individuals than do income rights.

43. Berle and Means, *The Modern Corporation*, pp. 119–25. My discussion here owes much to Stephen Munzer's comprehensive treatment of these issues in *A Theory of Property*, chap. 12. I also follow Munzer in some terminological divergence from the Berle and Means text (see Munzer, p. 320, n. 2).

44. Eugene Fama and Michael Jensen, "Separation of Ownership and Control."

45. Robert Clark, "The Four Stages of Capitalism: Reflections on Investment Management Treatises." Clark's claim, however, is actually a historical one, where he argues that capitalism has expanded in the functions it demands of capital managers, from the simple entrepreneur, to the professional business manager (made prominent by Berle and Means), to the portfolio manager, and finally to the savings planner (a role still in its infancy).

46. See, e.g., R. H. Coase, "The Nature of the Firm"; Armen Alchian and Harold Demsetz, "Production, Information Costs, and Economic Organization"; and Steven S. Cheung, "The Contractual Nature of the Firm." For discussion, see Munzer, *A Theory of Property*, pp. 348ff.

One untidy implication of the contracts view, however, is that, on that model, it is no longer clear what a firm *is*, since there is no principled distinction between the contracts internal to the firm's operations and those the firm makes with others, such as a subcontractor: see Cheung for an argument to this effect.

47. Harold Demsetz, "The Structure of Ownership and the Theory of the Firm," pp. 380–81.

48. Deuteronomy 23: 20–21 and Leviticus 25: 35–37. For discussion, see Benjamin Nelson, *The Idea of Usury*.

49. See Richard Schlatter, *Property: The History of an Idea*, pp. 30–70.

50. Mill, *On Liberty*, p. 88. Marx also made a distinction roughly parallel to this in distinguishing use value from exchange value. Also, he utilized the distinction in predicting that in developed capitalism there will be an increasing separation between control and ownership, and this separation serves to exacerbate the already entrenched alienation intrinsic to the capitalist order (*Capital*, vol. 3, chap. 27).

51. David Miller has argued that there are two contrasting sources for the justification of property rights: one is individual rights and the other is principles of distributive justice ("Liberty and Property"). The distinction I defend suggests that these two strategies essentially have different objects: the former is control rights and the latter is income rights.

Chapter 8

1. John Rawls, for example, sees talents and skills as socially owned, and Ronald Dworkin presses for the compensation of the talentless by the skilled in his egalitarian scheme; see Rawls, *A Theory of Justice*, pp. 101–2, and Dworkin, "What Is Equality? Part 2: Equality of Resources."

2. See G. A. Cohen, "Self Ownership, World Ownership and Equality" and "Self Ownership, World Ownership and Equality Part II." Richard Arneson also has scrutinized the notion of self-ownership and argues for the abandonment of the principle: see "Lockean Self Ownership: Towards a Demolition."

3. Or at least such equality of benefits will be one of the fundamental goals of the economic structures of the society. Egalitarianism does not rule out other economic goals that are consistent with the abstract equality principle (as I argue in section III). Whether this requires equality of resources or equality of welfare as the ideal is left open at this point (though see chapter 9).

4. See, for example, Alec Nove, *The Economics of Feasible Socialism*. I discuss such socialist policies in the next chapter.

5. See, for example, Harry Frankfurt, "Equality as a Moral Ideal."

6. Jeremy Waldron, *The Right to Private Property*, p. 398; see also, pp. 400f.

7. See John Simmons, "Inalienable Rights and Locke's Treatises," for a discussion.

8. Arneson, "Lockean Self-Ownership: Towards a Demolition," p. 36. Arneson contrasts this principle with what he calls the "self-benefit" principle, which states "moral rules should be so constructed that, if the rules are obeyed, the acts of each person benefit or harm only himself, except as he himself chooses to confer or exchange the benefits of his acts" (p. 37). The principle is borrowed from Alan Gibbard, "Natural Property Rights," p. 84.

9. See G. W. F. Hegel, *The Philosophy of Right*. See also Charles Taylor, *Hegel and Modern Society*, and Jeremy Waldron, *The Right to Private Property*, chap. 10 for discussion.

10. For a (critical) discussion of the intellectual development in that tradition, see Isaiah Berlin, "Two Concepts of Liberty."

11. Arneson himself does not defend this principle or these implications. He is quite critical of the self-ownership postulate as a primary distributive principle.

12. For a similar argument, see C. Edwin Baker, "Property and Its Relation to Constitutionally Protected Liberty," pp. 804–16.

13. I do not believe, in the end, that the attitude in question should be seen as identification but rather something a bit more complicated. See John Christman, "Autonomy and Personal History," for explanation. But for present purposes the term expresses the crucial idea in this debate.

14. For a general discussion, see John Christman, "Constructing the Inner Citadel: Recent Work on the Concept of Autonomy."

15. For discussion see the essays in John Christman, ed. *The Inner Citadel: Essays on Individual Autonomy*. See also Gerald Dworkin, *The Theory and Practice of Autonomy*. For my own view, see Christman, "Autonomy and Personal History."

16. See Joseph Raz, *The Morality of Freedom*, pp. 369–95.

17. Cf. Christman, "Autonomy and Personal History." In that work I framed this view as an alternative to Gerald Dworkin's theory of autonomy (*The Theory and Practice of Autonomy*, chap. 1) which I criticized. I have now been convinced that the differences between our positions are minimal.

18. Raz, *The Morality of Freedom*, pp. 373–78.

19. Raz, *The Morality of Freedom*, p. 375.

20. *Woman in the Dunes*, directed by Hiroshi Teshigahara (Japan, 1969), is based on the novel by Kobo Abe.

21. For an explanation of such neutrality, see Gerald Dworkin, *The Theory and Practice of Autonomy*, chap. 1, and Christman, Introduction to *The Inner Citadel*, p. 14.

22. For further elaboration and qualifications of this claim, see Christman, "Liberalism and Individual Positive Freedom."

23. Cohen, "Self-Ownership, World Ownership and Equality, Part II."

24. Laws governing the donation of organs (and prohibiting their sale) are clear expressions of the intuition here. See Alan Ryan, *Property*, p. 111. See also David Gauthier, *Morals by Agreement*, pp. 272ff.

25. For a general discussion of this issue, see Deborah Satz, "Markets in Women's Reproductive Labor."

26. Richard Arneson has discussed a similar suggestion in a different context and raised the objection that such a scheme would lack essential incentives to *develop* one's talents. See "Lockean Self Ownership." This effect could be offset, though, with a pool of resources raised to subsidize education to facilitate the development of all talents.

27. This proposal could be illustrated by imagining that the central planner lacks information concerning Able's and Infirm's preferences for labor and leisure. Hence control rights are protected since economic policy is set independent of individual decisions. For a similar suggestion, see John Roemer, "A Public Ownership Solution of the Tragedy of the Commons." The difference with Roemer's model, however, is that he assumes full ownership of talents.

28. Extreme scarcity of skills, to a degree that does not allow individual subsistence, is often simply assumed away on the Humean grounds that such conditions prevent the possibility of imposing principles of justice at all.

29. Or is it? Robert Lane proffers substantial evidence that labor, in most situations and at many levels, is not a source of disutility for workers but rather a source of their sense of self-worth. See *The Market Experience*.

30. Several related problems are elided here. For example, the right to withhold talents elicits a strong incentive to strategically misrepresent one's skills (in order to benefit from an incentive system).

Chapter 9

1. As we will see, sometimes "autonomy" is used as a "threshold conception," where it would make no sense to say it is increased.

2. Here I resist the general analysis used by Gary Becker and George Stigler in "De Gustibus Non Est Disputandum."

3. To demand more—for example, that one's beliefs (upon which conditional desires rest) be confirmed by objectively relevant evidence—would make the property of autonomy divergent from the idea of *self*-government that provides its intuitive base. For requiring such rationality conditions implies that people will not be considered autonomous even if they are acting on well-formed, considered, and consistent reasons for action. For consideration of this question, see Richard Lindley, *Autonomy*, pp. 20ff, and Lawrence Haworth, *Autonomy: An Essay in Philosophical Psychology and Ethics*, Part 1. The points I make here are developed further in John Christman, "Autonomy and Personal History," pp. 13–16.

4. This is not to reverse my claim, made in the last chapter, that the condition of independence is thoroughly derivative from the condition of authenticity. I am making a contingent assumption here about the existence of a consistent range of life plans for which these resources will be necessary for agents to achieve authenticity.

5. For an argument that parallels this one, see George Brenkert, *Political Freedom*, pp. 205–42.

6. This last phrase indicates that the ideal of autonomy cannot be fully defined outside of a robust theory of just social relations. Cf. Brenkert, *Political Freedom*, pp. 171–205.

7. This recalls the issues surrounding the "full disaggregation" view of ownership I considered in chapter 1.

8. Russell Hardin disagrees with this and argues that the value of autonomy is largely ephemeral; see "Autonomy, Identity, and Welfare." For critical discussion of his position, see John Christman's Introduction to *The Inner Citadel*, pp. 15–18.

9. For discussion, see Lita Furby, "Possessions: Toward a Theory of Their Meaning and Function throughout the Life Cycle," pp. 324–25.

10. See Jon Elster, *Sour Grapes*, pp. 109–40.

11. See Robert Lane, *The Market Experience*, pp. 43–57.

12. See Amartya Sen, *On Ethics and Economics*, p. 41.

13. For a discussion of this claim within the rubric of "needs" analysis, see Len Doyal and Ian Gough, *A Theory of Human Needs*, pp. 59–75.

14. See Lita Furby, "Possessions in Humans: An Exploratory Study of Its Meaning and Motivation," pp. 49–65; Kate Loewental, "Property," pp. 343–51.

As I discussed in chapter 7, however, when these investigators speak of property ownership, it is clear that they are referring uniquely to possession and control of the goods in question rather than transfer and income retrieval. Recall that when Kate Loewental discusses the concept of property, basing it on a general meaning of the verb "to have," she claims that it involves the idea that "it is permissible for X to use O, and if X consents, it is permissible for others to use O" ("Property," p. 344).

15. Furby, "Possessions: Toward a Theory," pp. 322–23.

16. Furby, "Possessions: Toward a Theory," pp. 320–24. For a philosophical argument connecting property and "personhood," see Margaret Jane Radin, "Property and Personhood," pp. 957–1015.

17. George Brenkert, *Political Freedom*, p. 109. Brenkert cites Herbert Marcuse, *An Essay on Liberation*, pp. 13–15.

18. A personality type that would stand as a counterexample to my view might be called a "single-minded Social Darwinist": a person who wants her character to be molded *only* by success or failure in the market; all other factors would render her resulting profile, in her own eyes, inauthentic. I assume, however, that this is not a typical personality profile.

19. Lane, *The Market Experience*, chap. 9.

20. Brian Barry, "The Welfare State Versus the Relief of Poverty," pp. 73–74.

21. See Alan Gibbard, "What Is Morally Special about Free Exchange?"

22. Also, as J. Donald Moon points out ("The Moral Basis of the Welfare State," p. 32), where state programs are designed to benefit only those already poor, welfare recipients often suffer from losses of self-esteem, because the provision of such benefits is often contingent on being a "failure" in the game of market competition.

23. See Charles Reich, "The New Property."

24. Quoted by Reich, p. 741. Some frightening recent decisions of the U.S. Supreme Court illustrate this, where the court upheld state and congressional restrictions on abortion counselling and funding to those who receive public assistance (where public assistance is construed in a chillingly broad sense). These decisions were made when there existed (presumably) a fully protected right to an abortion in the general population. For a general discussion of the court's treatment of the relative weight of property claims, see John Brigham, *Property and the Politics of Entitlement*.

25. See, for example, John Rawls, *A Theory of Justice*, pp. 90–95; Ronald Dworkin, "What is Equality? Part 1: Equality of Welfare" and "What Is Equality? Part 2: Equality of Resources"; Richard Arneson, "Equality and Equal Opportunity for Welfare"; G. A. Cohen, "On the Currency of Egalitarian Justice"; and Amartya Sen, "Equality of What?" and *Inequality Reexamined*.

26. This claim is, of course, not uncontroversial, as many claim that the satisfaction of

a person's actual desires is neither necessary nor always sufficient for advancing her good. For a discussion, see James Griffin, *Well Being*.

27. John Rawls uses just these considerations to motivate the use of primary goods as the metric for equality. Ronald Dworkin uses these points to reject equality of welfare and to adopt equality of resources, and Amartya Sen opts for "capabilities" as the standard. Others, such as Richard Arneson, think that welfare could still be used as the measure of equality but only if it is understood as "opportunity" for securing welfare. See note 25 for references. For a general discussion, see Cohen, "On the Currency of Egalitarian Justice."

28. Cohen, "On the Currency of Egalitarian Justice," pp. 916–44.

29. However, if the person refused to participate in such revitalizing programs, *that* choice might be considered the autonomous one and the person would be made to bear the costs of continued addiction.

30. Sen's "equality of basic capabilities" standard is largely consistent with the arguments presented here. See "Equality of What?," "Well Being, Agency and Freedom," pp. 198–203, and *Inequality Reexamined*.

31. See Bruce Landesman, "Egalitarianism," pp. 39–49, for an argument similar to this. Also, for a discussion of the complex nature of well-being, see Robert Lane, *The Market Experience*, Part 7.

32. This follows some of John Rawls's more recent views: see "The Idea of an Overlapping Consensus."

33. For an argument for this premise, see George Brenkert, *Political Freedom*, pp. 224–42.

34. For a study that brings out the importance of gender for theories of distributive justice, see Susan Moller Okin, *Justice, Gender and the Family*.

35. See, e.g., Alec Nove, *The Economics of Feasible Socialism*. For an alternative approach to market socialism, see David Miller, *Market, State and Community*.

36. John Roemer, "The Morality and Efficiency of Market Socialism," p. 452; see also J. Roemer, I. Ortuño-Ortin, and J. Silvestre, "Investment Planning in Market Socialism."

37. The phrase comes from Oskar Lange, see *On the Economic Theory of Socialism*, p. 83.

38. Even some who are generally sympathetic to egalitarianism think it may not: see Richard Arneson, "Is Socialism Dead? A Comment on Market Socialism and Basic Income Capitalism."

39. Again, I use "workplace" to denote that area of one's life where one's projects and activities are carried out. This may well be one's own home. In such a case, by the way, being abused or battered or not having equal status in domestic decision making will defeat autonomy.

40. See Stephen Munzer, *A Theory of Property*, chap. 12.

Bibliography

Ackerman, Bruce. (1977). *Private Property and the Constitution*. New Haven, CT: Yale University Press.

———. (1980). "Four Questions for Legal Theory" in *Nomos*, vol. 22: *Property*, J. R. Pennock and J. Chapman, eds. New York: New York University Press, 351–75.

Alchian, Armen, and Harold Demsetz. (1972). "Production, Information Costs, and Economic Organization," *American Economic Review* 62, 777–95.

Anderson, Elizabeth. (1990). "The Ethical Limitations of the Market," *Economics and Philosophy* 6, 179–205.

Aristotle. (1946). *The Politics of Aristotle*, trans. Ernest Barker. Oxford: Oxford University Press.

———. (1953). *The Ethics of Aristotle*, trans. J.A.K. Thomson. Harmondsworth, UK: Penguin.

Arneson, Richard. (1985). "Freedom and Desire," *Canadian Journal of Philosophy* 15, 425–48.

———. (1989). "Equality and Equal Opportunity for Welfare," *Philosophical Studies* 56, no. 1 (May), 77–93.

———. (1991). "A Defense of Equal Opportunity for Welfare," *Philosophical Studies* 62, no. 2 (May), 187–95.

———. (1991). "Lockean Self Ownership: Towards a Demolition," *Political Studies* 39 (March), 36–54.

———. (1992). "Is Socialism Dead? A Comment on Market Socialism and Basic Income Capitalism," *Ethics* 102, no. 3 (April), 485–511.

———. (1992). "Property Rights in Persons," *Social Philosophy and Policy* 9, no. 1, 201–30.

Arnold, N. Scott. (1987). "Why Profits Are Deserved," *Ethics* 97, no. 2 (January), 387–402.

Atiyah, Patrick. (1979). *The Rise and Fall of Freedom of Contract*. Oxford: Clarendon Press.

Austin, John. (1969). *Lectures on Jurisprudence*, 3rd ed. 3 vols. R. Campbell, ed. London: John Murray.

Baker, C. Edwin. (1985). "Property and Its Relation to Constitutionally Protected Liberty," *University of Pennsylvania Law Review* 134, no. 4 (April), 741–816.

Baker, John. (1987). *Arguing for Equality*. London: Verso Press.

Barone, E. (1935). "The Ministry of Production in the Collectivist State," in *Collectivist Economic Planning*, F. A. Hayek, ed. London: Routledge and Kegan Paul, 245–90.

Barry, Brian. (1990). "The Welfare State Versus the Relief of Poverty" in *Needs and Welfare*, A. Ware and R. Goodin, eds. London: Sage Press, 73–103.

Barzel, Yoram. (1989). *Economic Analysis of Property Rights*. Cambridge: Cambridge University Press.

Becker, Gary. (1981). *A Treatise on the Family*. Cambridge, MA: Harvard University Press.

Becker, Gary, and George Stigler. (1990). "De Gustubus Non Est Disputandum," in *The Limits of Rationality*, Karen Schweers Cook and Margaret Levi, eds. Chicago: University of Chicago Press, pp. 191–216.

Becker, Lawrence. (1977). *Property Rights: Philosophical Foundations*. Boston: Routledge and Kegan Paul.

———. (1980). "The Moral Basis of Property Rights," in *Nomos*, vol. 22: *Property*, J. R. Pennock and J. Chapman, eds. New York: New York University Press, 187–220.

Benn, S. I., and R. S. Peters. (1959). *The Principles of Political Thought*. New York: Collier Books.

Bentham, Jeremy. (1962). *The Principles of Morals and Legislation*, in John Bowring, ed., *The Works of Jeremy Bentham* 9 vols. New York: Russell and Russell.

Berle, Adolf, and Gardiner Means. (1991). *The Modern Corporation and Private Property*. New Brunswick, NJ: Transaction Publishers. (Originally published 1932).

Berlin, Isaiah. (1969). "Two Concepts of Liberty," in *Four Essays on Liberty*, 118–72.

———. (1969). *Four Essays on Liberty*. Oxford: Oxford University Press.

Blackstone, Sir William. (1962). *Commentaries on the Laws of England*, 11th ed. 4 vols. Boston: Beacon Press.

Blumenfeld, Samuel L., ed. (1974). *Property in a Humane Economy*. La Salle, IL: Open Court Press.

Bogart, John. (1986). "Lockean Provisos and State of Nature Theories," *Ethics* 96, no. 4 (July), 828–36.

Brandt, Richard. (1979). *A Theory of the Good and the Right*. Oxford: Oxford University Press.

Brenkert, George. (1991). *Political Freedom*. London: Routledge and Kegan Paul.

Brigham, John. (1990). *Property and the Politics of Entitlement*. Philadelphia, PA: Temple University Press.

Buchanan, Allen. (1985). *Ethics, Efficiency and the Market*. Totowa, NJ: Rowman and Allenheld.

Calabresi, Guido, and A. Douglas Melamed. (1972). "Property Rules, Liability Rules and Inalienability: One View of the Cathedral," *Harvard Law Review* 85, no. 6 (April), 1089–1128.

Carens, Joseph. (1981). *Equality, Moral Incentives, and the Market*. Chicago: University of Chicago Press.

Cheung, Steven S. (1983). "The Contractual Nature of the Firm," *Journal of Law and Economics* 26 (April), 1–21.

Christiano, Thomas. (1991). "Difficulties with the Principles of Equal Opportunity for Welfare," *Philosophical Studies* 62, no. 2 (May), 178–86.

Christman, John. (1986). "Can Full Ownership Be Justified by Natural Rights?" *Philosophy and Public Affairs* 15, no. 2 (Spring), 156–77.

———. (1988). "Constructing the Inner Citadel: Recent Work on the Concept of Autonomy," *Ethics* 99, no. 1 (October), 109–24.

———. (1988). "Entrepreneurs, Profits and Deserving Market Shares," *Social Philosophy and Policy* 6, no. 1 (Autumn), 1–16.

———. (1991). "Autonomy and Personal History," *Canadian Journal of Philosophy* 21, no. 1 (March), 1–24.

———. (1991). "Liberalism and Individual Positive Freedom," *Ethics* 101, no. 2 (January), 343–59.

———. (1991). "Self-Ownership, Equality, and the Structure of Property Rights," *Political Theory* 19, no. 1 (February), 28–46.

———. (1989). ed. *The Inner Citadel: Essays on Individual Autonomy*. New York: Oxford University Press.

Clark, Robert. (1981). "The Four Stages of Capitalism: Reflections on Investment Management Treatises," *Harvard Law Review* 94, 561–82.

Coase, R. H. (1937). "The Nature of the Firm," *Economica* 4, 386–405.

———. (1960). "The Problem of Social Costs," *Journal of Law and Economics* 3 (October), 1–44.

Cohen, G. A. (1977). "Robert Nozick and Wilt Chamberlain: How Patterns Preserve Liberty," *Erkenntnis* 11, 5–23.

———. (1979). "Capitalism, Freedom and the Proletariate," in *The Idea of Freedom*, Alan Ryan, ed. Oxford: Oxford University Press, 9–26.

———. (1983). "The Structure of Proletarian Unfreedom," *Philosophy and Public Affairs* 12, no. 1 (Winter), 3–33.

———. (1983). "Self Ownership, World Ownership and Equality, Part II," *Social Philosophy and Policy* 3, no. 2, 77–96.

———. (1986). "Self Ownership, World Ownership and Equality," in *Justice and Equality Here and Now*, Frank S. Lucash, ed. Ithaca, NY: Cornell University Press, 108–35.

———. (1989). "On the Currency of Egalitarian Justice," *Ethics* 99, no. 4 (July), 906–44.

Coleman, Jules. (1988). *Markets, Morals and the Law*. Cambridge: Cambridge University Press.

Connolly, William. (1983). *The Terms of Political Discourse*. Princeton, NJ: Princeton University Press.

Crocker, Lawrence. (1980). *Positive Liberty*. Netherlands: Martinus Nijhoff.

Crystal, Graef S. (1991). *In Search of Excess: The Overcompensation of the American Executive*. New York: Norton.

Demsetz, Harold. (1974). "Toward a Theory of Property Rights," in *The Economics of Property Rights*, Eric Furubotn and Svetozar Pejovich, eds. Cambridge, MA: Ballinger, 31–42.

———. (1982). "Professor Michelman's Unnecessary and Futile Search for the Philosopher's Touchstone," in *Nomos*, vol. 24: *Ethics, Economics and the Law*, J. R. Pennock and J. Chapman, eds. New York: New York University Press, 41–47.

———. (1983). "The Structure of Ownership and the Theory of the Firm," *Journal of Law and Economics* 26 (June), 375–90.

Dias, R. W. M. (1976). *Jurisprudence*. London: Butterworths.

Donahue, Charles, Jr. (1980). "The Future of the Concept of Property Predicted from Its Past," in *Nomos*, vol. 22: *Property*, J. R. Pennock and J. Chapman, eds. New York: New York University Press, 28–68.

Dosi, Giovanni. (1984). *Technical Change and Industrial Transformation*. London: Macmillan.

Doyal, Len, and Ian Gough. (1991). *A Theory of Human Needs*. New York: Guilford Press.

Duncan-Jones, Richard. (1990). *Structure and Scale of the Roman Economy*. Cambridge: Cambridge University Press.

Dworkin, Gerald. (1968). "Compulsion and Moral Concepts," *Ethics* 78 (April), 227–33.

———. (1988). *The Theory and Practice of Autonomy*. Cambridge: Cambridge University Press.

Dworkin, Ronald. (1981). "What Is Equality? Part 1: Equality of Welfare," *Philosophy and Public Affairs* 10, no. 3 (Spring), 185–246.

———. (1981). "What Is Equality? Part 2: Equality of Resources," *Philosophy and Public Affairs* 10, no. 4 (Fall), 283–345.

———. (1987). "What Is Equality? Part 3: The Place of Liberty," *Iowa Law Review* 73, no. 1 (October), 1–54.

———. (1990). "Foundations of Liberal Equality," in *Tanner Lectures on Human Value*, vol. 11. Grethe Peterson, ed. Salt Lake City: University of Utah Press, 1–119.

Eggertsson, Thrainn. (1990). *Economic Behavior and Institutions*. New York: Cambridge University Press.

Ellis, Lee. (1985). "On the Rudiments of Possessions and Property," *Social Science Information* 24, no. 1, 113–43.

Elster, Jon. (1983). *Sour Grapes*. Cambridge: Cambridge University Press.

———. (1983). *Explaining Technical Change*. New York: Cambridge University Press.

———, ed. (1986). *Rational Choice*. New York: New York University Press.

Elster, Jon, and Karl Ove Moene. (1989). *Alternatives to Capitalism*. New York: Cambridge University Press.

Epstein, Richard. (1985). *Takings: Private Property and the Power of Eminent Domain*. Cambridge, MA: Harvard University Press.

Fama, Eugene, and Michael Jensen. (1983). "The Separation of Ownership and Control," *Journal of Law and Economics* 26 (June), 301–25.

Faulkner, William. (1973). *Go Down, Moses*. New York: Vintage.

Feinberg, Joel. (1970). "Justice and Personal Desert," in *Doing and Deserving*. Princeton, NJ: Princeton University Press, 55–94.

———. (1973). *Social Philosophy*. Englewood Cliffs, NJ: Prentice Hall.

———. (1980). "The Nature and Value of Rights," in *Rights Justice and the Bounds of Liberty*. Princeton, NJ: Princeton University Press, 143–58.

Flathman, Richard. (1987). *The Philosophy and Politics of Freedom*. Chicago: University of Chicago Press.

Frankel Paul, Ellen, and Howard Dickman, eds. (1989). *Liberty, Property, and the Foundations of the American Constitution*. Albany, NY: SUNY Press.

Frankfurt, Harry. (1987). "Equality as a Moral Ideal," *Ethics* 98, no. 1 (October), 21–49.

Freidman, Milton. (1962). *Capitalism and Freedom*. Chicago: University of Chicago Press.

Furby, Lita. (1978). "Possession in Humans: An Exploratory Study of Its Meaning and Motivation," *Social Behavior and Personality* 6, no. 1, 49–65.

———. (1978). "Possessions: Toward a Theory of Their Meaning and Function throughout the Life Cycle," in *Life Span Development and Behavior*, P. B. Baltes, ed. New York: Academy Press, 297–336.

Furubotn, Eric, and Svetozar Pejovich, eds. (1974). *The Economics of Property Rights*. Cambridge, MA: Ballinger.

Gauss, Gerald. (1990). *Value and Justification*. Cambridge: Cambridge University Press.

Gauthier, David. (1986). *Morals by Agreement*. Oxford: Oxford University Press.

Gibbard, Alan. (1976). "Natural Property Rights," *Nous* 10, 77–88.

———. (1985). "What Is Morally Special about Free Exchange?" *Social Philosophy and Policy* 2, no. 2 (Spring), 20–28.

Goodin, Robert. (1986). "Laundering Preferences," in *Foundations of Social Choice Theory*, Jon Elster and Aanund Hyland, eds. Cambridge: Cambridge University Press, 75–102.

Gould, Carol. (1988). *Rethinking Democracy*. Cambridge: Cambridge University Press.

Grey, Thomas. (1980). "The Disintegration of Property," in *Nomos*, vol. 22: *Property*, J. R. Pennock and J. Chapman, eds. New York: New York University Press, 69–85.

Griffin, James. (1986). *Well Being*. Oxford: Clarendon Press.

Grunebaum, James O. (1980). "Property Rules and Property Rights," *Pacific Philosophical Quarterly* 61, 422–32.

———. (1987). *Private Ownership*. London: Routledge and Kegan Paul.

Gurin, Gerald, and Patricia Gurin. (1976). "Personal Efficacy and the Ideology of Individual Responsibility," in *Economic Means for Human Needs*, Burkhard Strumpel, ed. Ann Arbor, MI: Institute for Social Research, 131–57.

Gutmann, Amy. (1988). *Democracy and the Welfare State*. Princeton, NJ: Princeton University Press.

Hallowell, Irving. (1955). *Culture and Experience*. Philadelphia: University of Pennsylvania Press.

Hardin, Garret, and John Baden, eds. (1977). *Managing the Commons*. San Francisco, CA: W. H. Freeman.

Hardin, Russell. (1982). *Collective Action*. Baltimore, MD: Johns Hopkins University Press.

———. (1988). *Morality within the Limits of Reason*. Chicago: University of Chicago Press.

———. (1989). "Autonomy, Identity, and Welfare," in *The Inner Citadel: Essays on Individual Autonomy*, John Christman, ed. New York: Oxford University Press, 189–99.

Hart, H.L.A. (1979). "Are There Any Natural Rights?" in *Rights*, David Lyons, ed. Belmont, CA: Wadsworth, 14–25.

Harrison, A.R.W. (1968, 1971). *The Law of Athens*. 2 vols. Oxford: Clarendon Press.

Hausman, Daniel. (1992). "When Jack and Jill Make a Deal," *Social Philosophy and Policy* 9, no. 1 (Winter), 95–113.

Haworth, Lawrence. (1986). *Autonomy: An Essay in Philosophical Psychology and Ethics*. New Haven, CT: Yale University Press.

Hayek, F. A., ed. (1935). *Collectivist Economic Planning*. London: Routledge and Kegan Paul.

Hegel, G. W. F. (1952). *The Philosophy of Right*, trans. T. M. Knox. New York: Oxford University Press.

Hettinger, Edwin. (1989). "Justifying Intellectual Property," *Philosophy and Public Affairs* 18, no. 1 (Winter), 31–52.

Hicks, J. (1946). *Value and Capital*. New York: Oxford University Press.

Hirsch, Fred. (1976). *The Social Limits to Growth*. Cambridge, MA: Harvard University Press.

Hobbes, Thomas. (1968). *Leviathan*. Harmondsworth, UK: Penguin.

Hobhouse, L. T. (1964). *Liberalism*. New York: Oxford University Press.

Hohfeld, Wesley. (1919). *Fundamental Legal Conceptions*. New Haven, CT: Yale University Press.

Honore, A.M.A. (1961). "Ownership," in *Oxford Essays in Jurisprudence*, A. Guest, ed. Oxford: Clarendon Press, 107–47.

Hospers, John. (1961). *Human Conduct: An Introduction to the Problems of Ethics*. New York: Harcourt Brace, 433–46.

———. (1980). "Socialism and Liberty," in *Justice*, James Sterba, ed. Belmont, CA: Wadsworth, 231–36.

Hume, David. (1978). *A Treatise of Human Nature*, 2nd ed., ed. L. A. Selby-Bigge. Oxford: Clarendon Press.

Kaldor, Nicholas. (1939). "Welfare Propositions in Economics and Interpersonal Comparisons of Utility," *Economic Journal* 49, 349–52.

Kamien, Morton, and Nancy Schwartz. (1975). "Market Structure and Innovation: A Survey," *Journal of Economic Literature* 13, no. 1 (March), 1–37.

Kearl, J. R. (1977). "Do Entitlements Imply That Taxation Is Theft?" *Philosophy and Public Affairs* 6, no. 1 (Winter), 74–81.

Kirzner, Israel. (1973). *Competition and Entrepreneurship*. Chicago: Chicago University Press.

Kleining, John. (1971). "The Concept of Desert," *American Philosophical Quarterly* 8, no. 1 (January), 71–78.

Knight, Frank. (1957). *Risk, Uncertainty and Profit*. New York: Kelly and Millman.

Landesman, Bruce. (1983). "Egalitarianism," *Canadian Journal of Philosophy* 13, 27–56.

Lane, Robert. (1991). *The Market Experience*. Cambridge: Cambridge University Press.

Lange, Oskar. (1938). *On the Economic Theory of Socialism*. Benjamin Lippincott, ed. New York: McGraw Hill.

Lawson, F. H., and Bernard Rudden. (1982). *The Law of Property*. Oxford: Clarendon Press.

Letwin, William. (1989). "The Economic Policy of the Constitution," in *Liberty, Property, and the Foundations of the American Constitution*, Ellen Frankel Paul, et al., eds. Albany, NY: SUNY Press, 121–40.

Levin, Michael. (1985). "Negative Liberty" in *Liberty and Equality*, Ellen Frankel Paul, et al., eds. Oxford: Basil Blackwell, 84–100.

Levine, Andrew. (1988). *Arguing for Socialism*. London: Verso Press.

Lindley, Richard. (1986). *Autonomy*. New York: Macmillan.

Lipsey, R. G., and R. K. Lancaster. (1956). "The General Theory of Second Best," *Review of Economic Studies* 24, no. 63, 11–32.

Locke, John. (1958). *Essays on the Law of Nature*, ed. W. von Leiden. Oxford: Oxford University Press.

———. (1960). *Two Treatises of Government*, ed. Peter Laslett. Cambridge: Cambridge University Press.

Loewental, Kate. (1973). "Property," *European Journal of Social Psychology* 3, no. 3, 343–51.

Lukes, Stephen. (1980). "Socialism and Equality," in *Justice*, James Sterba, ed. Belmont, CA: Wadsworth, 211–30.

Lyons, David, ed. (1979). *Rights*. Belmont, CA: Wadsworth.

MacCallum, Gerald. (1967). "Negative and Positive Freedom," *Philosophical Review* 76, no. 3 (July), 312–35.

Mack, Eric. (1983). "Distributive Justice and the Tensions of Lockeanism," *Social Philosophy and Policy* 1, no. 1 (Autumn), 132–50.

Mackie, J. L. (1977). *Ethics: Inventing Right and Wrong*. Harmondsworth, UK: Penguin.

Macpherson, C. B. (1962). *The Political Theory of Possessive Individualism*. Oxford: Clarendon Press.

———. (1978). *Property: Mainstream and Critical Positions*. Toronto: University of Toronto Press.

———. (1985). *The Rise and Fall of Economic Justice*. New York: Oxford.

Maine, Henry Sumner. (1986). *Ancient Law*. London: Dorset Press.

Marcuse, Herbert. (1969). *An Essay on Liberation*. Boston: Beacon Press.

Marx, Karl. (1936). *Capital*. 3 vols. New York: Modern Library.

Mavrodes, George. (1974). "Property," in *Property in a Humane Economy*, Samuel L. Blumenfeld, ed. La Salle, IL: Open Court Press, 181–208.

Merryman, J. H. (1974). "Ownership and Estate," *Tulane Law Review* 48, 916–45.

Michelman, Frank. (1982). "Ethics, Economics, and the Law of Property," in *Nomos*, vol. 24: *Ethics, Economics and the Law*, J. R. Pennock and J. Chapman, eds. New York: New York University Press, 3–40.

Milenkovitch, Deborah Duff. (1984). "Is Market Socialism Efficient?" in *Comparative Economic Systems: Present Views*, Andrew Zimbalist, ed. Boston: Kluwer Nijhoff, 65–109.

Mill, John Stuart. (1900). *Principles of Political Economy*. New York: Colonial Press.

———. (1975). *On Liberty*, ed. David Spitz. New York: Norton.

Miller, David. (1980). "Liberty and Property," *Ratio*, 22, 1–14.

———. (1983). "Constraints on Freedom," *Ethics* 93, no. 4 (July), 66–86.

———. (1989). *Market, State and Community*. Oxford: Clarendon Press.

Minogue, Kenneth. (1980). "The Concept of Property and Its Contemporary Significance," in *Nomos*, vol. 22: *Property*, J. R. Pennock and J. Chapman, eds. New York: New York University Press, 3–27.

Mises, L. von. (1935). "Economic Calculation in the Socialist Commonwealth," in *Collectivist Economic Planning*, F. A. Hayek, ed. London: Routledge and Kegan Paul, 87–130.

Moon, J. Donald (1988). "The Moral Basis of the Welfare State," in *Democracy and the Welfare State*, Amy Gutmann ed., Princeton, NJ: Princeton University Press, 27–52.

Munzer, Stephen. (1990). *A Theory of Property*. Cambridge: Cambridge University Press.

Murphy, Jeffrie, and Jules Coleman. (1984). *The Philosophy of Law*. Totowa, NJ: Rowman and Littlefield.

Narveson, Jan. (1984). "Equality vs. Liberty: Advantage Liberty," *Social Philosophy and Policy* 2, no. 1 (Autumn), 33–60.

———. (1988). *The Libertarian Idea*. Philadelphia, PA: Temple University Press.

Nath, S. K. (1969). *A Reappraisal of Welfare Economics*. London: Routledge and Kegan Paul.

Nedelsky, Jennifer. (1990). *Private Property and the Limits of American Constitutionalism*. Chicago: University of Chicago Press.

Nell, Edward. (1987). "On Deserving Profits," *Ethics* 97, no. 2 (January), 403–10.

Nelson, Benjamin. (1969). *The Idea of Usury*. Chicago: University of Chicago Press.

Nelson, Richard. (1981). "Research on Productivity Growth and Productivity Differences: Dead Ends and New Departures," *Journal of Economic Literature* 19 (September), 1029–64.

Nelson, William. (1984). "Equal Opportunity," *Social Theory and Practice* 10, no. 1, 157–84.

Nicholas, Barry. (1962). *An Introduction to Roman Law*. Oxford: Clarendon Press.

Nove, Alec. (1984). "Some Observations on Intersystemic Comparisons," in *Comparative Economic Systems: Present Views*, Andrew Zimbalist, ed. Boston: Kluwer Nijhoff, 47–64.

———. (1983). *The Economics of Feasible Socialism*. London: Allen and Unwin.

Nozick, Robert. (1969). "Coercion," in *Philosophy, Science and Method*, Sidney Morgenbesser, Patrick Suppes and Morton White, eds. New York: St. Martin's Press, 440–72.

———. (1974). *Anarchy, State, and Utopia*. New York: Basic Books.

Okin, Susan Moller. (1989). *Justice, Gender and the Family*. New York: Basic Books.

Parent, W. A. (1974). "Some Recent Work on the Concept of Liberty," *American Philosophical Quarterly* 11, 149–67.

———. (1983). "Some Recent Work on the Concept of Privacy," *American Philosophical Quarterly* 20, no. 4 (October), 341–55.

Pejovich, Svetozar. (1974). "Towards a General Theory of Property Rights," in *The Economics of Property Rights*, E. Furubotn and S. Pejovich, eds. Cambridge, MA: Ballinger, 341–54.

Pejovich, Svetozar, and Eric Furubotn. (1972). "Property Rights and Economic Theory: A Survey of Recent Literature," *Journal of Economic Literature* 10, 1137–62.

Pennock, Roland J., and John W. Chapman, eds. (1980). *Nomos*, vol. 22: *Property*. New York: New York University Press.

———. (1982). *Nomos*, vol. 24: *Ethics, Economics and the Law*. New York: New York University Press.

Posner, Richard. (1972). *The Economic Analysis of Law*. Boston: Little Brown.

Proudhon, P.-J. (1969). *Selected Writings of P.-J. Proudhon*, ed. Stewart Edwards, trans. by Elizabeth Fraser. Garden City, NY: Doubleday.

———. (1970). *What Is Property?* trans. Benjamin Tucker. New York: Dover Publications.

Pryor, Frederic L. (1973). *Property and Industrial Organization in Communist and Capitalist Nations*. Bloomington: Indiana University Press.

Putterman, L. (1982). "Some Behavioral Perspectives on the Dominance of Hierarchical over Democratic Forms of Enterprise," *Journal of Economic Behavior and Organization* 3, 139–60.

Radin, Margaret Jane. (1982). "Property and Personhood," *Stanford Law Review* 34, no. 5 (May), 957–1015.

———. (1988). "The Liberal Conception of Property: Currents in the Jurisprudence of Takings," *Columbia Law Review* 88, 1667–96.

Rawls, John. (1955). "Two Concepts of Rules," *Philosophical Review* 64, 3–32.

———. (1971). *A Theory of Justice*. Cambridge, MA: Harvard University Press.

———. (1982). "The Basic Liberties and Their Priority," in *Tanner Lectures on Human Value*, vol. 3, Sterling McMurrin ed. Salt Lake City: University of Utah Press, 1–87.

———. (1987). "The Idea of an Overlapping Consensus," *Oxford Journal of Legal Studies* 7, 1–25.

Raz, Joseph. (1986). *The Morality of Freedom*. Oxford: Clarendon Press.

Reeve, Andrew. (1986). *Property*. Atlantic Highlands, NJ: Humanities Press.

Reich, Charles. (1964). "The New Property," *Yale Law Journal* 73, no. 5 (April), 733–87.

Roemer, John. (1986). "The Mismarriage of Bargaining Theory and Distributive Justice," *Ethics* 97, no. 1 (October), 88–110.

———. (1988). "A Challenge to Neo-Lockeanism," *Canadian Journal of Philosophy* 18 (December), 697–710.

———. (1988). "A Public Ownership Solution of the Tragedy of the Commons," *Social Philosophy and Policy* 6, no. 2, 74–92.

———. (1992). "The Morality and Efficiency of Market Socialism," *Ethics* 102, no. 3 (April), 448–64.

Roemer, John, with I. Ortuño-Ortin and J. Silvestre. (1993). "Investment Planning in Market Socialism," in *Democracy and Markets: Participation, Accountability and Efficiency*, S. Bowles, H. Gintis, and B. Gustafsson, eds. Cambridge: Cambridge University Press, 279–305.

Rose-Ackerman, Susan. (1985). "Inalienability and the Theory of Property Rights," *Columbia Law Review* 85 (June), 931–69.

Rothbard, Murray. (1974). "Justice and Property Rights," in *Property in a Humane Economy*, Samuel L. Blumenfeld, ed. La Salle, Il: Open Court Press, 101–22.

———. (1978). *For a New Liberty*. New York: Libertarian Review Foundation.

Rousseau, J. J. (1987). "Discourse on the Origin of Inequality," in *The Basic Political Writings*, trans. by Donald Cress. Indianapolis, IN: Hackett, 25–110.

Ryan, Alan. (1979). *The Idea of Freedom: Essays in Honor of Isaiah Berlin*. Oxford: Oxford University Press.

———. (1984). *Property and Political Theory*. Oxford: Basil Blackwell.

———. (1987). *Property*. Minneapolis: University of Minnesota Press.

Ryan, Cheyney. (1977). "Yours, Mine and Ours: Property Rights and Individual Liberty," *Ethics* 87, no. 2 (January), 126–41.

Sagoff, Mark. (1984). "Ethics and Economics in Environmental Law," in *Earthbound*, Tom Regan, ed. Philadelphia, PA: Temple University Press, 147–78.

Samuelson, Paul. (1967). *Economics*. New York: McGraw Hill.

Saraydar, Edward. (1989). "The Conflation of Productivity and Efficiency in Economics and Economic History," *Economics and Philosophy* 5, 55–67.

Satz, Deborah. (1992). "Markets in Women's Reproductive Labor," *Philosophy and Public Affairs* 21, no. 2 (Spring), 107–31.

Scanlon, T. M. (1980). "Comments on Ackerman's *Private Property and the Constitution*," in *Nomos*, vol. 22: *Property*, J. R. Pennock and J. Chapman, eds. New York: New York University Press, 341–50.

———. (1981). "Nozick on Rights, Liberty and Justice," in *Reading Nozick*, J. Paul, ed. Totowa, NJ: Rowman and Littlefield, 107–29.

Schlatter, Richard. (1957). *Private Property: The History of an Idea*. New Brunswick, NJ: Rutgers University Press.

Schmidd, A. Allen. (1978). *Property, Power and Public Choice*. New York: Praeger.

Schumpeter, Joseph. (1950). *Capitalism, Socialism, and Democracy*. New York: Harper.

———. (1962). *The Theory of Economic Development*. Cambridge, MA: Harvard University Press.

Scitovsky, T. (1941). "A Note on Welfare Propositions in Economics," *Review of Economic Studies* 8 (November), 77–88.

Sen, Amartya. (1977). "Rational Fools: A Critique of the Behavioral Foundations of Economic Theory," *Philosophy and Public Affairs* 6, 317–44.

———. (1979). "Utilitarianism and Welfarism," *Journal of Philosophy* 76, no. 9, 463–89.

———. (1980). "Equality of What?" in *Tanner Lectures on Human Values*, vol. 1, S. McMurrin, ed. Cambridge: Cambridge University Press, 197–220.

———. (1981). *Poverty and Famines: An Essay on Entitlement and Deprivation*. Oxford: Clarendon Press.

———. (1984). "Well Being, Agency and Freedom: The Dewey Lectures," *Journal of Philosophy* 82, 169–221.

———. (1987). *On Ethics and Economics*. Oxford: Basil Blackwell.

———. (1992). *Inequality Reexamined*. Cambridge, MA: Harvard University Press.

Sen, Amartya, and Bernard Williams, eds. (1982). *Utilitarianism and Beyond*. Cambridge: Cambridge University Press.

Simmons, John. (1983). "Inalienable Rights and Locke's Treatises," *Philosophy and Public Affairs* 12, no. 3 (Summer), 175–204.

Snare, Frank. (1972). "The Concept of Property," *American Philosophical Quarterly* 9 (April), 200–206.

Snyder David. (1986). "Locke on Natural Law and Property Rights," *Canadian Journal of Philosophy* 16, no. 4 (December), 723–50.

Steiner, Hillel. (1975). "Individual Liberty," *Proceedings of the Aristotelian Society* 75, 33–50.

———. (1977). "The Natural Right to the Means of Production," *Philosophical Quarterly* 27 (January), 41–49.

———. (1983). "How Free: Computing Personal Liberty," in *Of Liberty*, A. Phillips Griffiths, ed. Cambridge: Cambridge University Press, 73–89.

Tawney, R. H. (1920). *The Acquisitive Society*. New York: Harcourt Brace Jovanovich.

———. (1964). *Equality*. London: Allen and Unwin.

Taylor, Charles. (1979). *Hegel and Modern Society*. Cambridge: Cambridge University Press.

———. (1979). "What Is Wrong with Negative Liberty?" in *The Idea of Freedom*, Alan Ryan, ed. Oxford: Oxford University Press, 175–94.

Thomson, Judith Jarvis. (1975). "The Right to Privacy," *Philosophy and Public Affairs* 4, 295–331.

Tully, James. (1980). *A Discourse on Property: John Locke and His Adversaries*. Cambridge: Cambridge University Press.

Tversky, Amos, and Daniel Kahneman. (1990). "Rational Choice and the Framing of Decisions," in *The Limits of Rationality*, Karen Schweers Cook and Margaret Levi, eds. Chicago: University of Chicago Press, 60–89.

Varian, Hal. (1984). *Microeconomic Analysis*. New York: Norton.

Waldron, Jeremy. (1988). *The Right to Private Property*. Oxford: Clarendon Press.

Ware, Alan, and Robert Goodin, eds. (1990). *Needs and Welfare*. London: Sage Press.

Westen, Peter. (1990). *Speaking of Equality*. Princeton, NJ: Princeton University Press.

Whelan, Frederick. (1980). "Property as Artifice: Hume and Blackstone," in *Nomos*, vol 22: *Property*, J. R. Pennock and J. Chapman, eds. New York: New York University Press, 101–29.

Wheeler, Sam. (1980). "Natural Property Rights as Body Rights," *Nous*, 14, 171–93.

Wilson, G. P. (1957). "Jurisprudence and the Discussion of Ownership," *Cambridge Law Journal*, 15, 216–229.

Zaitchick, Alan. (1977). "On Deserving to Deserve," *Philosophy and Public Affairs* 6, no. 4 (Fall), 370–88.

Zimbalist, Andrew, ed. (1984). *Comparative Economic Systems: Present Views*. Boston: Kluwer Nijhoff.

Zimmerman, David. (1981). "Coercive Wage Offers," *Philosophy and Public Affairs* 10, no. 2 (Spring), 121–45.

Index